about the author

Colin Evans is the author of several crime-related books, including *Killer Doctors* (Michael O'Mara) and *The Casebook of Forensic Detection: How Science Solved 100 of the World's Most Baffling Crimes* (Wiley). His articles frequently appear in the *Fort Lauderdale Sun-Sentinal* and he has contributed both to Visible Ink's *Great American Trials* and *Great World Trials*.

also from visible ink press

Great World Trials As riveting as a courtroom potboiler, *Great World Trials* brings you right into the jury box with gripping accounts of 100 important legal battles waged outside the United States. Coverage includes cases involving Martin Guerre (1560), Oscar Wilde (1895), Adolf Eichmann (1961), the Tiananmen Square Dissidents (1991) and Yigal Amir (1996). *Great World Trials* provides background information, case details, verdicts, and impact analysis.

Edward W. Knappman • 7 x 9 • paperback • 450 pages • 90 photos • 1997 • ISBN 1-57859-001-9

Great American Trials From Salem Witchcraft to Rodney King "An extraordinary introduction for anyone contemplating a legal career; for the rest of us it is a fine reference and a delight to read." — *Chicago Tribune*

Two hundred historically significant, legally important and notorious trials that have captured the interest of the world are recalled through lively text and captivating photos. Included are brief and accurate summaries of such trials as Dred Scott • Lizzy Borden • Leopold and Loeb • Brown v. Board of Education • Charles Manson • Roe v. Wade • Jim Bakker • Ted Bundy • and Oliver North.

Edward W. Knappman • 7 x 9 • paperback • 872 pages • 175 photos • 1996 • ISBN 0-7876-0937-4

Criminal Quotes The 1,001 Most Bizarre Things Ever Said by History's Outlaws, Gangsters, Despots, and Other Evil-doers For anyone who's ever marveled at what they've read in the paper or heard on the news at 11, Criminal Quotes will make for some mighty interesting—if gasp-inspiring—reading. Yes, these 1,000 quotes are real. No matter how diabolical, egomaniacal, bizarre and even grisly the sentiments might be, they were all spoken or written down by outlaws, gangsters, despots and other evil doers throughout the ages—from John Dillinger to Jeffrey Dahmer. For true crime fans, lovers of dark humor and curious observers.

Andrew Chesler and H. Amanda Robb • 5 x 8 • paperback • 175 pages • 1996 • ISBN 0-7876-0937-4

america's courtroom celebrities

Super Lawyers

america's courtroom celebrities

Super Lawyers

40 top lawyers and the cases that made them famous

Colin Evans

DETROIT • NEW YORK • TORONTO • LONDON

america's courtroom celebrities
SuperLawyers

Published by Visible Ink Press™
a division of Gale Research
835 Penobscot Building
Detroit, MI 48226-4094

Visible Ink Press™ is a trademark of Gale Research

Most Visible Ink Press™ books are available at special quantity discounts when purchased in bulk by corporations, organizations, or groups. Customized printings, special imprints, messages, and excerpts can be produced to meet your needs. For more information, contact the Special Markets Manager at the above address. Or call 1-800-877-4253.

Art Director: Tracey Rowens
Typesetting: LM Design
Images on the cover and interior pages of the courthouse steps are from PhotoDisc, Inc., ©1997.

ISBN 1-57859-004-3

Library of Congress Cataloging-in-Publication Data

Evans, Colin, 1948-
Superlawyers : America's courtroom celebrities / by Colin Evans.
p. cm.
Includes index.
ISBN 1-57859-004-3
1. Lawyers—United States—Biography. I. Title.
KF372.E94 1997
340'.092'2—dc21 97-37401
[B] CIP

Printed in the United States of America

10 9 8 7 6 5 4 3 2 1

SuperLawyers

america's courtroom celebrities

Contents

Introduction
(Colin Evans)

America has always been fascinated by headline criminal trials. In the early twentieth century, goaded on by press barons like William Randolph Hearst, huge crowds would flock to newsstands, desperate for details of the latest courtroom spectacular. When radio became the primary source of national information, it, too, recognized the insatiable public appetite for real-life human drama, and often covered big trials in the minutest detail. The advent of television only broadened this coverage; and now, with Court TV, gavel-to-gavel action is beamed right into our own living room. Hand-in-hand with this progress has gone the public acclamation of top trial attorneys. These modern-day equivalents of the Wild West gunslinger-for-hire have always fascinated the American public: now they bask in the kind of media limelight previously reserved for the likes of movie stars, sporting heroes, and politicians. As O.J. Simpson pondered his fate in court, there must have been times when he felt transported back to his gridiron days, surrounded as he was by so much highly trained and well-paid humanity. But just how good were his defenders, the so-called "Dream Team?" And how do they compare with the great lawyers of the past, or even other attorneys currently practicing? Within these pages you will get a chance to draw your own conclusions as we examine the lives and cases of the *SuperLawyers*, the twentieth century's top forty American advocates.

The great lawyer, the really great lawyer, is a rare jewel. America has more attorneys than the rest of the world combined—658,000 approximately in 1994, estimated to rise to 839,000 in 2005 (U.S. Department of Labor statistics, 1997)—and yet only a handful achieve any kind of fame outside their own office. Why is this? The main reason is that most law school graduates hardly ever set foot in a courtroom, preferring instead the dry complexities and greater financial certainty of corporate law. They may be fine attorneys but we don't get to hear about them. And for those that do test the often risky waters of trial law, there is the sheer size of America to contend with. The regional genius might earn a prodigious reputation in his or her own neck of the legal woods, yet never make it to the majors. The reader can rest assured that they won't find any bush leaguers here. Every lawyer discussed within these pages is right out of the top drawer, blessed with that magical something, that spark of brilliance that elevates them from the pack and into the spotlight. Some, like Johnnie Cochran, are household names. Others are half-forgotten. A couple were even downright shady. But all are legal giants, larger than life, prepared to fight tooth and nail for their client.

It is this sense of personal involvement that makes the American lawyer so unique and fascinating. More than any other country, they identify with their client. Whenever the likes of Leslie Abramson or Gerry Spence bare their souls before a jury, it is impossible not to feel their intensity and burning commitment; in stark contrast to the cooler, more detached air of British courtrooms, say, where the outcome of most trials would probably be unaffected even if the opposing lawyers were to switch sides halfway through. This would be unthinkable in a great American trial. When Clarence Darrow pleaded for the lives of teenage killers Nathan Leopold and Richard Loeb, he did so out of a deep-seated loathing for capital punishment. The millions who devoured his speeches in stop-press editions all across the nation were left in no doubt that this remarkable counselor put his heart and soul into every word.

Another trait that Darrow shared with all the *SuperLawyers* was his ability to dominate courtroom and jury alike. Reduced to its essence, adversarial trial advocacy is all about salesmanship: the attorney who presents the better case to the jury usually wins, and the *SuperLawyers* win more often than most. Such success is clearly addictive as most of these legal mega-stars spent their entire careers in trial practice. A few trifled with politics—one came within a whisker of the presidency—but it can be no coincidence that only one went on to become a judge. After the adrenalin rush of supercharged advocacy, dispassionate rulings from the bench must seem like very warm beer.

For ease of reference the profiles have been arranged alphabetically. They include brief details of each lawyer's life and career, and then a single case is explored in-depth. The selections are, of course, purely subjective, but having said that, few serious legal students would dispute that of all those included, each one fully merits its place in a book of this type. Where disagreement is more likely to surface is over those many fine lawyers who have, through constraints of space and scope, been omitted; and to all those who wonder why "so and so" was left out, I offer my sincere apologies.

So let's get to it, and learn more about the *SuperLawyers*, those men and women who have plied their trade and gained their hardwon reputations in the toughest and most unpredictable workplace of all—the American courtroom.

Leslie Abramson
(1944-)

I. Career

Ever since 1870, when Ada H. Kepley made history by becoming America's first female lawyer, women have struggled to gain recognition in the legal arena. Only in recent years have they begun to take center-stage in this most male-dominated of environments, and none has benefited more from this belated revolution than California attorney Leslie Abramson.

At an inch under five feet tall, this pocket-sized firecracker has become one of the most celebrated lawyers in America. She has achieved this prominence, not through any quota system or by being bubbly and cute in front of the TV cameras, but simply by getting the job done. Her record is remarkable: of the fifteen capital cases she has defended, only one client has received the death penalty. When the "Queen of Miracles" goes to bat for a defendant, she brings to her argument a level of hot-blooded commitment and passion that others can only dream of emulating. Abramson doesn't just have cases, she creates causes.

As a self-appointed icon for the misunderstood, she has had to endure a hailstorm of barbs and taunts. Arguably many of the wounds have been self-inflicted—her combativeness and lacerating tongue are not universally appreciated—

Abramson during the retrial for Erik and Lyle Menendez. (AP Wide World/Nick Ut)

but few can doubt her sincerity. "I'm drawn to cases where very nice people and very good people are accused of crimes because the law lags behind psychology," she explains. "I am drawn to these people because they need me."

Abramson knows first-hand the pain of rejection. Her own childhood in New York was an emotional rollercoaster. When she was age six her father left home, a trauma that Abramson coped with by first burying herself in a passion for comic books, then in what she described as "obsessive" college cheerleading. In her adolescent years she was inspired by the activism of her grandmother, Fanny Kaprow, a left-wing organizer for the International Garment Workers Union. Abramson's instincts led her down a different path: after obtaining a law degree at UCLA in 1969, she joined the public defender's office.

Her entry into private practice eight years later coincided with California's decision to reintroduce the death penalty after a decade-long moratorium. She was tailor-made for such high pressure cases. The same impulsiveness that made her once accuse prosecutors of "killing" a client who died in custody because he did not receive his diabetes medication, can also have a spellbinding effect on juries in capital trials. She speaks a simple language, high on visceral appeal, always searching for the common thread that will bind her to the jury's collective consciousness. Usually she finds it. When she doesn't the emotional fallout can be spectacular.

When Harvey Giss, a deputy district attorney, described Abramson as "pompous, arrogant, and self-righteous . . . nothing but a glamorous spin doctor," he was venting an animosity that stemmed from a 1980 capital case when he had defeated his blonde nemesis. In typical fashion, Abramson fired back with both barrels, "This particular person only . . . lives as a paragraph in a story about me. He's not worthy of my comment. He's nothing. Who is this guy?"

This shoot-from-the-lip belligerence can often obscure what is a very genuine legal talent, for as Abramson has demonstrated on dozens of occasions, when it comes to getting juries to see things her way, she is unique.

II. Peter Chan (1988)

It was a rainy December day in 1984 when officers Duane Johnson and Archie Nagoa left their Los Angeles substation in response to a silent alarm triggered by the owner of the Jin Hing jewelry store on nearby Bamboo Street. The two officers covered the half-block journey on foot. Beneath their yellow rain slickers they wore holstered guns, though there was little indication that weapons would be needed when they reached the store. Everything pointed to a false alarm. An apparent customer admitted the officers, who gave the store a cursory once-over and, finding nothing untoward, turned to leave. Suddenly gunfire erupted. The "customer" turned out to be just one of four would-be robbers. In the next chaotic few seconds a wild shootout left two of the robbers dead on the floor. Beside them lay Officer Johnson.

Cop-killers who get caught can expect little leniency from the law. The grim specter of a police officer cut down in the line of duty usually provides a powerful incentive for the state to go all out for a death sentence. Eventually, in 1988, after years of wrangling, Hau Cheong (Peter) Chan, aged thirty-two, and Sam Nam Chinh, twenty-two, stood separate trials, charged with first-degree murder. A further suspect, Thong Huynh, earlier acquitted of harboring Chinh after the robbery, agreed to testify for the prosecution about how the theft was allegedly planned. Chinh's conviction and subsequent life sentence meant that the state's sole surviving chance of securing a death penalty rested in its prosecution of Chan.

And he was defended by Leslie Abramson.

The omens did not look good. Apart from first-degree murder, Chan faced numerous other counts, including the attempted murder of Officer Nagoa, and there was plenty of eyewitness testimony to refute his claim that he had never set foot in the store. Leon and Robert Lee, father and son owners of the jewelry store, and other customers who were held up, all identified Chan as one of the robbers who had fled after the shootout.

Chan hotly denied this, claiming that he was merely a getaway driver for the other thieves. Even if this were true, it would not definitely save him. Under California law a suspect can be found guilty of crimes actually committed by others, as long as the jury believes he acted in concert with them and without coercion. This meant that even if Chan had just chauffeured the other gang members to the store, if the collective intent was robbery, and this led to murder, he was equally culpable. To Abramson fell the task of undermining this interpretation.

A. Doubts Begin to Surface

Skillfully, she lured the jury away from the notion of first-degree murder, highlighting minor discrepancies in state witnesses' testimony in such a way as to make them seem dangerously suspicious. Just as adroitly, Deputy District Attorney Lawrence Longo hammered home the senseless brutality of the slayings; how the gang had burst in at gunpoint, then began filling black plastic bags with jewelry, oblivious to the fact that Leon Lee had tripped a silent alarm hooked into the nearby police station. According to Longo, it was Chinh who lost his head and opened fire for no reason, killing Johnson and wounding Nagoa, before he and Chan fled for their lives. Now Longo was asking the jury to send Chan—the alleged mastermind of the bungled robbery, the man who had staked-out the jewelry store a few days beforehand and then led his gang on its deadly mission—to the gas chamber.

Abramson fought like a tiger. Reminding the jury of eyewitness fallibility, she delivered an impassioned plea on Chan's behalf, one which sowed enough seeds of doubt for Superior Court Judge Jean Matusinka to make abundantly clear in her instructions to the jury that a verdict of second-degree murder would not be inconsistent with the evidence.

B. A Month of Deliberation

On March 14, 1988, the jury retired. For almost a month, deliberating on and off, they wrestled with their consciences, until, on April 11, they returned a second-degree murder conviction. They also found Chan guilty of two counts of attempted murder, assault with a deadly weapon, and first-degree robbery. He was acquitted of the remaining charges.

Abramson was jubilant. "I'm in seventh heaven," she cried. "All I want is justice and justice is done." By contrast, Longo thought the verdict "a terrible miscarriage of justice." In the spectator's gallery, Officer Johnson's widow heard the verdict in silence, then left the court without comment.

Jurors confirmed Abramson had been the key. It was her incisive questioning, they said, that had raised sufficient doubts as to whether Chan had actually been in the store.

But the "Queen of Miracles" wasn't through yet. She filed successfully for a delay in sentencing because probation reports contained "quadruple levels of hearsay going back twelve years." Even Judge Matusinka described the report as "very, very one-sided." When Longo wanted prosecution testimony placed into the probation report, Abramson erupted. Dismissing Longo's request as "theories" and "rejected facts," she argued that they should have no place in the report. For one and a half days opposing lawyers pored over the report, haggling over every detail.

At the end of it all, on September 27, 1988, Chan was jailed for thirty-eight years-to-life, a sentence that a very disgruntled Officer Nagoa described as "better than nothing." Before leaving the courtroom he clashed angrily with Abramson, ending with "He's alive!" to which she replied, "So are you!"

"But Duane isn't!" retorted Nagoa bitterly, storming from the court.

C. Stoking Controversy

Such skirmishes are an almost daily occurrence to Abramson. She arouses powerful emotions, both for and against. Just recently her handling of the Menendez brothers' defense stoked up yet more controversy. After the second trial, in which the brothers were convicted of killing their parents, Abramson found herself facing allegations that she had doctored evidence by ordering a defense psychiatrist, Dr. William Vicary, to extensively alter the notes he used to testify, upon pain of dismissal from the case if he disobeyed.

Although Abramson denied Vicary's charge, she did admit asking him to clarify ambiguous statements and to seal notes that infringed on doctor-patient privilege or concerned subjects barred by the judge. When quizzed about the matter, on April 9, 1996, Abramson twice invoked her Fifth Amendment right to silence. She later waived her right against self-incrimination but still refused to talk, citing attorney-client privilege.

The controversy shows no sign of abating. On November 16, 1996, the State Bar of California and the Los Angeles district attorney announced a joint investigation of Abramson's alleged misconduct. As of this writing, the investigation is still pending.

OTHER NOTABLE CASES:

Ricardo Sanders (1982); Arnel Salvatierra (1988);
Erik Menendez (1993–96)

F. Lee Bailey
(1933-)

I. Career

The element of luck in advocacy is impossible to overstate, and anyone entering this most demanding of professions needs all the help Dame Fortune can spare. A big case, early in one's career, can make all the difference between success and failure. Geography, too, plays its part. It is no coincidence that the overwhelming majority of lawyers featured in these pages hung out their shingles in the major metropolitan areas; after all, this is where most crimes occur and where the most sensational cases are to be found. When the Greek shipping magnate, Aristotle Onassis, observed that, in business, to "catch big fish, you have to fish in deep waters," he might equally have been describing the law. Who knows how many Clarence Darrows have languished in relative obscurity because they opted to practice in some rural backwater? The ambitious head for the big city.

Francis Lee Bailey didn't have far to travel. Born in Waltham, Massachusetts, almost within sight of downtown Boston, he was already on the outskirts of a major American crime battlefield. But before joining the skirmish there were other hurdles to clear. Two undistinguished years at Harvard confirmed his belief

A young F. Lee Bailey. (UPI-Archive Photos)

that he was unsuited for academia and led to his enlistment in the Navy. Besides flying Sabrejets for the Marines, he acted as squadron legal officer, and it was here that he gained his first taste of the law. It proved addictive. Upon his discharge in 1956 he went to work as an investigator, ferreting out background information for trial lawyers, first for his mentor, Harvey Hamilton, then expanding to include a wide range of law firms.

Not only did this investigative bureau fund his own progress through law school, but it gave him an invaluable insight into the courtroom process. Contact with so many trial lawyers—studying and dissecting disparate techniques of cross-examination, learning to evaluate evidence, assessing witnesses—convinced Bailey that this was where his future lay. Heeding Hamilton's advice, he spent every available moment in the courtroom. He had no shortage of talent and matched that with self-confidence to spare. On November 16, 1960, he was admitted to the Massachusetts bar.

One year and one day later the brash young lawyer, who had already begun to amass an enviable reputation in the Boston area, flew to Cleveland on a journey that would change his life. The next day he drove southwest to the city of Marion, to interview an inmate at the Ohio State Correctional Institution.

The man sitting across the table from Bailey that day was no ordinary prisoner. Six years earlier his handsome face had been emblazoned across every front page in America and hundreds more overseas. Prison life had etched a definite gauntness into the matinee idol looks but had done nothing to diminish the passion in his eyes, as he told the improbable-sounding story he had told so many times before. Even before he was finished, he had converted Bailey to his cause. A handshake sealed the deal.

When the young attorney left Marion prison that raw November day he had no way of knowing that this case would dominate the next five years of his life and make him the most talked-about lawyer in America. Other cases—big cases—would intervene, but nothing could deflect F. Lee Bailey from an unshakeable belief that Dr. Samuel Sheppard had been wrongly convicted of murder.

II. Samuel Sheppard (1966)

The facts of the case, briefly, were these: In the early hours of July 4, 1954, someone murdered Marilyn Sheppard at her home on the shores of Lake Erie. Her husband, Dr. Samuel Sheppard, an affluent thirty-year-old osteopath, claimed to have been dozing on the living room couch when he was awakened by a loud moan or scream from upstairs. According to Sheppard, after rushing upstairs and finding his wife motionless on the bed, he was attacked himself and knocked unconscious. Later, he had come to and fought with the assailant, "a man with bushy hair," on the beach at the foot of his garden, until again blacking out. When he regained consciousness, he found himself immersed in the waters of Lake Erie. Groggily, he staggered back to the house and phoned for help.

When the police arrived they found Marilyn, battered and lifeless in a pool of blood, the apparent victim of a botched robbery. Downstairs, a writing desk had been ransacked and the contents of Sheppard's medical bag lay strewn across the floor. Sheppard, meanwhile, had been whisked away by his two brothers to their family-owned hospital, prompting the first murmurings from the press that the wealthy "Sheppard Boys" had closed ranks to protect their own.

With the discovery at the house of a canvas bag, containing Sheppard's wristwatch, key chain and key, and a fraternity ring, came suspicions that the doctor had faked a robbery in order to conceal murder. When it became known that Sheppard had been enmeshed in a long-running extra-marital affair, Cleveland's press-barons threw the Constitution out the window—or those parts that didn't suit them. Finally, goaded on by a blizzard of savage editorials, the police arrested Sheppard and charged him with murder.

The trial, in October 1954, was a shambles. Judge Edward Blythin, with both eyes firmly set on re-election in the forthcoming November ballot, cast legal probity to the wind and concentrated on some hardcore campaigning. He let the press run rampant, issuing handwritten passes for the elite like Dorothy Kilgallen and Bob Considine, and even providing them a special table at which to sit. Overcome, it seemed, by so many popping flashbulbs and celebrity reporters, Blythin seemed oblivious to the fact that a man was on trial for his life.

A. Guilty!

The ugliness drew to a shabby close on December 21, 1954, when, without a scrap of evidence to connect him to any crime, Sheppard was convicted of second-degree murder and imprisoned for life. His stunned supporters tried every legal avenue open to them, but every appeal, every motion, every petition foundered in a sea of apathy. Behind bars, Sheppard watched his life dribble away one hour at a time. But he never lost hope. And then one day the prison guard told him that he had a visitor, some hotshot young lawyer named F. Lee Bailey.

On a purely selfish level, Bailey realized that here was an opportunity offered to very few young advocates—get Sheppard acquitted and the future was limitless. Underpinning that realization was a genuinely held belief that the State of Ohio hadn't come close to proving its case beyond a reasonable doubt. With that in mind, and without any definite prospects of remuneration beyond a vague verbal agreement, Bailey plunged headlong into the fray, logging thousands of miles on his client's behalf, most at considerable expense to himself.

In order to drum up publicity, he loudly trumpeted his client's willingness to take a polygraph test. An ardent believer in the polygraph's ability to detect untruthfulness, Bailey took this request to the courts. This posed problems. At the time of his arrest Sheppard had repeatedly—and quite legally—declined all police requests to take a polygraph. Now he was pleading for a chance to be tested by his own attorney. Perhaps mindful of his earlier intractability, on December 27, 1962, the Ohio Supreme Court denied the motion. Undeterred, Bailey went back to the TV and radio talkshow circuit, pleading his case in the court of public opinion. Slowly a groundswell of support for Sheppard began to build. But still the courts would not listen and Sam Sheppard remained behind bars.

In true Hollywood fashion, Bailey's big break came from the most freakish of circumstances. On March 17, 1964, purely by chance, he attended a meeting in Manhattan of the Overseas Press Club, and among those present was noted journalist, Dorothy Kilgallen, who had covered the Sheppard trial. As the conversation turned to talk of miscarriages of justice, Kilgallen aired her belief that Sam Sheppard had not received a fair trial. Bolstering this view was her revelation that during Sheppard's trial, the judge, the late Edward Blythin, gave her his off-the-record opinion that the defendant was "guilty as hell." Bailey's legal antennae began to twitch—this was appeal court gold-dust! Accusations, if substantiated, of judicial prejudice might well be grounds for a new trial. Corroboration came in a hurry, when investigators learned that Judge Blythin's indiscretions had been repeated in the presence of various court employees. By a strange twist of fate, the very man who had done so much to victimize Sam Sheppard would also secure his liberty from jail.

That happy day came just four months later, when a judge ordered Sheppard freed on bail, saying that carnival conditions surrounding his trial " . . . fell far below the minimum requirements for due process."

The following year Bailey argued his case before the Supreme Court, claiming that Blythin had displayed prejudice and allowed the trial to be conducted in a manner unbecoming a legal action. The Court agreed. On June 6, 1965, they handed down their landmark decision that Sheppard's 1954 conviction be set aside, because Blythin ". . . did not fulfill his duty to protect Sheppard from inherently prejudicial publicity which saturated the county."

B. Roman Circus

It was a decision well-received by most of the media. The *New York Times* summed up the general mood: "A complaisant judge, irresponsible police offi-

F. Lee Bailey leaving the courthouse after his drunk-driving charge. (UPI Corbis-Bettmann)

cials, and a sensationalist press combined to turn the trial of Dr. Samuel Sheppard into a latter day Roman circus."

Not everyone was thrilled. Cleveland newspapers groused about a decision that had forced the State of Ohio into a corner. If the DA's office backed down now it would be an admission of gross incompetence; too many reputations had been made on the Sheppard case—reputations that needed protecting. Stubbornly, it was decided to try Sheppard again, although this time on a charge of second-degree murder, a bondable offense which meant the defendant would remain at liberty to jail pending trial.

An entirely different attitude permeated the courtroom during the second trial. Media interest remained high but restrained. Prosecution witnesses, telling essentially the same story that they told over a decade earlier, now faced an attorney at the peak of his powers. Bailey picked their testimony clean of prejudice and opinion and left a very skinny skeleton of facts, indeed. The detectives, so confident and assured first time around, were reduced to tight-lipped humiliation as their evidence was demolished. By its conclusion the prosecution's case had been reduced, in Bailey's words, to "ten pounds of hogwash in a five pound bag."

On December 16, 1966, less than twelve hours of jury deliberation ended Sam Sheppard's twelve-year ordeal. But it was liberty at a price. His health broken, Sam Sheppard died in 1970. The attorney-client relationship survived to the end as Bailey helped carry Sheppard's coffin to its final resting place.

During the interim, the attorney from Boston became a courtroom superstar. The pugnacity and machine-gun delivery of facts and questions that got him noticed so quickly on the Massachusetts judicial circuit soon gained him entrance to courtrooms all across America. His rugged style isn't to everyone's taste, but he is no mere heavyweight verbal slugger. Early on, through his investigative bureau, he realized the value of preparation, and it is this attention to detail that still forms the backbone of his criminal practice. Few lawyers in history have entered the courtroom so well-prepared. Better than most, Bailey knows that the advocate who rises to his feet without a firm grasp of every fact of the case is either an incurable optimist or destined for obscurity.

After so long at the peak of his profession he continues to grab headlines, and not always for the right reasons. In 1982, following a two-week trial, he was cleared of a drunk-driving charge in San Francisco. The biggest sensation of all came on March 7, 1996, when a Florida judge imprisoned Bailey for six months for refusing to hand over to the government $3 million in cash and stock worth $20 million, drug-related assets garnisheed from one of his clients, Claude Duboc.[1] It was merely the latest extraordinary chapter in an extraordinary career.

OTHER NOTABLE CASES:

Willard Page (1961); Albert DeSalvo (1966); Ernest Medina (1971); Patty Hearst (1976); O.J. Simpson (1995)

---

[1] *Bailey was freed on April 19, 1996, after spending forty-four days in prison. He is currently in litigation over the legal costs incurred in this matter.*

Stephen C. Baldwin
(1864-1923)

I. Career

There can have been very few attorneys whose abilities were so extraordinarily precocious as to merit unique attention within the law, and yet this is precisely what happened to Stephen Baldwin, one of this century's titans in the field of civil litigation. At the age of twenty, and still legally a minor, he made a special application to the U.S. Supreme Court, so that he might gain admittance to the bar. They made the order without demur—even at this tender age, Baldwin's intellect was an object of wonderment.

He began his education early, and by age eleven, he received a thorough grounding in the Latin classics. He studied under the personal tuition of his father, Reverend Stephen L. Baldwin, a Methodist missionary who spent most of his life in China, and who passed on his detailed experience of that mysterious country in a series of widely read books. Stephen Jr. was born in Foochow (Fuzhou), a large city in southeastern China, about 500 miles north of Hong Kong.

Before reaching his fifteenth birthday he had twice circumnavigated the globe, at a time when foreign travel was still an unknown and often dangerous experience. Then it was off to Europe where he completed his education. In his late teens he returned to America, where his father had taken up a post as Secretary of the Missionary Society of the Methodist Episcopalian Church. Baldwin intended to go to Yale, but there seemed little point: already the law beckoned. After the special petition to the Supreme Court, Baldwin plunged into private practice and was immediately successful as a jury lawyer in the courts of New York.

An early landmark came when he won a $15,000 judgment against a tramcar company for a broken ankle sustained by a young woman named Jeannie Mitchell. This was a stupendous award for the time, and boosted Baldwin's name and reputation into the very top flight of his profession.

Inevitably, as a New York lawyer specializing in corporate and civil actions, he became embroiled in that city's political infighting. When City Mayor William Gaynor and Police Commissioner Theodore Bingham had a big falling-out, accusation and counter accusation cut through the smoke-filled Tammany backrooms. Finally the gibes stung Gaynor into filing a $100,000 libel suit, and it took some serious lobbying on Baldwin's part to persuade his bluff client to withdraw the action, which he was sure would lead to Gaynor's downfall. Baldwin did save Gaynor temporarily, only for the mayor to be rejected by his own party in 1913.

Baldwin climbed from one success to another. In 1914, he was appointed by Governor Martin Glynn to investigate the disgraceful conditions endured by inmates of Sing Sing. Baldwin's report, bitter in its condemnation of what amounted to institutionalized sadism by the prison officials, led to the removal of Warden Thomas J. McCormick.

But it was in 1916 that Stephen Baldwin wrote his name indelibly into the annals of legal history, when he earned for himself the kind of jaw-dropping fee that made other lawyers gasp.

II. Guggenheim v. Guggenheim (1916)

In 1847, a Swiss immigrant named Meyer Guggenheim arrived in Philadelphia and founded a business importing lace from his home country. With his seven sons, he later established the large smelting and refining plants that would form the core of his immense business empire. When he died in 1905 Guggenheim was one of the richest men in the world, and he passed his money-making instincts on to his sons, who soon diversified into other areas of com-

Stephen Baldwin in court. (UPI-Corbis-Bettmann)

merce. The bedrock of their fortune always remained the minerals industry, and it was this core business that led to one of the most bitter and divisive civil suits to come before an American court in the first half of the twentieth century.

Baldwin had been briefed by William Guggenheim to sue his brothers, Isaac, Daniel, Morris, Solomon, and Simon, to recover $10 million in profits to which William said he was entitled as a member of the family firm. The dispute had arisen over a trio of subsidiary companies, set up by the defendants to mine for minerals in Chile.

The case opened June 20, 1916, before Justice Stephen Callaghan in the Supreme Court in Brooklyn. Baldwin briefly outlined the suit. It all hinged around a meeting on January 4, 1912, when William and another brother Benjamin—who later that year was killed in the *Titanic* disaster—had been asked by the remaining brothers to sign an agreement waiving any participation in profits that might arise from the operation of the "Chuquicamata Prospect" mining venture in Chile. Having been assured that this was an exploratory project with unquantifiable chances of success, both men, whose ties with the family company had been loosened but not severed in recent years, duly signed the proffered document. That same day, with the ink hardly dry on the paper, the other brothers entered into an agreement to operate the Chile mining properties in the name of Meyer Guggenheim's Sons.

Within a matter of months it became apparent that the Chuquicamata Prospect was a fantastically rich source of copper. According to Baldwin, between 1912–16 it had realized $60 million in profits, and his client was asking the court to award him one sixth of these profits as recompense for the shameful manner in which he had been misled. For it was Baldwin's contention that the brothers had deliberately taken advantage of William's admitted business naivete. Fully cognizant of the mine's true worth, they bilked their own flesh and blood out of his rightful share.

A. Fraud Denied

Through their counsel, Samuel Untermyer, the defendants denied any attempt to defraud. William, they admitted, did lack business acumen which had contributed towards his departure from the company in 1900, but that had not been the main reason. That lay in his alleged profligacy. According to the defendants, despite having an annual income of $250,000, their errant brother was permanently strapped for cash; further evidence, they said, of his unfitness for commerce. And yet, in 1912, for no apparent reason, they had readmitted him to the company on a non-participatory basis.

As Baldwin soon made plain, it required little flexing of the imagination to wonder if such largess owed more to financial rather than familial considerations. He forced Daniel to admit that, at the time of the signing, he and his brothers were in possession of a report indicating that the Chuquicamata Prospect was very rich indeed; a suspicion borne out by a second survey, in 1913, filled with glowing predictions that the mine would last for forty-one years and produce millions of tons of top grade copper.

Next, Baldwin called Pope Yeatman, a mining engineer, and his testimony was devastating. In 1911, he went to Chile to search out mineral deposits for the Guggenheims. He sent back a stream of information, and there could be no doubt that his preliminary reports on the Chuquicamata Prospect, highlighting the fantastic abundance of its copper reserves, was on Daniel's desk long before the January 4, 1912 agreement.

B. Settlement Rumors

With rumors of a settlement in the air, the judge called Baldwin and Untermyer into his chambers. Baldwin wanted to introduce the Yeatman report which, he claimed, substantiated William's story. An already dire situation for the defense slid downhill even faster when, suddenly, Baldwin obtained a second report from Yeatman in which he called the Chuquicamata Prospect "the greatest known copper deposit in the world." Once Baldwin studied the figures that were being bandied about in this report, he at once threatened to increase the claim for damages to $26 million.

On June 26, 1916, the trial was brought to an abrupt conclusion. "For personal reasons," said a triumphant Baldwin. Publicly he was reticent about claims that a settlement had been reached. Off the record an associate told eager reporters that a deal was in the offing and that William Guggenheim would not accept any less than $5 million.

The exact settlement details were never revealed. And neither was the size of Baldwin's fee. Some put the figure at $500,000; others insisted it was closer to a million. The most commonly quoted sum is $800,000. What is certain is that, allowing for the corrosive effects of inflation, no lawyer in history has been so well recompensed for a single week in court.

Until his premature death in 1923, Stephen Baldwin reigned supreme among the civil litigators of his time. He was a colossus of the courtroom, blessed with every gift that Nature could bestow, a large handsome man, unfailingly courteous, and with a quickness of wit that could reduce his opponents to limp silence. Above all, he had the enviable and rare ability of being able to hack away the dross of a case to reveal its essence. And when it came to presenting that essence to a jury, Stephen Baldwin had no superiors and very few peers.

OTHER NOTABLE CASES:

Jeannie Mitchell (1903); William Gaynor v. Theodore A. Bingham (1912); Edward Grout (1916); John Dillon (1919); David Lamar (1921)

Melvin Belli
(1907–1996)

I. Career

Melvin Belli did not believe in understatement. From the tips of his snake-skin cowboy boots, up past the double-breasted suits with red silk linings, to the halo of snowy-white marcelled hair that crowned his head, there was not an inch of him that had not been expressly prepared for public consumption. He lived his life in the spotlight, appearing to love every minute, and like most publicity hounds, he thrived on controversy. Belli was prepared to take on the world. Coca-Cola, General Motors, and the Hershey chocolate company were just a few of the global giants he tackled in a career that began in the Great Depression and ended four years shy of the millennium. In that time he made and lost millions of dollars. He also left a trail of wives behind him. About the only constant in his life was an unswerving belief in his own ability.

"I don't know if there are any better lawyers than I am," he once declared, "but I'd dispute it if anyone said so." It was this brash arrogance that kept Melvin Belli in the headlines and made him one of the very few lawyers whose name transcended the courtroom and was recognized all across America and beyond.

Melvin Belli in his San Francisco office.
(AP Wide World)

In 1954 *TIME* magazine dubbed him "The King of Torts," because of his phenomenal success in liability and personal injury cases. But there was more to Belli than just a hunger for multi-million dollar settlements; after all, this was a lawyer who had learned his trade representing death row inmates in San Quentin.

He was always unconventional. In 1933, fresh out of the University of California's Boalt School of Law, he joined a federal program set up to study the effects of the Depression on America's poor. Belli volunteered to travel the country as an indigent, jumping boxcars and getting first-hand knowledge of how vagrants really lived. His findings were written in a report that was later used as the basis for nationwide transit relief programs.

It was soon after this that Belli, at the behest of a Catholic priest, undertook to provide counsel for the inmates of San Quentin. It was harrowing work. Early on he watched two of his clients die on the gallows. The memory never left him. Later, as technology advanced, he lost others to the gas chamber.

There were triumphs, though. When one inmate was brought into court on charges of murdering a fellow prisoner, Belli, demonstrating the flair for showmanship and vivid exhibits that lasted throughout his career, confronted the jury and flung open a bag of knives that had been confiscated from other prisoners. After inspecting this murderous collection of hardware at close range, jurors had little trouble accepting Belli's plea that his client had acted in self-defense, and duly acquitted him.

Gradually, he weaned himself off criminal cases, turning more to personal injury and medical-malpractice suits. He was especially tough on incompetent doctors, a toughness dictated by his belief that the medical profession did such a poor job of policing itself. And he could be just as tough on big business, as one San Francisco company found out to its cost.

II. Jeffers v. Municipal Railroad (1942)

One day in 1941, a young mother named Katherine Jeffers stepped off a San Francisco trolley bus on Market Street and got knocked down by another passing streetcar that sheered off her right leg, just below the knee. In an instant Katherine Jeffers' life had changed forever. The wife of a navy commander, she hired Belli to represent her interests and he filed suit against the Municipal Railroad. In the ensuing court case, Katherine Jeffers was awarded damages amounting to $65,000, a sizable sum for the time, and one which prompted attorneys for the railroad to move for a new trial on grounds it was excessive. Nobody, they argued, had ever received such an amount for the loss of a leg; furthermore, recent technical advances in the construction of artificial limbs had made such a disability far less onerous than in previous times. Weighing these considerations in tandem, the judge set aside the verdict as excessive.

Belli went to trial again. This time, aware of what to expect, he came armed with something far more compelling than mere argument: he brought an exhibit. All eyes were on Belli as he hefted the bulky parcel into court, and they continued watching his every move as he placed it on the counsel's table in front of him. By this time the young attorney's use of bizarre exhibits was becoming a regular feature of his civil cases, and chief railroad counsel, John Moran, studied the L-shaped parcel closely indeed, wondering what it contained. Wrapped in cheap yellow wrapping paper and tied with string, the parcel stood out like a beacon on Belli's desk. Most courtroom spectators recognized the yellow paper as the kind used by butchers to wrap meat; though none could hazard a guess as to what Belli was up to.

All through that first day Belli did nothing to satisfy that curiosity. He would move the parcel from time to time, always with a maximum of fuss, yet without ever making an attempt to open it. The next day, it was the same; he brought the package into court, arranged it on his desk, and once again ignored it. By the third day, interest in the parcel had neared a climax and Belli sensed that the psychological moment was near.

This peak coincided with Moran's peroration. It was sensitive, of course, and filled with the railroad company's regret that this young woman had lost a leg, but, he argued, sentiment should never be allowed to influence the size of the award. Not only were the previous damages excessive, claimed Moran, but with one of these marvelous new artificial limbs Katherine Jeffers could do almost anything she would before: drive cars, play with her kids, swim, dance with her husband, make love.

To hear Moran say it, Katherine Jeffers had suffered little more than a mild hiccup in her life. Jurors switched their gaze to the defendant. Demurely dressed in a gingham frock, she had been positioned by Belli so that her one good leg, encased in a black stocking, was toward them.

And all the time Belli kept manipulating the parcel in front of him.

A. All Is Revealed!

At last it was his turn to speak. Drawing on his massive reserves of showmanship, he rose slowly to his feet and reached for the mysterious parcel. At first the knots in the string seemed to give him trouble, but when a court bailiff hurried forward brandishing a pair of scissors, Belli graciously waved him away, insisting that he could untie the knots by hand. With a final wrench, the string came free. So too did the yellow butcher's paper. Belli let it fall to the floor. Everyone in court craned for a better view. But all they saw was a second layer of yellow paper. Belli was in no rush. Another half a minute passed. Only when he had milked the incident of every ounce of dramatic effort, did he suddenly rip off the paper, turn to the jury and raise aloft the contents of the parcel. Moran began to mouth an objection, then fell silent.

Clasped in Belli's hand was Katherine Jeffers' artificial limb!

Somehow Belli seemed to invest the prosthesis with all the menace of a medieval weapon of war. The lacings and the straps hung loose, the metal joints glistened wickedly, as he first thrust the cold plastic shaft out before him, then approached the jury.

"Ladies and gentlemen of the jury," he said, getting ever closer, "this is what my pretty young client will wear for the rest of her life. Take it." He dropped the prosthesis into the lap of the first juror, who jolted backward with shock. "Feel the warmth of life in the soft tissues of its flesh, feel the pulse of blood as it flows through the veins, feel the marvelous smooth articulation of the new joint, and touch the rippling muscles of the calf."

At Belli's request the jury began to pass the artificial limb along the row, each examining it closely. "Don't be alarmed by all the harnesses and straps and creaking of the metal," Belli implored. "My client is no longer frightened. She will wear this artificial leg for the rest of her life in exchange for that limb which God gave her as she started life, and which she should have worn for the rest of her days."

For twenty minutes the jury-members pored over the prosthesis, weighing Belli's words, hardening their expressions toward the team of strangely mute railroad attorneys. When they had finished, Belli took the artificial limb and passed it to the judge. He examined it, too.

Throughout the trial Katherine Jeffers had shown immense dignity and fortitude: she wasn't asking for sympathy, she just wanted justice. When the jury came back, they gave it to her—$100,000, a massive increase over the first trial. Moran again asked for a new trial on grounds of excessive verdict. Considering the outcome of this ill-judged venture, he was probably relieved when the judge denied the motion.

This trial marked a quantum leap forward in the assessment of damages for personal injury. Ten years earlier, loss of leg below the knee might have been

Jack Ruby, center, confers with his attorneys Melvin Belli, right, and Joe Tonnehill, left, in District Court in Dallas, on January 20, 1964. (AP Wide World)

worth $1,000, $5,000, maybe $10,000. Belli's revolutionary use of exhibits changed all that. His argument was profoundly simple: inflation had driven the price of everything through the roof, but the courts had not kept pace. They were still computing the cost of human pain and suffering based on figures almost half a century old.

It was a string of successes like this that established Belli's reputation in the 1940s and 1950s as a fighter for the underdog. In one memorable suit, he persuaded a woman claiming damages for botched breast surgery to strip off in the judge's chambers, while jurors, one by one, trooped through to personally view the grotesque outcome. The poor woman's red-faced embarrassment gave way to wracking sobs during her ordeal but Belli won the suit, and with it a $115,000 award.

B. Courtroom Revolution

Other attorneys soon began to ape Belli's courtroom tactics, but none could match the master. He wrote about his successes in numerous books, explaining his methods. Belli set the ground rules, introducing the use of dramatic evidence such as graphic photographs of accident victims and charts specially prepared for juries that are today's standard procedure in civil damage suits. And how many lawyers had a skeleton affectionately known as "Elmer" hanging up in their office, ready to be offered into evidence should the need arise?

In later life Belli concentrated almost exclusively on civil actions. A rare interruption to this lucrative regimen came in 1964 when he defended Jack Ruby, the killer of alleged presidential assassin Lee Harvey Oswald. After that it was back to the big time and the big bucks, handling such diverse clients as Mae West, Errol Flynn, Tony Curtis, Lenny Bruce, Mickey Rooney, Lana Turner, Muhammad Ali, and the Rolling Stones.

Over the course of his long career, Belli claimed to have won more than $350 million for his clients, and it was this kind of money that enabled him to live the California good life and brought him a $7 million mansion overlooking San Francisco Bay.

In his final years Melvin Belli began making headlines for all the wrong reasons, with allegations of malpractice and an acrimonious struggle with the IRS over claims that he owed millions in back taxes. In 1988 he divorced his fifth wife Lia, moved out of the family home and onto his 105-foot yacht, "Adequate Award," where he lived alone with four dogs, feeding them from bone china and sterling silver.

In December 1995, Belli's law firm filed for bankruptcy protection, ironically because of costs the firm incurred in representing clients who sued Dow Corning Inc. over breast implants. Just over six months later, on July 9, 1996, Melvin Belli died of pneumonia. Among the bequests in his soon-to-be hotly contested will was an amount of $10,000 for his collection of dogs.

In his heyday, San Francisco tour buses used to slow down outside Belli's ground-level office on Montgomery Street, where he was a daily fixture until well past his 80th birthday. Tour guides used to announce him as "the most famous lawyer in America." Beyond the window, surrounded by the souvenirs and memorabilia from too many trials to remember, this son of a California pioneer family could be seen at his desk studying his latest case. Always attuned to the importance of good public relations, Belli would give the tourists a wave and the bus would carry on its way, with most of the passengers wondering what a nice white-haired old man like that was doing with a skeleton hanging up in his office.

OTHER NOTABLE CASES:

Chester Bryant (1938); William Riker (1944); Maureen Connolly (1955); Jack Ruby (1964); Winnie Judd (1969); Martha Mitchell (1974); Soledad Brothers (1975)

Roy Black

(1945-)

I. Career

Each year a tidal wave of money floods into South Florida. Most flows up through the Caribbean and into the glittering tower-blocks of Miami, where soberly dressed executives in wood-paneled boardrooms decide on its future destination. Clean or legitimate funds get absorbed into the local economy; the rest—the unwashed element—goes in search of a good laundering service, usually offshore. No one knows for certain how much is involved but suffice to say that no other financial market in America reaps such an annual harvest. Vast wealth naturally attracts big commerce, and such commerce naturally attracts lawyers, thousands of them. Within the tri-county area of Dade, Broward, and Palm Beach, are to be found some of the ablest attorneys in the nation. Most make a good living, some make a fortune, others crop up regularly in the media, a tiny few fall by the wayside, disgraced and disbarred. Picking one's way through the South Florida legal minefield is no task for the faint-hearted, but those that do are almost universal in the opinion that, when it comes to mastering every aspect of modern-day trial procedure, Miami's Roy Black is in a league of his own.

Colleagues and foes alike know him as "The Professor," due in part to his studious, academic appearance, but mainly because of the teaching duties he performs at the University of Miami. Passing on the knowledge gleaned from countless trials to each fresh generation of aspiring hopefuls is something he does very well. For the awestruck students, it is their chance to glimpse the workings of a superlative legal brain. They recall his kid-glove handling of Patricia Bowman during the William Kennedy Smith rape trial—surely one of the deftest, most intelligent cross-examinations yet caught by the TV cameras—and wonder if such subtlety can be acquired, or if it is merely the preserve of a fortunate few. Those searching for clues to Black's ability could do worse than study his cosmopolitan background, an unusual mix of the traditional and the progressive, the kind that often makes for a well-rounded personality.

He was born in New York, but grew up an only child in Stamford, Connecticut. When his mother remarried, Black gained an English stepfather who was not only the great grandson of the Archbishop of Canterbury, but also an ex-Formula One Grand Prix racing driver. It was this paradox of parental identities that first led to Black attending a strict English preparatory school, and then, at age fourteen, his being whisked off to the tropics when his stepfather decided to uproot the family and move to Jamaica. Black spent much of his youth in the Caribbean, honing his watersport skills to such a pitch that he was offered a swimming scholarship at the University of Miami, where he eventually entered their law school. A brilliant pupil, when he took the Florida bar exam in 1970, he received the highest score in the state.

Like many fledgling lawyers intent on a career in criminal law, Black cut his teeth at the public defender's office. And it didn't take him long to get noticed. When he was just thirty-years-old, and handling a caseload of the indigent and the dispossessed, *The Miami Herald* named him one of the ten best criminal defense lawyers in the city. No mean feat, considering that Black was toiling daily in one of America's most competitive markets, switching from folksy country lawyer to hard-nosed cross-examiner in the twinkling of an eye.

During his time at the public defender's office, Black demonstrated the same workaholic tendencies that hallmark his current activities. There was little

Roy Black and William Kennedy Smith talk with reporters outside the Palm Beach County Courthouse. (AP Wide World/Kathy Willens)

or no time for leisure pursuits. Much later, after he had achieved a string of triumphs in private practice, he explained the reason for his success: "I think that somebody once said that the will to win doesn't mean anything because everybody wants to win. It's the will to prepare to win that makes the difference." Fellow Miami attorney, H.T. Smith, who worked alongside Black during his public defender days, sees it in simpler terms, describing Black as "someone who takes on all challengers and challenges." At the end of 1982 there came a trial that would provide Black with the biggest challenge yet in his career, and springboard him into the front rank of American trial lawyers.

II. Luis Alvarez (1983)

As cases go, it was depressingly routine for South Florida in the early 1980s: a black male, shot by a white police officer in dubious circumstances. What raised this killing out of the ordinary was the civil unrest it ignited. For two days and nights the Overtown district of Miami was a combat zone, as angry residents took to the streets to vent their belief that Miami Police Department officers were operating a shoot-to-kill policy against blacks. Before the riot was over, one person lay dead, almost thirty were injured, and thirty-seven had been arrested.

Against this backdrop, on February 16, 1983, a grand jury indictment was returned against twenty-three-year-old Luis Alvarez, a Miami police officer with eighteen months experience, charging him with manslaughter. By the time he came to court, Alvarez was the fourth South Florida officer in less than a year to stand trial for killing a black man.

This was the first time that Black had defended a police officer on such serious charges, and his immediate response was to file a motion requesting a change of venue. Alvarez, he said, could not get a fair trial in Miami. Six times Black tried to have the trial moved, and six times he was denied.

Undeterred, he applied himself to the critical task of picking a jury. This is an area in which Black excels and, like his predecessors in the three previous trials involving police officers, he succeeded in seating an all-white panel. As was his right, he twice used preemptories to excuse black jurors, a ploy that did little to alleviate suspicion in the black community that he was trying to pack the jury with sympathetic ears.

Black is renowned for his ability to bond with a jury, and this was evident in his opening statement, "Luis Alvarez is accused of doing nothing more than his duty," he quietly told the jury, initiating a theme that he would hammer home every chance he got during the trial: without the selfless dedication of officers like Luis Alvarez, the streets of South Florida would become a jungle. It was an appeal to emotion more than reason, because, as Black knew all too well, much of the evidence against his client cast a considerable pall over Alvarez's version of events.

A. Arcade Shootout

It had started at a video arcade in Overtown on December 28, 1982. Official reports had Alvarez entering the arcade with Louis Cruz, a police trainee, intending to demonstrate how to conduct a routine check. While there he had reason to suspect that Nevell Johnson, a twenty-year-old black man who was playing a video game, was carrying a concealed weapon. During the search Alvarez's service revolver accidentally discharged, killing Johnson.

That was the official version. Other witnesses at the arcade didn't see it that way at all, claiming Alvarez had gunned down Johnson for no reason at all. Even Sergeant Robert Hill of the Miami PD conceded that Alvarez had flouted rules by cocking his gun, holding it too close to Johnson's head, not giving Johnson clear commands, and not communicating directly with Patrolman Cruz. Neither was Cruz much help to the defense. He testified that Alvarez noticed a suspicious bulge in the rear waistband of Johnson's slacks, and asked what it was. When Johnson replied that it was a gun, Alvarez ordered Cruz to remove it. When Cruz, covered by Alvarez, reached for the gun, Johnson turned sharply, and Alvarez fired without hesitation. Cruz further admitted that at no time did he see Johnson go for the gun. Yet another state witness, firearms expert Harry Sefried, said the gun had been modified to fire more quickly.

The prosecution's abrupt decision to rest caught Black momentarily off-guard. "In a six-week trial, one would expect to see more than one day of eyewitness testimony," he said. If he was blind-sided then it was only temporary, for he immediately went onto the offensive. Alvarez, he said vehemently, had fired only in self-defense because Johnson *did* go for his gun.

On the stand, Alvarez echoed this claim. "I shot because I had to shoot." He denied state witness claims that he had deliberately cocked his gun and that he was a "macho" policeman. Using Black as victim, Alvarez acted out the deadly events in front of the jury, holding the revolver alongside Black's head. It was gripping stuff. Some idea of his agitation can be gauged from his statement that, at the time, he thought Johnson had actually fired at him. Only later, on picking up the pistol, did he realize that the victim had not fired a shot.

On March 8, 1984, Black finished his summation and the case went to the jury. At 9:17 P.M. on March 15, they returned a verdict of not guilty. Miami exploded. By midnight, 200 arrests had been made, and things only got worse. Throughout the weekend 550 people were taken into custody, yet no deaths or serious injuries were reported.

Black was soon in the position of having to defend his victory. Of the four officers charged with killing black men, only one was convicted, prompting calls to eliminate all-white juries in such cases. Black decried the proposed jury selection changes as short-sighted. "I have been involved in hundreds of criminal trials, and one of the most important rights the defendants had was to use their preemptory rights to exclude people who would not admit their prejudices." He cited a case in which he used a preemptory challenge to get a white woman off a jury that was trying a sixteen-year-old black youth for murder. The youth was acquitted by a jury with two black members.

B. Rise to the Top

On September 11, 1984, U.S. Attorney General Stanley Marcus announced that Alvarez would not be charged with civil rights violations. This closed the book on Luis Alvarez, but it was to be the opening chapter on Roy Black's rise to the top. Along the way he handled politicians, businessmen, and drug barons. In 1989, he defended yet another Miami police officer, William Lozano, who had killed a black motorcyclist and his passenger in a roadside incident. This episode triggered a further three days of rioting in Miami. Black was unimpressed. "I'm going to do whatever I can to get this guy off," he said. "If the town burns down because of it, so be it."

On this occasion, Black lost first-time around only to have Lozano's conviction overturned on appeal. At a second trial in Orlando, the jury returned an acquittal. A week later, on June 2, 1993, Black, who had had his client declared an indigent, billed the city manager's office for his services. They blanched at the figures—$710,000—and said it would have to be renegotiated.

The size of his fees soon became a topic for comment. Miami prosecutor, Michael Band, remarked acidly, "Roy represents people who can afford him . . . You're basically innocent until proven broke."

The numbers kept growing. By the end of the 1980s, he reigned supreme in the South Florida retainer league. After his defense of William Kennedy Smith, he faced the howling media to answer reports that Smith's defense had cost $2 million—of which Black's fee was rumored to be at least $250,000. Black smiled insouciantly, "My mother told me never to mention money in polite company."

"How about talking about it with us?" fired back one reporter.

"Touché," the elegant lawyer replied, before retiring gracefully, probably to read his next brief.

OTHER NOTABLE CASES:

William Lozano (1989); William Kennedy Smith (1991); Alex Dauod (1992)

Vincent Bugliosi
(1934-)

I. Career

Whatever else Vincent Bugliosi does or achieves in his life, history will remember him first and foremost as the prosecutor who put the Manson Family behind bars. Because of their sheer scale and horror, the Manson atrocities have assumed a unique position in the American psyche, and it is sometimes easy to forget that at no time were multiple convictions a foregone conclusion in this most convoluted of trials. When the world read *Helter Skelter,* Bugliosi's epic account of the case, it gained an insight into the legal jousting that had dogged the prosecution. And it came to appreciate how one man refused to be sidetracked by defense shenanigans, determined that justice would prevail.

The son of a grocery store owner in Hibbing, Minnesota, who later worked as a conductor on the railroad, Bugliosi's background is grass-roots Midwest, and conservative to the core. While he was still young the family moved to California. All that West Coast sunshine did wonders for Bugliosi's backhand, so much so that after graduating from Hollywood High, the only court that interested him was one with tramlines and a net. His prowess with a tennis racket earned him a scholarship to the University of Miami. Only later did he take up law at UCLA. In 1964 he was president of his graduating class, and that same year joined the Los Angeles County District Attorney's Office.

His flamboyant courtroom manner—a legacy, he says, of his Italian ancestry—made him a natural stand-out in the courtroom, and he soon found bigger and more sensational cases passing across his desk. Before the Manson case he had tried a dozen homicide trials, winning convictions in all, and by the time he left the DA's office the box-score read 105-1 in felony trials. On top of his duties as deputy DA, he was a professor of criminal law at the Beverly School of Law, Los Angeles.

In Hollywood the nexus between the movie industry and the legal profession has always been strong, and as Bugliosi's fame grew, so did his marketability. His exploits provided the impetus for Robert Conrad's starring role in the TV series "The DA." By then, though, Bugliosi had forsaken public office for private practice. During his eight-year career in public service he tried close to 1,000 felony and misdemeanor court and jury trials. It was the kind of record that allowed F. Lee Bailey (q.v.) to dub him "the quintessential prosecutor."

But Bugliosi was no one-string fiddle. And it was as a defender that he gained arguably his greatest triumph, in a case so bizarre as to almost defy belief.

II. Stephanie Stearns (1986)

For years Malcolm "Mac" Graham had dreamed of quitting the California corporate treadmill and sailing the Pacific in his thirty-eight-foot ketch *Sea Wind.* When a company upheaval led to his redundancy in 1974, he decided that the moment had come at last. His wife, Eleanor, known as "Muff," was less enthusiastic, and only abandoned her busy San Diego social life with the greatest reluctance. With widely differing expectations the couple set sail. Their destination was a minuscule island called Palmyra, a deserted atoll approximately 1,000 miles south of Honolulu.

For several months it was idyllic. Palmyra turned out to be everything that Mac Graham had expected, a tiny scrap of paradise set in an endless azure ocean. Even Muff found it bearable. Until the visitors arrived.

Buck Walker and Stephanie Stearns were polar opposites to the well-organized and well-provisioned Grahams. Walker, an ex-jailbird, was fleeing an arrest warrant in Hawaii; Stearns was a hippie with bad taste in men. They had limped into Palmyra aboard a leaky wreck called the *Iola,* half-starved and broke. At first the Grahams took them under their wing, but soon animosities began to surface.

Emotions climaxed on the night of August 28, 1974. While Mac Graham was making his usual weekly radio call to an acquaintance in Hawaii, the friend overheard a commotion. Graham explained wearily that it was just Muff and Stephanie "making a truce." Then he hung up. He has never been heard from since.

In October 1974, repainted and renamed, the *Sea Wind* sailed into Ala Wai Yacht Harbor near Waikiki. At the helm were Walker and Stearns. They explained to skeptical coastguard officers that the Grahams had drowned while fishing on Palmyra, so they had commandeered the *Sea Wind*. Minus any trace of the Grahams, all the authorities could do was level charges of theft on the high seas. Walker, with his lengthy record, received a ten-year sentence: Stephanie got two years and a term of probation.

And there things languished until 1981 when a beachcomber on Palmyra discovered an aluminum trunk that had washed ashore. Inside were the remains of a female skeleton that was later identified as Muff Graham.

By now Stearns was back in San Francisco, working at a travel agency: Walker was still in prison. Both were charged with murdering Muff Graham. After years of wrangling they were granted separate trials in San Francisco, because of local hostility against them in Hawaii. On June 11, 1985, after a two-week trial, Walker was convicted of murder and later sentenced to life imprisonment.

But had Stephanie Stearns been an accomplice to that murder?

The Government said yes, and in February 1986, she faced her accusers at the Federal Courthouse in San Francisco. By this time Bugliosi had taken charge of her defense, drafted in by Stearns' original lawyer Leonard Whitehead, who ordinarily specialized in political cases.

Early on Bugliosi gained a significant victory, when visiting Judge Samuel King from Honolulu dismissed one felony count of murder, citing government failure to prove that a killing was committed during the act of stealing the Grahams' boat.

A. Remains Identified

Despite being wholly circumstantial, the evidence against Stearns was deadly. A string of expert witnesses left no doubt that the remains found in the trunk belonged to Muff Graham. According to one pathologist, the jawbone had been split from the skull by something like a hammer, and the skull showed signs of having been burnt, possibly by an acetylene torch, one of which happened to be aboard the *Sea Wind*. The arms and legs had been deliberately broken to make them fit into the trunk.

The prosecution contended that all the murderous activities—fetching the acetylene burner and two aluminum chests from the *Sea Wind*, burning the bodies in the containers, loading a 180-pound man and a 120-pound woman onto a rubber dinghy, then sailing that dinghy into a lagoon where the bodies were dumped, before returning to the *Sea Wind*—had to have been carried out with Stearns' knowledge.

Other visitors to the island testified to the tension that existed between the Grahams and their often hungry neighbors. The ham radio operator repeated his story about a "commotion," until Bugliosi pointed out that when first questioned by the FBI in 1974 he had made no mention of the so-called disturbance. Further doubts were introduced when it was found that no tapes or notes had been made of Stearns' original interview with the coastguard.

At the end of a strong prosecution case, Bugliosi was faced with the eternal dilemma that plagues every defense attorney—should he put his client on the stand? Whitehead said no. And yet, gut instinct told Bugliosi that if she didn't testify, Stearns was doomed.

She had already been troublesome, acting flirtatiously in court, frustrating Bugliosi at every turn. For his client to have any chance at all, Bugliosi had to concede that Walker had murdered Muff Graham, and yet Stearns not only insisted that Walker was innocent, she also refused to accept that Muff Graham had been murdered.

Eventually, Bugliosi's reasoning won out and Stearns took the stand. She described how she and Walker were intending to leave Palmyra and had been invited aboard the *Sea Wind* as dinner guests of the Grahams on August 30, 1974. When they arrived the boat was deserted. Walker explained that the Grahams, who had gone fishing, told him to help himself if they were not back. All night long the hungry couple gorged themselves on the food and drink. When they awoke the next morning, there was still no sign of the Grahams. Later that day, a search of the tiny island revealed their capsized dinghy on a beach.

"Sharks were everywhere," said Stearns. "They were very aggressive. I knew there was no hope of finding them." That day she and Buck moved onto the

Sea Wind and began eating the food. She denied all knowledge of any killings, and under Bugliosi's gentle cajoling came across as gullible to the point of recklessness. She admitted lying repeatedly on Buck's behalf. First, during her interview with the coastguard in Hawaii, and again at the boat theft trial, when she said they had towed the *Iola,* and that it foundered on a reef. Now, she confessed that Buck deliberately sank the *Iola.*

She was questioned about several entries in her diary. One, dated September 4, 1974, read: "We grow fatter and fatter . . . The dogs feast on corned beef hash." (A reference to the dogs that she and Walker kept). "The words seem callous, I know," she said, wiping away a tear. "After they were gone I didn't think it was so bad to eat their food." She claimed that Walker had threatened to abandon her on Palmyra unless she went with him.

B. Stunning Revelation

For assistant U.S. Attorney Elliott Enoki, the notion of Stephanie Stearns as gullible dupe was total nonsense. She was, he said, a woman of the world, who, after getting out of jail in 1975, began associating with yet another fugitive, someone fleeing a California murder charge.

This revelation, entirely unexpected, stung Bugliosi into a massive damage limitation exercise. In a superb peroration he argued that the prosecution had attempted to shift the burden of proof onto the defense, forcing Stearns to prove that she "did not commit the murder."

"What we have here is a real murder mystery," he said, "one that only Agatha Christie could conjure up in her most inspired moments." He conceded that Muff Graham had been murdered but pinned the entire blame on Buck Walker, "a human monster." Comparing his client and Walker to Adolf Hitler and Eva Braun, he said that no one had ever accused Braun of any crimes just because of her association with Hitler.

Rather less colorfully, Bugliosi argued that Stearns' own actions provided the strongest evidence of innocence. In 1974 she had told the authorities where she found the dinghy, and seven years later the remains of Muff Graham turned up in that very place. Why, asked Bugliosi, with all of the Pacific available, dump the bodies in the lagoon? Answer—because Walker acted alone. He not only had to hide the bodies from the authorities, "he had to hide them from Stephanie Stearns." Bugliosi concluded, "There is only one verdict consistent with the evidence in this case, and that is a verdict of not guilty—not guilty!"

Vincent Bugliosi, left, the chief prosecutor of Charles Manson and three female followers in the Sharon Tate murder trial, holds a conference with a defense attorney, Paul Fitzgerald, outside the Los Angeles courtroom. (AP Wide World)

For days the jury deadlocked at 6-6. Then it was 10-2. Finally, after further instructions from the judge, on February 28, 1986, they found Stephanie Stearns not guilty.

Malcolm Graham's body has never been found.

Like all top trial attorneys, Bugliosi realizes the value of a strong summation. By trial time he usually has at least half of this critical argument already sketched out. As soon as he receives a case, he finds the strengths and weaknesses, and steers everything toward that all-important final address to the jury. Everything is down to preparation.

Nowadays, Bugliosi is almost as renowned for his writing as for his cases. *Helter Skelter* remains the biggest selling true crime book ever and while that remains on the shelves, he is unlikely to shed the title of the "prosecutor who nailed Charlie Manson."

OTHER NOTABLE CASES:

Palliko & Stockton (1968–69); Perveler & Cromwell (1969); Charles Manson & Others (1970)

Marcia Clark
(1953-)

I. Career

No lawyer in history has been more heavily scrutinized than Marcia Clark. From the moment it was announced that this thirteen-year veteran of the Los Angeles District Attorney's Office was to lead the criminal prosecution of O.J. Simpson, every aspect of her life and appearance was placed under the media microscope and analyzed as if she were some kind of laboratory specimen. Her hair, her dress, her manner of speaking, her courtroom tactics, her marital situation, her fitness as a mother, all these and more became the stuff of endless speculation across America. So, too, were her occasional flashes of pique, most often when she felt that opposing counsel had transcended the limits of acceptable advocacy and lurched into the realm of personal attack. For a woman who had previously guarded her privacy with a messianic zeal those eighteen months were merciless. Most onlookers could only marvel that the outbursts were so sporadic.

She was always tough. And unconventional. Back in the early 1980s hard-bitten L.A. cops became used to the rookie prosecutor hanging round after hours, matching them drink for drink, able to hold her own in any cussing contest. They

Clark during the O.J. Simpson double-murder trial in Los Angeles. (AP Wide World/Vince Bucci)

recognized a kindred spirit. Right from joining the DA's office in 1981 there was no second-guessing Clark's courtroom stance: right behind the victims of crime. To her uncluttered way of thinking bad guys deserved to be behind bars, and the really bad guys should be on death row.

Opposing lawyers are mixed in their opinions of Clark. "Marcia is an outstanding trial lawyer, effective in all phases of trial work," says Barry Levin, a defense attorney who fought Clark in a lengthy murder trial and lost. "She is what a prosecutor should be. She is tough, she is fair, and you can't intimidate her. I know. I tried to do that many times." Others, less complimentary, describe her as "hard as nails" and "in your face." None, though, at least before the Simpson case, ever questioned her ability.

She was raised as Marcia Kleks in a liberal Jewish home in Berkeley, California. It was a nomadic family and by age fourteen, she had lived in Texas, Washington, Michigan, Maryland, Staten Island, as well as all over California. Two years spent studying theater at Susan Wagner High in New York, where she worked after hours in Greenwich Village boutiques, were followed by a return to California and UCLA, to study dance and political science. There she met and married Gabriel Horowitz, an ex-member of the Israeli air force and professional backgammon player.

After graduating in 1974, she put all career aspirations on hold to travel the international backgammon circuit with her husband. Although the venues were exotic—Monaco, London, Puerto Rico, and Las Vegas—the marriage was not, and the couple divorced. (Tragically, years later Horowitz was accidentally shot in the head and crippled.) Clark resumed her studies, and in 1979 received her law degree from Southwestern University School of Law. That same year she passed the bar exam. Twelve months later she married Gordon Clark, an employee of the Church of Scientology, who later switched careers and moved into computer programming. The following year, after an unhappy flirtation with private practice—she was mortified when a motion she had drafted for an obviously guilty client succeeded and he was set free—Clark joined the prosecutor's office, taking the step that would make her the most famous female lawyer ever.

During the next decade she learned to juggle the disparate roles of wife, prosecutor, and mother with uncommon skill, and as her career zoomed ever upwards, she began to take on higher-profile cases. One of the most notorious came in 1991. It involved a relatively recent development in criminal activity, one that Clark loathed, and one that gave her a vivid opportunity to remind the judicial system that, no matter how fine the point of law, at the heart of every criminal act there is a victim.

II. Robert Bardo (1991)

Stalking is amongst the most cowardly of crimes. When practiced over a period of months or years, this form of remote-controlled sadism can wound more deeply than any physical weapon and leave its victim scarred forever. Rebecca Schaeffer wasn't even that lucky. At the end of her two-year ordeal, this young actress lay dead in a pool of blood. According to the twisted rationale of Robert Bardo, a nineteen-year-old ninth-grade dropout from Tucson, Arizona, and the man who ended Schaeffer's brief life, it was all her fault, the penalty she paid for being "callous."

Bardo's obsession with Schaeffer began in 1987, when she was co-starring in the TV sitcom *My Sister Sam*. Simple fan worship soon escalated into a non-stop torrent of letters and messages to the studio where she worked. It was not an exclusive affair. During this same period Bardo also doted on singer Debbie Gibson, and in 1988 had traveled to New York City, intent on tracking her down. When thwarted in that desire, Bardo contented himself with a visit to the Dakota, the ultra-rich apartment block overlooking Central Park, home to John Lennon and the site of his murder in December 1980 at the hands of another so-called "fan."

Bardo was a man who took his stalking seriously, reading everything he could about the subject. It was from one such magazine article that he learned how a fellow stalker, who had attacked his victim, had hired a private investigator to find out the victim's address. The Anthony Agency in Tucson was equally efficient. Bardo showed them a photo of Schaeffer, said he was an old friend who wanted to get in touch, and handed over $250. All it took was a couple of phone calls to the California Department of Motor Vehicles (DMV) and Bardo had Rebecca Schaeffer's home address. It was that easy.

Bardo's campaign soon entered a more sinister phase. He wrote his sister in Knoxville, Tennessee, saying that if he could not have Schaeffer then nobody would. And then, on the morning of July 18, 1989, Schaeffer received a phone call from Bardo. He was, he said, less than two blocks from her home at 120 North Sweetzer Avenue, in the Fairfax district of Los Angeles.

At 10:15 A.M. a neighbor heard a single gunshot, followed by two loud screams. He ran out to find the twenty-one-year-old Schaeffer lying dead in the doorway of her apartment. Down the street a yellow-shirted man could be seen trotting unhurriedly away.

The next day Tucson police were astonished when a man they had arrested for running wildly on the freeway, apparently intent on committing suicide, suddenly blurted out that he had shot Rebecca Schaeffer. For good measure Bardo also revealed where L.A. police might find the yellow shirt and a copy of *Catcher in the Rye*[1] that he had dropped shortly after the killing.

---

[1]*Mark Chapman, after murdering John Lennon, sat quietly reading this very same book while waiting to be arrested.*

As part of a plea-bargain that automatically excluded the death penalty, Bardo agreed to a non-jury trial. The presiding judge was Dino Fulgoni, a former prosecutor, and to him fell the task of evaluating the evidence and deciding whether Bardo was guilty of first- or second-degree murder. The distinction was critical. If convicted of murder in the first-degree, Bardo faced life imprisonment without parole: a second-degree conviction opened the disturbing possibility that he could be back on the streets in a matter of years.

Marcia Clark, prosecuting the most important case of her career, was determined that Bardo should spend the rest of his life behind bars. Equally determined, Stephen Gallindo, Bardo's public defender, refused to enter a plea for his client, protesting the fact that Bardo had been brought to Los Angeles without an extradition hearing. Furthermore, he claimed that his client's obsession stemmed from a long-standing mental illness, requiring treatment, not permanent incarceration.

A. Cold-blooded Murder

Clark would have none of it. Bardo was, she said, fully aware of his actions. "After years of fantasizing about violence," he had committed a murder that was the result of "carefully controlled, methodical planning." It was hard to dispute her reasoning, especially when presented with the chilling evidence of a videotaped confession made by the defendant just after his arrest.

The confession contained a graphic account of his visit to Schaeffer's apartment. When Schaeffer answered the door, Bardo asked if she had received a postcard he had sent her recently. According to Schaeffer, she not only remembered the card, but spent several minutes discussing it with him. Then, when it was time for him to leave, she shook his hand, smiled and said, "Please take care."

Some time later, realizing that he had forgotten to give her a letter and a CD intended as a gift, he retraced his steps and again knocked at the door. This time Schaeffer was in her bathrobe. "Hurry up," she said. "I don't have much time."

"I thought that was a very callous thing to say to a fan," said Bardo. He then described pulling a .357 magnum out from the shopping bag he was carrying and firing, mimicking her screams—"Why? Why?"—as the bullet struck its mark. Yet he claimed to have "almost had a heart attack" when he heard on TV that night that she was dead; odder still from someone who now said that his "mission" was complete.

Clark, quite naturally, pointed out that the sole basis for this alleged course of events was the defendant himself. Underpinning everything, she said, was Bardo's desire to achieve notoriety. She read from a letter that he had written to his sister: "I have an obsession with the unobtainable, and I have to eliminate [something] I cannot have." Conceding that this behavior was bizarre, Clark agreed that "a normal person does not stalk and murder someone he does not know," but she told Fulgoni, "this was less than full psychosis" and therefore deserving of a first-degree conviction.

Corroboration for Clark's view came from a security guard at Warner Brothers. John Egger testified that Bardo had turned up one day with a giant teddy bear and flowers, asking to see Schaeffer. He seemed very lucid. Such was Bardo's despondency when refused admittance, that Egger gave him a ride back to his Hollywood hotel. As he dropped him off, Egger suggested to Bardo that he return to Tucson. Bardo had said, "I'm going to do that."

On October 29, 1991, Judge Fulgoni rejected defense claims that Bardo had acted impulsively after a brief encounter with Schaeffer, and found the defendant guilty of first-degree murder. The killing, he said, had been planned and willful, and he had not ruled out the possibility that Bardo may even have ambushed Schaeffer as she answered the door.

On December 20, 1991, Bardo was sentenced to life without parole. As a result of this trial, access to DMV records has been restricted.

After the trial Judge Fulgoni paid tribute to Clark's performance, particularly the manner in which she cross-examined Dr. Park Elliott Dietz, a nationally renowned psychiatrist with long experience in obsessive disorders. It was his contention that Bardo had been mentally ill since childhood, and had been raised, along with a disturbed brother and other siblings, by a mentally ill mother. Clark accused Dietz of passively accepting Bardo's version of the killing, without challenging its veracity.

"It was quite obvious," said Fulgoni, "that when [Dietz] would try to divert her, she not only understood what he was doing, but she was way ahead of him and had a counter tactic."

B. Concern for the Victim

Such preparation has seen Clark through sixty jury trials, of which twenty have been homicides, and also there is that concern for the victim. One lawyer, Madelynne Kopple of Santa Monica, recalls the double homicide in a drug deal gone wrong, the sort of case where nobody usually cares too much about the victims. Clark's vivid re-creation of the last twenty minutes of the victims' lives secured death sentences for both killers. And all while she was eight months pregnant! "She gave the most powerful argument I ever heard to a jury," said Kopple.

Clark continues to surprise. Visitors who stare askance at the life-sized Jim Morrison poster on her office wall and another of Jimi Hendrix at her home, tend to overlook the eighteen-hour days that are regularly part of her calendar. It is a grueling schedule, one that exacts a toll. In January 1994, she separated from her husband. The ensuing custody battle for their two children, fought against the backdrop of O.J. Simpson, was a bloody affair. But she survived, and in November 1995, she signed a $4.2 million book deal to tell her side of the "trial of the century." Agents said the frenzied auction for the manuscript was inspired because Clark is "a single mother, a professional battling sexism in the workplace," someone who has "coped with the media onslaught." And only Marcia Clark knows just how great those pressures really are.

OTHER NOTABLE CASES:

James Hawkins, Jr. (1985); Albert Lewis & Anthony Oliver (1993); O.J. Simpson (1995)

Johnnie Cochran, Jr.
(1937–)

I. Career

Fifteen years before becoming one of the most recognizable lawyers on earth, Johnnie Cochran was at the wheel of his Rolls Royce, cruising down Sunset Boulevard, just minding his own business, when he spotted a flashing blue light in the rear-view mirror. Unaware of having committed any traffic violation, he pulled off to the side and waited for the two Los Angeles Police Department officers to approach. In the back seat of Cochran's car were two of his children, and it was for them that he was concerned, especially when the tone of the officers made it brutally apparent what they thought of Afro-Americans driving such luxurious vehicles. Cochran let the aggressive questioning run on for a few minutes, then flashed the card that showed him to be the third highest ranking officer at the L.A. District Attorney's Office.

The transformation was instant. These cops had been caught harassing one of the city's most powerful black figures, and both knew what that could mean to their immediate job prospects. Falling over themselves in embarrassment, they waved the millionaire attorney on his way. Cochran, blood boiling with rage, drove off.

In this grotesque vignette can be found the raison d'être for Cochran's life: a quest for justice. He knows, at bitter personal cost, the problems of being black in America. "When you drive down the street," he explains, "and people say, 'Johnnie, please save Michael.' 'Please save O.J.,' there is a sense that if it can happen to Michael Jackson or O.J., it can happen to any of us."

For more than thirty years he has made his livelihood out of fighting for the underdog. If nowadays more of those underdogs wear designer suits than they once did, then that is merely a reflection of Cochran's prowess. He is extraordinarily good at what he does. And he never stops fighting.

That struggle began for Cochran in his hometown of Shreveport, Louisiana. When he was five years old his sharecropper parents moved to California, eventually settling in Los Angeles. After working in the shipyards, his father became a salesman for Golden State Mutual Life Insurance, then one of the nation's largest black-owned companies, eventually rising to become chief of the company's training program. His improved economic status allowed him to move his family out of the public housing projects and into the West Adams neighborhood of Central L.A. Reaping the benefit of the changing socio-political climate, Johnnie Cochran became one of the first black students at Los Angeles High School, and then at UCLA and Loyola Law School, from where he graduated in 1962.

Defense attorney Johnnie Cochran Jr. addresses Superior Court Judge Lance Ito during the Simpson double-murder trial. (AP Wide World/Reed Saxon)

For the next three years he flexed his legal muscles in the Los Angeles city attorney's office. As one of very few black lawyers on the staff, besides his normal caseload, he also investigated and prosecuted racism and corruption in the LAPD. The problem seemed endemic and in the wake of the 1965 Watts riots, Cochran quit the attorneys' office to join the law firm of Gerald Lenoir. One year later he represented the family of black motorist Leonard Deadwyler, shot dead by a police officer during a routine traffic violation, in a civil action against the LAPD. Cochran didn't win the televised trial but his fiery courtroom performance marked him as a man with a future.

Over the next decade he confirmed that promise, amassing a considerable private practice, mostly built around suing various California municipal authorities. Then came a brief stint in the L.A. County District Attorney's Office as the top administrator. In an ironic twist, he was Gil Garcetti's boss for a while. Garcetti, who would later endure a brutal public mauling for his perceived mismanagement of the O.J. Simpson trial, was originally fulsome in his praise of Cochran, describing him as "a great trial lawyer." (What he thought later is less well-documented!)

By 1980 Cochran was back working for himself and once again making huge media waves. This time it concerned Cal-State-Long Beach football star Ron Settles, arrested for speeding and later found hanging in his jail cell in the Signal Hill Station. Though authorities insisted that Settles had committed suicide, Cochran forced an exhumation and new autopsy which suggested that Settles had probably died from a choke hold.

This case marked a watershed for Cochran. "It was the most remarkable civics lesson you could learn," he later noted. "When I started trying cases thirty-one years ago, you would be almost held in contempt of court if you said a police officer was lying." Not only did Cochran win a $760,000 award for the Settles family—at that time the largest-ever settlement in a cell death case—he was instrumental in bringing about a change in police procedure, as LAPD officers were barred from employing the carotid choke hold.

In his career Cochran has enjoyed so many victories that attempting to isolate just one for closer examination poses considerable difficulties. However, in 1989, he not only pulled off what many still regard as his greatest triumph, he may well have saved his client's life, as well.

II. Todd Bridges (1989)

For several months police had kept the vacant house on the 300 block of West 65th Street in South-Central L.A. under tight surveillance. Emergency calls to that address were such a common occurrence that no one was unduly surprised when, on February 2, 1989, reports came in of a shooting at this suspected "crack house."

The first officers on the scene found Kenneth "Tex" Clay, 25, lying on the ground, bleeding from eight bullet wounds. Miraculously none of the injuries was life-threatening and Clay was able to furnish a description of his two assailants and the car they were driving; so good, in fact, that officers were able to make arrests almost at once.

It wasn't the first time that actor Todd Bridges had been picked up following an incident at the West 65th address. Just one week earlier he had been arrested there on suspicion of possessing cocaine. For twenty-three-year-old Bridges this was just the latest glitch in an incident-packed life. Between 1978–86 he played the part of Gary Coleman's brother on the hit TV series *Diff'rent Strokes.* The program made him famous and put money in his pocket: the trade-off came in that he couldn't stay out of trouble with the law. In 1983 he was arrested in Beverly Hills for carrying a loaded, concealed .45 handgun in his car. After pleading guilty, he was fined $240 and given one year's probation.

A marked escalation in his erratic behavior came in 1986 when he was charged with making a bomb threat against a San Fernando Valley car customizer. The dispute had arisen after the businessman demanded payment in advance before carrying out any work on Bridges' car. (In recent weeks the actor had bounced numerous checks and the dealer wanted to be sure of getting his money.) When a homemade pipe bomb exploded in a car belonging to the dealer, Bridges was arrested and subsequently given a one-year jail term. Because of possible deleterious effects on his show business career the sentence was suspended, although he was fined $2,500 and ordered to make $6,000 restitution.

But with this latest incident, he was staring at serious jail time. That probability increased further still when Harvey Duckett, his companion at the time of the shooting, agreed to testify against Bridges after pleading no contest to charges of being an accomplice to the attack. Facing charges of attempted murder, Bridges made his first smart move in years—he hired Johnnie Cochran to defend him.

Cochran's first course of action was to get Bridges' bail reduced from $2 million to half that sum. Next, Cochran examined the case against his client. It seemed watertight: not only were there two strong eyewitnesses—one of whom was the victim—but the .22 handgun used to shoot Clay was found in Bridges' car, together with a shotgun.

Todd Bridges, right, stands with his lawyer, Johnnie Cochran in a Los Angeles courtroom as it is announced that the former child actor is acquitted of attempted murder and attempted voluntary manslaughter. (AP Wide World/Nick Ut)

A. Drug-Binge Blackout

Confronted by these stark realities, Cochran did some hard thinking. The defense he eventually presented to the jury was that Bridges had no recollection of the shooting; it had been carried out in the haze of a four-day drug binge. Far from being a reckless gunman, said Cochran, his client was a victim, someone to be pitied, not despised, and someone in desperate need of help.

The chief prosecution witness was Kenneth Clay himself. He testified that he had been taking care of the vacant house on behalf of a friend, and that he had gone there because neighbors had phoned him to report "burglars." Upon his arrival he found Bridges, whom he knew, with another man. When he threw them out, trouble erupted. Clay said that the two men kicked open the door and

Bridges burst in, firing rounds from a small caliber handgun, all the while yelling, "I told you, Tex! I told you, Tex!" Clay described hearing the hammer click on the empty chamber. Then the two attackers fled.

Fortunately for Cochran, Clay was a man with a past. Back in his homestate of Texas he had convictions for drug offenses, and it was easy to portray him as a "crack house janitor" who had become enmeshed in a drug-related argument.

When Bridges took the stand he was suitably vague. Asked by Cochran if he had shot Clay, he replied, "I don't think I did. I don't know who did." Then came a vivid and harrowing account of a fourteen grams a day coke-habit that had left him so "based-out," he could not remember what had happened.

Bridges told his story well, and on November 7, 1989, he was acquitted on charges of attempted murder and attempted involuntary manslaughter. A mistrial was declared when, after further deliberation, the jury deadlocked 8-4 in favor of acquittal, on a third charge of assault with a deadly weapon. Jurors later said they found the state witnesses "hard to believe" and decided to give Bridges the benefit of the doubt. His girlfriend, Becky San Felipo, announced that Bridges intended "to work on an anti-drugs . . . campaign for kids."

"Todd feels great," Cochran confirmed to waiting reporters. "What we've said all along is that Todd, after going to the house, blacked out . . . Needless to say, Todd has a lot of faith in the American system of justice." Describing the trial as "a cathartic experience" for an actor who had found himself "at the depths of life" during Christmas 1988, Cochran went on to illuminate Bridges' situation at the time of the shooting. "He was out of work and wanted to kill himself . . . this incident was the culmination [of his drug-abuse.]"

B. Steering the "Dream Team"

Once again, Cochran had displayed his remarkable knack of making jurors see things his way. It was a talent that the whole world came to marvel at in the O.J. Simpson trial. Never before had such a high-priced gathering of legal talent been assembled in one courtroom; yet few doubted whose hand was at the tiller, steering the "Dream Team" to victory.

As the most successful Afro-American lawyer ever, Cochran has lectured in America and Europe on the significance of race in the courtroom. He is uniquely qualified on the subject. In his career it is estimated that he has won $40-43 million from various Californian municipalities in police cases, and this had inevitably provoked complaints that he's after money and nothing else.

For all those who sneeringly deride Cochran as nothing more than an avaricious "gun for hire," there is the case of Elmer "Geronimo" Pratt to set the record straight. In 1972 this member of the Black Panthers was charged with shooting a white schoolteacher during an $18 robbery at a Santa Monica tennis court. Pratt claimed he was in Oakland at the time, attending a meeting of the central committee of the Panthers. Despite the fact that the victim's husband had identified another suspect as the gunman, Pratt was convicted and sent to prison for life. Cochran insists that Pratt was framed by the FBI as part of a policy to destabilize radical political groups.

There is no money in this case and precious little kudos, and yet Cochran continued to toil for Pratt's release. On June 21, 1997, Pratt was released from prison after Superior Court Judge Everett Dickey ruled that prosecutors had improperly witheld information at the original trial. A decision on whether to retry Pratt has yet to be made. As he says, "It taught me that you can work within the system and believe in it, but if the government wants to get you, they can go out and get you," adding in that familiar steely tone, "It also taught me that you never stop fighting."

OTHER NOTABLE CASES:

Leonard Deadwyler (1966); Philip Eric Johns (1975); Patricia Diaz (1992); Reginald Denny (1992); Michael Jackson (1993); Tupac Shakur (1995); O.J. Simpson (1995)

Roy Cohn
(1927–1986)

I. Career

At the time of his death in 1986, Roy Cohn was one of America's best-known lawyers. For the most part his fame came not from courtroom achievement, though there was plenty of that, but through the society pages. Whenever New York's glitzy power-crowd converged on Studio 54 for yet another soiree, Cohn always made sure he could be seen schmoozing with the likes of Calvin Klein, Andy Warhol, Truman Capote, and Frank Sinatra, trading gossip, filing away little nuggets of information for future reference. It was this thirst for self-promotion that fueled his success. Ever since first surging to prominence in the anti-Red hysteria that swept postwar America, Cohn had never been off the front pages for long. Few lawyers have courted the press quite so assiduously, first to make his reputation in the legal field, then to heighten public awareness of him as an "insider." Later, those same media contacts would rally to Cohn's side and help him suppress details of his outlandish private life.

How he managed to avoid personal catastrophe is a mystery, but somehow Cohn journeyed unscathed through one of the darkest periods of American history, much of which he helped to create. By the time he joined Senator Joseph

Roy Cohn seated at his desk. (UPI/Corbis-Bettman)

McCarthy's Committee on Un-American Activities in January 1953, the young prosecutor from Manhattan was already a practicing and not always discreet homosexual. But none of this seemed to matter. Television was good to him, making his earnest, pinched face famous from coast-to-coast. Viewers readily identified with his strident anti-Communist rhetoric, and came to regard Cohn as a valiant bulwark against the onslaught of Marxism, pushing him toward the kind of celebrity that he craved.

Perhaps because he was born and brought up in comfortable surroundings, he was unconcerned by the mere accumulation of money. Sure, he enjoyed the trappings of wealth, but he enjoyed the power more. His father was Albert Cohn, who after a career in the Bronx District Attorney's Office was raised to the New York Supreme Court as a judge. With such a pedigree, Roy Cohn took his choice of career for granted and entered Columbia University.

Thanks to the abbreviated wartime curriculum, he hurtled through college and law school in just over three years, and was admitted to the bar at the remarkably young age of twenty-one. Even his detractors had to admit, it was an astonishing display of intellectual rigor. Such precocity did not go unnoticed and in 1948 he was made an assistant U.S. attorney. With his active social life and fondness for tittle-tattle, he became a favorite of newspaper reporters who recognized good copy and always kept Cohn's name well to the fore in articles about up and coming young lawyers.

Just two years later came the chance that Cohn hungered for.

II. Ethel & Julius Rosenberg (1951)

Few incidents have so jolted American self-confidence as the dramatic 1949 revelation that the Soviet Union had exploded a nuclear device. Ever since World War II, Washington had confidently reassured its citizens that America's lead in the nuclear arms race was unassailable, at least for the next decade. Now, in just four years, that advantage had been eradicated. Many in the security services concluded that such an erosion must have resulted from one thing and one thing alone—someone had betrayed U.S. atomic secrets.

As events unfolded, this proved to be a remarkably accurate diagnosis, for it soon became clear that Communist sympathizers in the West had been passing sensitive information behind the Iron Curtain since 1944 and possibly earlier. In America an exhaustive FBI inquiry led to the doorstep of David Greenglass, a laboratory technician at the top-secret Los Alamos research installation in New Mexico, where the first atomic weapons had been designed. Under interrogation he admitted drawing crude diagrams of critical parts of the atomic explosive device, which he then passed to his brother-in-law, Julius Rosenberg, for onward transmission to the Soviet Union. As the FBI net tightened, other members of an apparent spy-cell—Rosenberg's wife, Ethel, and his former college classmate, Morton Sobell—were also arrested and charged with conspiracy to commit wartime espionage.

Their subsequent trial, coming at the peak of the anti-Communist hysteria in post-war America, provided Roy Cohn with his first opportunity to shine on the international stage. Although just an assistant on the prosecution team, he soon became its most effective and visible member. (He later boasted that he had written chief prosecutor Irving Saypol's opening and closing statements, and mapped out the overall strategy.)

An incident early in the trial highlights Cohn's ruthless pragmatism. It involved a surprise witness, Max Elitcher, an acquaintance of the Rosenbergs, who, although an avowed Communist, agreed to testify against them because he did not approve of spying. However, he wanted it stated that he was still a Communist party member. Cohn, unable to countenance a self-confessed Marxist testifying for the government, hurriedly entered into negotiations with the lawyer who had found Elitcher, O. John Rogge. After some prodigious arm-twisting by Cohn, Rogge went back to Elitcher. The two men talked in private for an hour. Finally, Rogge emerged to announce, "Max has left the Communist Party."

Cohn's air of gloating accomplishment sickened some onlookers. If many found his conduct of the trial hard to stomach, others suspected a hidden agenda. Cohn was acutely conscious of the fact that many of those under scrutiny for alleged Communist sympathies were Jewish; some felt that, being Jewish himself, he was driven by a subconscious urge to redress the balance. Only this, they argued, could explain such zealotry.

A. Ferocious Attack

Whatever the motivation, Cohn pursued his prey like a hungry jackal. Not everything was a clean catch and kill, though. Many government officials were wary of him, fearing he was a loose cannon, a suspicion enhanced by his performance when he conducted the direct examination of Greenglass, who by this time had agreed to give evidence for the prosecution. Although Greenglass had been carefully schooled in his responses by anxious prosecutors, Cohn was unable to keep him to the script. In his eagerness to please, Greenglass began blurting out rambling and irrelevant responses to Cohn's questions. Anxiously, Cohn sought to steer the wayward witness back on the desired track. "What else [did Julius Rosenberg want?]"

At last, Greenglass remembered the plot "He told me to write it up, to write up anything I knew about the atomic bomb."

Cohn breathed a sigh of relief as he finally got the answer he had been desperate for. But that night he had to endure a savage roasting from his colleagues, most of whom thought he'd nearly blown it. Writing years later, Cohn recalled those momentous events in rather a different light. "I knew that I was twenty-three years old, and this in itself was pretty dramatic, for here I was standing alone without props or assistants. . . . I was a twenty-three-year-old kid up there against the world and I knew that my youth was the key to the drama . . . As I concluded the two-day direct examination of Greenglass without tripping once, I took my seat at the government table. Suddenly I was in the limelight. I did more than accept it. I liked it."

On a technical level Cohn's trial conduct was masterly. Not once, throughout two days of questioning, did he refer to a piece of paper. He always despised lawyers who lugged heavy cases into court and only spoke after consulting reams of documents. "I do have a retentive mind," he said, "but I think things out in advance. I . . . do not need notes."

Other aspects of Cohn's trial performance were less laudable. He campaigned to bug Julius Rosenberg's cell in order to get a recording of his voice for a government witness to identify. Cohn's denial of this charge, "When I prosecuted the Rosenberg case . . . at no time did I ever order or use a mail interception or wiretap," pointedly neglects to mention that this was only because his superiors had already vetoed the suggestion.

As it transpired, there was no need for such misconduct. Both Rosenbergs were sentenced to death and Morton Sobell received thirty years imprisonment. Cohn wallowed in his triumph, so pleased at the outcome that he gleefully invited friends in to hear the sentencing.

While the weight of evidence suggests that Julius Rosenberg and Sobell were guilty, doubts at the time about Ethel's guilt have persisted to the present day. Cohn gave short shrift to such circumspection. He always maintained that Ethel was the driving force behind the spy ring. "I never had any doubt, not only about her guilt, but I feel she was the strong one among the two of them and belonged in that case as much as he did, if not more."[1]

Nor was he in any doubt that the Rosenbergs got what they deserved. "There are lots of things in my younger life as a prosecutor—the McCarthy hearings, for instance—that I might have done differently, but the Rosenberg case is one thing I have never had two seconds' doubt about."

---

[1]*In 1997, Aleksander Feklisov, the KGB agent who "ran" the Rosenberg ring, refuted all allegations of Ethel's involvement.*

B. Bar Investigation

Fallout from the Rosenberg trial continued to haunt Cohn. Rumors that he had privately lobbied trial judge Irving Kaufman for exemplary death penalties refused to go away, and in 1977 led to an investigation by the American Bar Association. When their report exonerated Cohn, critics alleged he had been pulling strings behind the scenes again.

It was an accusation leveled against Cohn throughout his career. Few attorneys have wielded such political clout. How much of this was real or imagined is unimportant; all that mattered was the perception, and the perception was that Roy Cohn mattered.

His prominence during the McCarthy hearings led to a huge and lucrative upsurge in other civil litigation cases. Some called him a shameless opportunist, an accusation often leveled against the super-successful, but in Cohn's case the charge is undeniably valid. He was a great user of people. Clients were his entree into the gossip columns of the New York press; so that when he found himself fighting off disbarment proceedings following a 1963 accusation of perjury, all he had to do was pick up the phone and call *The New York Times* or *The Wall Street Journal* to get favorable headlines. Right to the end his legendary media connections bailed him out.

And it was during the 1960s that he needed all the help he could get, as he spent most of the decade defending himself against a litany of charges. Scandal, too, was an ever-present nightmare, and how much he relied on his close friendship with FBI Director J. Edgar Hoover, to paper over the more dangerous cracks in his public facade, is unknowable.

Through it all, Cohn prospered. In later years he drew accusations of sloppiness and unpreparedness, too ready to fall back on the hope that his magnetic personality would carry the day; whilst others pointed to his tendency in civil litigation to avoid trial at all costs, always believing that he could negotiate everything. Cohn put most of the criticism down to jealousy.

Professionally, he dodged the slings and arrows with the surefootedness of a mountain goat, but one thing he could not fight were the consequences of his riotous lifestyle, and on July 22, 1986, he died from AIDS-related cancer.

Earlier, mention was made of Cohn's pragmatism, and it was a trait that never deserted him. When, late in life, he applied for membership of the Connecticut bar, he leered to an office colleague, "When I take the ethics exam, I'll read the questions and whatever I would do, I'll put down the opposite answer." He was joking but only just. Roy Cohn had built his life on moral ambivalence. He knew that his actions were often wrong but he didn't care. With this incredible man, the end not only justified the means, it *was* the means.

OTHER NOTABLE CASES:

Bon Ami Co. v. Tel-A-Sign Inc. (1962); Iva Schlesinger (1966); Dewi Sukarno (1974); Anthony Salerno (1986)

Grant Cooper
(1903–1990)

I. Career

Had it not been for a bout of wretched seasickness, it is entirely possible that Grant Cooper might never have pursued the law as a career and the American courtroom would have been deprived of one of its premier performers. After dropping out of high school in his hometown of New York and a succession of odd jobs that appeared to be going nowhere, Cooper signed on with an oil-tanker bound for California. That voyage passed off well enough, but soon afterwards the young sailor found himself literally all-at-sea, caught in the kind of stomach-churning storm that brings about a radical reappraisal of one's suitability for the nautical life.

He couldn't wait to get back on terra firma, and when an uncle, himself a lawyer, invited Cooper to join the profession, the young man jumped at the opportunity. Because he lacked a high school diploma, his enrollment at Southwestern University was contingent upon his maintaining a grade average of at least eighty-five-percent. Shrugging off this arduous burden like it wasn't there, Cooper graduated from law school in 1926 and went straight into practice. One year later he was admitted to the California bar, having already won several criminal defense cases. At that time, bar membership was not a mandatory requirement for lawyers practicing in some courts.

After a period in private practice, he served as Chief Deputy District Attorney of Los Angeles, and later became assistant insurance commissioner for California. His early career was eventful, and not always for the right reasons. In the early 1940s he helped L.A. mayor Fletcher Bowron rid the city of a gambling syndicate. However, electronic eavesdropping methods were used to gather evidence and Cooper and others were indicted by a grand jury. The wiretapping was subsequently ruled legal and the indictments dropped.

Like many prosecutors who have sent men to their death, Cooper came to question the effectiveness of capital punishment, feeling that it failed to deter murder. Certainly one particular California couple was in no way deterred by the thought of a trip to San Quentin's green chamber, as they planned what became the most sensational murder to hit the Golden State in decades.

II. Bernard Finch (1960)

At some time before midnight on July 18, 1959, Barbara Finch was gunned down outside her home in West Covina, a suburb of Los Angeles. Within days her estranged husband, handsome, wealthy Dr. Bernard Finch, aged forty-two, and his young mistress Carole Tregoff, were arrested and charged with murder. The police believed that Finch, unwilling to divorce Barbara and lose at least half of his estimated $750,000 fortune, had engineered a homicidal conspiracy with the twenty-year-old Tregoff.

With its brooding overtones of sex, money, and hired hitmen, the case attracted huge headlines all across America. Once in custody, Tregoff spurned her former lover, and the couple were represented by separate counsel in court, with Cooper acting for Finch. In these volatile surroundings, Finch needed someone to defuse the situation, and nobody did that better than Cooper. With his movie-star handsome looks and commanding presence, he skillfully insinuated himself between his client and the jury, acting as a lightning rod for criticism, deflecting suspicion.

The first state witness was Marie Anne Lindholm, the Finches' Swedish maid. She had been indoors on the night of the shooting and had heard Barbara scream. Running out, she saw Finch, gun in hand, standing over his semi-conscious wife. After a struggle Barbara broke free and ran off, with Finch in mania-

Dr. Bernard Finch (far left) and Carole Tregoff talk with her attorneys in court. (AP Wide

cal pursuit. Moments later Marie heard a shot. She then called the police.

Cooper's cross-examination of Lindholm was gossamer light. There was no attempt to bully the young Swedish woman—her confusion was apparent to all—instead, he handled her quietly and with great consideration, obviously earning the respect and liking of the jury as he did so. In the process he also managed to cast just enough doubt on her recollection of events to make room for the surprise defense that he had prepared, which would be revealed later. First, Cooper had to deal with Marie Anne's claim that Finch had hired "someone in Las Vegas" to kill Barbara.

That someone turned out to be John Patrick Cody, an amiable jailbird who admitted swindling $1,200 out of Finch and Tregoff on the pretext that he would kill Barbara. Even Cooper struggled with this self-confessed thief, liar, and sponger, who, despite all these defects, still made an impact, especially with his claim that Tregoff had declared, "Jack, you can back out. But if you don't kill her, the doctor will; and if he doesn't, I will."

One month into the trial, Cooper at last rose to present the "surprise defense" that had been rumored ever since the trial began. He revealed it through the testimony of his client, Dr. Finch.

A. An Amazing Story

It had all been an accident, Finch explained glibly, caused by Barbara pulling a gun when he and Tregoff had arrived to discuss the divorce. Finch told of disarming his distraught wife, only for her to again grab the gun and run off. When he caught up with her she was taking dead aim at the cowering Tregoff. Finch snatched the gun and attempted to throw it away, only to stare in horror as the weapon discharged accidentally—hitting his fleeing wife between the shoulder blades. Tearfully, Finch brought this overwrought saga to an astonishing conclusion by claiming that, as she lay dying, Barbara had actually apologized for being so foolish as to get herself shot!

In running this defense, Cooper knew he was taking a chance, but Finch didn't miss a trick. He was smooth and he was loyal. By contrast, Tregoff came across as someone out to save her skin at all costs, ready to pile every scrap of available blame on her former lover.

Those who confidently predicted that Tregoff's treachery would send Finch to the gas chamber had reckoned without Grant Cooper. When he rose to make his summation the courtroom couldn't hold all the judges, lawyers, and reporters who wanted to hear him make his ultimate plea. Demand for seats was so great that even Cooper's own wife had difficulty finding a place. Throughout the trial he had demonstrated the skilled actor's trick of making the audience—in this case the jury—focus on him even when others were speaking. Now, he was center stage.

Cooper spoke quietly, in a low voice, balancing cadence and pitch with consummate ease. There were no histrionics, beyond an occasional use of his hands when some particular point needed emphasis. He affected regret that the jury had been so inconvenienced by the state's reliance on the testimony of John Cody. "The cast of characters in the alleged conspiracy wasn't chosen by the prosecution, of course. They are stuck with it . . . Cody was in jail for passing a bad check—that was a one-year sentence—and for breaking out of jail, another

Grant Cooper, chief of the team of defense attorneys in the trial of Sirhan Sirhan, discusses the verdict after the jury found Sirhan guilty of first-degree murder. (AP Wide World)

one-year sentence. He saw a chance for parole." Here, Cooper gave the jury a telling look. But it was in his portrayal of Dr. Bernard Finch, the unhappily married family man, that Cooper really excelled. Under his hypnotic spell, it was not always easy to remember that Finch was on trial for his life and not running for public office.

After eight days of bitter wrangling, the jury announced that they were unable to agree upon a verdict and a mistrial was declared.

A second trial again ended in deadlock, despite an extraordinary admonition to the jury by Judge LeRoy Dawson that they ought not to believe the evidence of either defendant. As the judge railed on, Cooper interrupted constantly, and was twice told to be silent. He was finally cited for contempt of court and later fined $500. Subsequently, the State of California set aside the conviction and reprimanded the judge.

On January 3, 1961, prosecutors tried for a third time to convict Finch and Tregoff. By now much of the earlier sensational coverage had dissipated as other scandals took their place, leaving a markedly calmer courtroom atmosphere. Of far greater importance to Finch was the fact that Cooper, citing pressure of work, delegated his role of defense counsel to an associate. How much this affected the outcome is conjecture, but what is certain is that Finch was convicted of first-degree murder, while Tregoff was found guilty in the second degree. Both were sentenced to life imprisonment.

B. The Price of Murder

Ironically, divorce would have been the cheaper option for the money-conscious physician. The three trials wiped him out financially. Cooper's retainer amounted to $25,000, plus $350 a day for each trial day. In order to cover these fees, Finch signed over his business assets, plus the deeds to his house, his cars, and a powerful speedboat.

Cooper left this case with his pockets and his reputation bulging. A past president and founding member of the American College of Trial Lawyers, he was rarely out of the news for long. In 1969 he was blasted for daring to defend Sirhan Sirhan, the killer of Senator Robert Kennedy; and in that same year he was fined $1,000 for contempt of court and publicly reprimanded by the State Supreme Court for illegally obtaining and using federal grand jury transcripts in the Friars Club card-cheating trial in which he had defended Maurice H. Friedman.

In his later years Grant Cooper tended to avoid the glare of public controversy, and remained in affluent obscurity until his death in 1990.

OTHER NOTABLE CASES:

Maurice Friedman (1969); Sirhan Sirhan (1969); Frank Fasi (1977)

Clarence S. Darrow

(1857–1938)

I. CAREER

No lawyer has been more defined by his courtroom utterances than Clarence Darrow. The millions of words that tumbled from his lips, in hundreds of trials, sound as fresh and as relevant now as the day they were first spoken, and it is for this reason that he remains the greatest American advocate of modern times. Others have matched his passion, some his eloquence, a few his record; none have come close to capturing the aura of nobility that shrouded this crumpled bear of a man. That was Darrow's secret. No matter what the case, he always managed to convey an invincible impression that his was the way of right and enlightenment. The causes that he championed—unions, the abolition of capital punishment, racial tolerance, and anti-Creationism—were not topics guaranteed to win him popularity in every American household, but he knew that if the war for change was to be won, then it would be through a series of small battles, and there was nobody better prepared for a long campaign.

No lawyer has been more publicly loathed. Millions denigrated him as "The Great Atheist," seeing in his shaggy, overhanging eyebrows and beetling gaze the work of the Devil. He preferred to think of himself as an agnostic, yet made no bones about his distaste for organized religion. The seeds of his skepticism were sown early. As a boy growing up near Kinsman, Ohio, his childhood was almost entirely free from dogma. Unusual for the times, neither parent attended church and neither forced religion upon their son. So Darrow grew up, very much thinking for himself. It was a habit he took to the grave.

Academically, there was little to suggest the philosophical giant to come. Two undistinguished years at the University of Michigan were followed by twelve months of law school, then came admittance to the Ohio bar in 1878. Privately, though, it was a different matter. He immersed himself in literature, Russian mostly, devouring a diet of Chekhov, Dostoevsky, and later Gorky, and in these great writers Darrow learned the mastery of words that would dazzle juries from coast-to-coast. Not that there was much call for such talents in his first position, city attorney for Ashtabula, a small town on the shores of Lake Erie. With little crime and even less civil litigation, Ashtabula's primary contribution to Darrow's development was as a place to polish his poker playing skills, and it was not long before he began looking further afield. His gaze fell on Chicago. At that time the city was growing at a frantic pace, with immigrants flocking in from around the globe. In 1887 Darrow joined the rush, and quickly found himself involved in attempts to free the participants in the Haymarket Riots.[1]

Three years later he was appointed city counsel. He also built up a prosperous corporate practice, only to abandon it in 1894 to defend railroad strike leader, Eugene Debs, thus forging his first links with the unions. These lasted until 1911 when Darrow traveled to Los Angeles to defend union agitators, John and James McNamara, on charges of dynamiting public buildings. By pleading them guilty, Darrow saved their lives and ruined his own. His union paymasters were incensed by the verdicts: they wanted martyrs not leniency, and Darrow had denied them. Viciously, America's labor unions turned their back on the man who had been their greatest champion.

This betrayal sent Darrow's career into a sharp decline that lasted until 1924 and the Leopold and Loeb case, when again he was the target of union wrath, this time for defending "two rich kids." The *Detroit Free Press* branded him "a high-priced emotional lawyer who makes a specialty of cheating the gallows."

---

[1]*In 1886, an explosion during a demonstration in Chicago's Haymarket Square killed eight police officers. Four men were later hanged for the outrage.*

Others harped on the fact that while Darrow was saving Leopold and Loeb from the gallows, an equally young murderer, Bernard Grant, was hanged, leading the *Cleveland Plain Dealer* to editorialize, with quite remarkable unoriginality, that there seemed to be "one law for the poor and another for the rich." On one point everyone agreed, though: Darrow's powerful performance in the Leopold and Loeb trial before a single judge silenced all those carping critics who sneered that he was only capable of winning verdicts from gullible jurors.

His reputation restored, Darrow next won acclaim for his 1925 defense of John Scopes, a Tennessee schoolteacher indicted on charges of teaching Darwin's theory of Evolution. This was an ideal forum for Darrow's agnosticism, and his demolition of thrice-defeated presidential candidate William Jennings Bryan on cross-examination has been quoted and requoted enough times not to need further repetition here, save to say that it remains a classic of its kind and would be immortalized in the play and subsequent movie *Inherit the Wind*. One year after this triumph, Darrow was again ruffling establishment feathers, this time in Detroit.

II. Ossian Sweet & Others (1926–27)

On a September evening in 1926 an angry mob converged on the intersection of Garland Street and Charlevoix Avenue in Detroit, outside the home of Dr. Ossian Sweet. Marching under the banner of the Improvement Association (IA), they gathered to protest the fact that Sweet, a successful black physician, purchased a house in what had hitherto been an exclusively white neighborhood. Behind the neatly curtained windows Sweet and his wife were entertaining a group of friends and family to dinner. Then the jeering mob arrived.

As they paraded outside Sweet's house, the mood got uglier, more violent, and soon cries of "Niggers! Get the niggers!" began to fill the night. With the situation deteriorating fast, suddenly a burst of gunfire—some 15-20 shots—rang out from the house. One of the mob fell injured; another, Leo Breiner, was killed. As the crowds scattered, the police moved in. After brief questioning, all eleven people in Sweet's house were arrested and charged with murder.

At first, three local black attorneys handled their defense, but on October 7 the National Association for the Advancement of Colored People (NAACP) wired Darrow, asking him to take charge. When Darrow arrived in Detroit, he raised hopes in the NAACP, only for these to be dampened by reports that some of Darrow's fund-raising speeches since arriving advanced the bizarre concept that slavery, for all its ills, at least introduced blacks to civilization! Those better placed to gauge public opinion hurriedly advised Darrow to set aside the proselytizing and stick to the matter in hand.

He saw the case in simple terms: Ossian Sweet and those present at his house were merely defending themselves. In order to counter this notion, state prosecutors paraded a trail of citizens through the court, all of whom claimed to have witnessed the attack, without having been any part of it. Darrow, dripping sarcasm, lambasted their claims to have been merely innocent bystanders, and compelled each to admit that the IA had been formed only in response to Sweet's purchase of a home in the neighborhood. The drubbing handed out to IA member, Eben B. Draper, was typical. Asked if Sweet's actions influenced his decision to join the IA, Draper shrugged, "Possibly."

"Did it?" pressed Darrow.

"Yes."

"You joined that club to aid in keeping that a white district?"

"Yes."

"At the meeting in the school was any reference made to keeping the district free from colored people?"

"Yes."

"How many people were present at that meeting?"

"Seven hundred," Draper admitted.

A. A Lightning Strike

For the next witness, Darrow was at his most avuncular, lobbing the most inoffensive questions, flattering almost. Once he had been softened up, the witness was caught entirely off-guard by Darrow's sudden shouted question, "Your interest was in keeping out Negroes to maintain the value of your property?'

Blindsided by the transformation, he blurted out "Yes" without really thinking.

Mostly, though, the state witnesses had been well-schooled, parroting the testimony of the local police inspector who denied that there had been a riot,

Clarence Darrow smokes a cigar and reviews his mail. (Library of Congress)

or anything resembling civil disorder, until the shots were fired from Sweet's window. Darrow must have despaired of making any inroads at all, when he was handed a golden opportunity by a fifteen-year-old youth.

"How many people were present?" asked Darrow.

"There was a great crowd—No, I won't say a great crowd, a large crowd—well, there were a few people and the officers were keeping them moving."

Darrow let this pass for a few seconds, allowing the boy to think he had moved on and regain his confidence, before inquiring abruptly, "Have you talked to anyone about the case?"

"Lieutenant Johnson [a high-ranking police officer]."

"And when you started to answer your question you forgot to say 'A few people,' didn't you?"

After a sheepish grin, the lad said, "Yes, sir."

Darrow waved him away contemptuously. "That's all. Step down."

For weeks the trial drifted. At its conclusion, Darrow spelled out the plight of the Afro-American in 1920s Detroit—a ready source of cheap labor for the auto assembly plants, yet denied basic human rights, including the right to live where they wished. No matter how compelling the content of Darrow's speech, it failed to convince everyone, and on November 27, 1926, the jury announced itself deadlocked and a mistrial was declared.

The second trial began on April 19, 1927. On this occasion Darrow spent what was for him an unusually long time on jury selection—more than a week—but by its conclusion he weeded out the more obvious bigots and felt confident of gaining a verdict. He also decided to broaden the range of his attack. Now it was the whole Afro-American race, eleven million people, which was demanding justice. Each day the court was thronged with black spectators, all feeling that their collective fate rested on the seventy-year-old shoulders of this remarkable man.

He did not let them down. The evidence was much as before, but what made the difference was Darrow's summation to the jury. It ranks amongst the most powerful and moving speeches ever made. Shorn of lofty rhetoric and expressed with a compassion that only the stoniest heart could have ignored, at its core throbbed the ever-present reality of being black in America:

"I imagine that they [the defendants] can't rub color off their faces, or rub it out of their minds. I imagine it is with them always. I imagine that the stories of lynchings, the stories of murders, the stories of oppression is a constant topic of conversation. I imagine that everything that appears in the newspapers on this subject is carried forward from one to another until every man knows what others know, upon the topic which is the most important of all to their lives."

B. Pulsating Oratory

Darrow then delivered a gut-wrenching litany of racial abuse, hatred and intolerance, incidents that had blighted every corner of America. He spared no one. When it was done he turned one last time to the jury:

"Gentlemen, what do you think is your duty in this case? I have watched day after day, these black, tense faces that have crowded this court. These black faces that now are looking to you twelve whites, feeling that the hopes and fears of a race are in your keeping. This case is about to end, gentlemen. To them, it is life. Not one of their color sits on this jury. Their fate is in the hands of twelve whites . . . I ask you, in the name of progress and of the human race, to return a verdict of not guilty in this case!"

Then Darrow slumped to his chair, exhausted. For seven hours he held the courtroom spellbound: now it was up to the jury. The next day, July 21, 1927, they acquitted every defendant.

Probably only Clarence Darrow could have won this verdict at this time in America. With simple, bitingly effective words, he almost dared the jury to deny him, in a breathtaking display of the kind of brinkmanship that was part and parcel of his life. By the late 1920s he had reached almost mythic status, touring the country advocating the closed shop and unrestricted freedom of expression, opposing Prohibition and the League of Nations. If the punishing schedule eventually broke his health, then the "Crash of '29" almost finished him off. Beset by money worries, it was mainly to recover his financial stock that he agreed to take the notorious Massie case in Hawaii.[2]

On March 13, 1938, Darrow died in his adopted hometown of Chicago. For two days and nights, crowds filed solemnly past his bier in a funeral home. They came to honor a man whose place in American history, not just that of the courts, is assured. He was opinionated and crusty, and some complained that he rarely laughed, as if burdened by the weight of the entire world. His mood swings were notorious. Someone who knew him well, the writer Lincoln Steffens, once said, "At three o'clock he is a hero for courage, nerve and calm judgment. But at 3:15 he might be a coward for fear, collapse, panicky mentality."

---

[2]*In 1932 American naval officer Thomas Massie and three others were convicted for killing Joe Kahahawai, after a court had been unable to decide whether the young islander and four friends had raped Massie's wife. Although convicted and sentenced to ten years imprisonment, Massie and his co-defendants were freed immediately.*

Anyone searching for an epitaph for Clarence Darrow need look no further than the words he himself uttered at the McNamara trial, when, with tears in his eyes, he stood before the jury and cried, "I have stood for the weak and the poor. I have stood for the men who toil!"

OTHER NOTABLE CASES:

Eugene Debs (1895); William Haywood (1907); McNamara Brothers (1911); Clarence Darrow (1912); Nathan Leopold & Richard Loeb (1924); John Scopes (1925); Cologero Greco & Donato Carillo (1927); Thomas Massie (1932)

Vincent J. Dermody
(1914–1992)

I. Career

It is a curious fact that prosecutors rarely achieve the kind of public acclaim routinely doled out to their opponents at the defense table. Had Vincent Dermody chosen a different path he might well have become one of America's best known lawyers; as it was, he had to settle for being one of the finest prosecutors New York City ever had. All too often state or federal office is just part of a carefully mapped-out strategy, a stepping-stone on the road to further political advancement; for a few like Dermody it is their life's work. When he retired from the New York District Attorney's Office in 1969, he had spent almost three decades trying to put the "bad guy" behind bars. The overwhelming majority of cases he tried were of little significance, other than to the interested parties, but all had to be prosecuted to the full extent of the law, and nobody did this better than Dermody. To see him, expression askance, hand querulously fingering the thin covering of sandy hair, was to witness pure skepticism at work.

Law enforcement was in his genes. He was born in the Bronx, the son of a NYPD police inspector who had charge of the mounted patrol. But there were no silver spoons along the way. Dermody got where he did by sheer hard work. In 1941 Thomas Dewey (q.v.) hired him straight out of Fordham Law School to become part of the famous "Gangbusters," charged with cleaning up New York's runaway organized crime. As an assistant district attorney,he was transferred to the homicide department in 1948.

Working in one of the world's murder capitals made for a hectic caseload during the 1950s, allowing Dermody to work his way steadily up through the hierarchy. When in 1963, a new capital crimes procedure was implemented whereby a jury decided between life imprisonment and the death penalty, he was the prosecutor who won the first decision for executions, against two men convicted of a double slaying in a liquor store robbery. Then came one of those sensational cases that knocks everything else off the front pages.

There is a saying in legal circles: "You can't convict a million dollars." Mostly this is true, but as Vincent Dermody demonstrated, rules are made to be broken.

II. Mark Fein (1964)

On November 8, 1963, the body of Rubin Markowitz, a middle-aged Brooklyn bookmaker was dragged from the Harlem River. He had been shot four times to the head and chest. Inquiries into the deceased's betting activities led detectives first to some prostitutes, then to millionaire businessman, Mark Fein, age thirty-two, who lived on Park Avenue with his heiress wife. It soon became clear that Fein had owed Markowitz $7,200 on a wager, and had been due to settle the obligation on October 10, 1963, the last day that anybody saw Markowitz alive.

Dermody took up the story in a Manhattan courtroom, telling the jury that on that October day, "Mark Fein shot and killed Markowitz in Fein's apartment at 406 East 63rd Street and . . . put his body in a trunk that Fein had purchased in Harlem."

This apartment was not, of course, the plush Park Avenue residence where Fein lived his respectable family life, but another where he indulged in a "second life," among girls and bookies, using a number of assumed names.

Dermody illuminated the defendant's relationship to Markowitz. "He stated that he [knew] the deceased as a bookmaker, and that he had, in fact, seen the deceased sometime between 3:30 and 4:00 P.M. on October 10 at a gas station at about 61st Street and First Avenue . . . and that he had paid him a large sum of money."

After a succession of witnesses passed through the courtroom to testify that Fein and Markowitz had done a great deal of sports betting together, it was time for Dermody to produce his star witness. She gave her name as Mrs. Carmela Lazarus, but after considerable confusion over the numerous aliases she had adopted at various times in her life, the thirty-seven-year-old red-head conceded that she was best known as Gloria Kendall, and this was the name that she testified under.

Dermody came straight to the point. "How old were you when you first started prostituting yourself?" Gloria thought it was probably at about age twenty-one, but had to admit, "I don't really remember."

She revealed how she had met Fein in 1960, "through a stockbroker customer of mine," and from then on saw him once every week or so. Sometimes he would take male friends to her apartment and Gloria would arrange other girls for the occasion, with Fein picking up the tab, "sometimes, $700 a month."

Dermody wanted to know, had Fein ever asked her to lend him money?

"Yes . . . because he had lost a lot of money . . . on baseball. And I said, well, maybe I could loan him something, a few hundred. And he said that would not help much because he had lost $60,000."

Gloria did, in fact, loan him "all my savings that I had," around $1,600. But by borrowing from "two other people" she was able to raise the loan to "close to $3,000."

In September 1963, she said, Fein repaid around $2,000 of the loan. One month beforehand he had leased an apartment on 63rd Street, a hideaway for their assignations, and it was from there that he telephoned her on October 10, 1963. "He said 'I'm at the apartment on 63rd Street, and I'd like to see you right away.'" When Gloria replied that she was busy and tried to put him off, Fein became more urgent, saying, "I can't wait, Gloria. I have to see you right away!"

Mark Fein, arraigned on a homicide charge in the death of Rubin Markowitz, an alleged bookie, stands next to detective Irving Gilmore, who arrested him. (AP Wide World)

A. Body in Trunk

Dermody asked Gloria what she had found at the apartment. "Mark was sat across the room from me, and I sat on the couch. He said to me, 'What do you think is in that case, Gloria?' Well, I said 'I have no idea.' [Then] he said 'It's the body of a dead man, my bookmaker, Ruby . . . I had to meet him this afternoon to pay him the money that we lost on the Series . . . we had words. And I shot him.' He said 'Please, Gloria, help me . . . there's nobody else I can turn to.'"

She described helping Fein to get Markowitz's body into a trunk that the defendant had bought earlier, then accompanying him to a garage where he rented a station wagon. Back at the apartment, "two boys"—friends of Gloria's—carried the trunk down to the station wagon. Leaving Fein on the sidewalk, she and her two friends "cruised around in the station wagon for about half an hour" until they found a "suitable" spot on the bank of the Harlem River, where "all three of us carried the trunk to the edge and pushed it over into the water."

In response, William Kleinman, chief defense attorney, made hay with Gloria's conflicting accounts to police. Had she not, on one occasion, stated that Fein did not kill Ruby, and that she had not seen what was in the trunk? Kleinman wondered if the DA's office had offered anything in return for her testimony?

Gloria lowered her head. "Yes. I was told that there would be three charges that I would have to answer for."

"And when were those charges to be made?" asked Kleinman.

"Whenever the time came that they thought it should be done [sic]."

As Gloria vacated the witness-stand, Dermody realized that this case was going down to the wire. Kleinman had done a first-rate job of undermining her credibility, and it was now up to Dermody to repair his tarnished witness in the eyes of the jury.

He began by spelling out the obvious, "She was the defendant's friend. She was his selection. He sought her out. He went to bed with her. He paid for her favors and paid for the favors she offered his friends. She was good enough for him in the privacy of a bedroom. He knew that he could come to her and she would help him out. She was dependable. It is a cute trick to argue that how can you possibly believe an old whore like Gloria. But this is the defendant's friend. We don't pick and choose the witnesses."

Next, Dermody demolished defense claims that someone as rich as Fein would deign to kill for such a paltry sum. Everyone, he told the jury, even a millionaire, has their breaking point and Fein had amassed total gambling debts of $60,000. It was motive enough.

B. Life in Prison

On November 25, 1964, Mark Fein was convicted of second-degree murder and later sentenced to a maximum of life imprisonment.

This case was a great personal triumph for Dermody and helped secure his promotion to head of the district attorney's homicide bureau in 1966. That same year also saw him prosecuting the killers of Black Muslim activist, Malcolm X. On that occasion, Dermody told the jury that the slaying "was an object lesson to Malcolm's followers, telling them that this is what can happen and will happen." All three defendants were sentenced to life.

On May 22, 1992, Dermody died at Lawrenceville Hospital in Bronxville, New York. The years in harness were long gone, but the legacy lived on. Vincent Dermody showed that public service can be more than a career expedient, it can be something intrinsically worthwhile.

OTHER NOTABLE CASES:

Talmadge Thayer & Norman 3X & Thomas 15X (1966)

Alan Dershowitz
(1938–)

I. Career

Appellate law is not for the thin-skinned. The omnipresent specter of defeat—fewer than five percent of appeals are successful—insures that the attorney who specializes in this arm of the law gets used to a diet of constant rejection and disappointment. Ironically, because those cases that do succeed often generate huge headlines, the public tends to believe that the judicial system is more lenient than is really the case. No one is more aware of this dichotomy than Alan Dershowitz. Since joining the faculty at Harvard Law School, this remarkable attorney and the team he supervises has mounted a whole string of appeals. Most have been refused and go largely unnoticed. Those that succeed end up on the nightly news, or in one extraordinary instance, Hollywood celluloid.

He has been called "the top lawyer of last resort in the country—a sort of judicial St. Jude." Civil liberties mean a lot to Dershowitz and so does the Constitution, and he is forever defending the one and testing the other. With his glittering academic record—at age twenty-eight he became the youngest full professor in the history of Harvard Law School—he could have easily opted for

Dershowitz addresses a symposium at Harvard University's Criminal Justice Institute. (AP Wide World/Steven Senne)

comfortable obscurity in the dry and dusty groves of academia. Instead, his appetite for confrontation has made him one of the nation's most respected and recognized legal figures.

His beginnings were unremarkable, a middle-class Brooklyn upbringing, the son of a hardworking father who ran a store on Manhattan's Lower East Side. It was at Brooklyn College that his superb legal brain blossomed, and from there he went to Yale Law School, where he was first in his class and editor-in-chief of the *Yale Law Journal*. After a short period clerking for Chief Judge David Bazelon and Justice Arthur Goldberg, at age twenty-five he was appointed to the Harvard faculty.

Since that time, besides teaching courses on virtually every aspect of criminal law, civil liberties and constitutional litigation, Dershowitz has taken on some of the most notorious cases in recent memory. He is no starry-eyed idealist, but someone who practices the law by three golden rules: "I never believe what the prosecutor or police say, I never believe what the media say, and I never believe what my client says." Aware that the vast majority of prisoners are guilty, he knows, too, that occasionally, an innocent person falls through the judicial cracks. Most often they are poor, overwhelmed by the enormous financial advantage that the state wields on behalf of its citizens. But not always. . . .

II. Claus Von Bülow (1984)

When Alan Dershowitz first entered the Claus Von Bülow case, one Rhode Island jury and most of America believed that this scion of the Danish nobility had attempted to murder his wife. Only a miracle, it seemed, could prevent Von Bülow from spending the next twenty years in prison, the sentence handed down by the court judge. While on bail he telephoned Dershowitz and asked him to organize his appeal. Dershowitz's knowledge of the prosecution's case stemmed from what he had read in the papers, and it appeared rock-solid.

Around Christmas 1979, Martha "Sunny" Von Bülow, a wealthy Rhode Island socialite, had been taken to the hospital in a coma. Eventually she was discharged without anyone learning the reason for her illness. On December 21, 1980, she again lapsed into unconsciousness and was rushed to Columbia Presbyterian Hospital in New York City, where she remains comatose to this day.

Following a family-inspired investigation, in March 1982, Claus Von Bülow was convicted of having twice attempted to murder Sunny by injecting her with insulin. The evidence of Sunny's amanuensis, Maria Schrallhammer, proved crucial. It had been her discovery of a black bag containing mysterious vials in a closet at the family home, and the subsequent discovery of yet another bag containing a hypodermic needle encrusted in insulin that brought about Von Bülow's downfall.

After reviewing the case notes, Dershowitz agreed to handle Von Bülow's appeal. A short while later, in May 1982, he met noted author Truman Capote. Besides being one of America's foremost writers, Capote was a world-class gossip, someone who moved easily in the circles that Sunny Von Bülow had inhabited. He knew Sunny very well and he astounded Dershowitz with his revelation that she had regularly injected herself with all manner of drugs, which directly contradicted the prosecution's contention that, in the Von Bülow household, only Claus knew how to use a hypodermic.

Independent corroboration for Capote's story came from David Marriott, a streetwise hustler who claimed that he had often delivered drugs to Sunny at the Von Bülow household. What might otherwise have been dismissed as fanciful speculation had to be taken more seriously when Catholic priest Philip Magaldi confirmed in a 1978 affidavit that Marriott had admitted delivering drugs to the Von Bülow home.

To Dershowitz's way of thinking, this suggested the strong possibility that Sunny's coma was self-induced, a hypothesis confirmed by acquaintances who cataloged Sunny's lifetime of drug and alcohol abuse, interspersed with mammoth food binges, a potentially lethal combination for a known reactive hypoglycemic (someone who suffers from low-blood sugar).

Dershowitz was also very suspicious about the insulin-encrusted hypodermic needle, especially when all the medical experts he consulted agreed that the act of withdrawing a needle from human flesh would effectively wipe the needle clean. This raised the suggestion that the needle had been deliberately dipped into insulin in order to create the illusion that it had been used lethally; for what reason, Dershowitz could only speculate.

Rounding out his doubts was a strong suspicion that the state's harvesting of evidence at the Von Bülow residence, in particular the bag that allegedly held the hypodermic, constituted illegal search and seizure. He itemized all of these objections in the longest and most complex appellate brief he had ever written. Filed on March 15, 1983, it ran to more than 50,000 words.

A. Team Goes to Work

While waiting on the court's decision, Dershowitz's eighteen-strong team, drawn from the very brightest of his Harvard students and other lawyers, continued searching for the evidence that would confirm their belief that no crime had been committed. Sunny's coma, they felt, had been a tragic accident, unwittingly self-inflicted, and now ruthlessly exploited by a family determined to see Von Bülow jailed at any price. At stake were millions of dollars. If convicted, Von Bülow would lose all claim to his wife's fortune and it would pass to the children of Sunny's first marriage. Neither they, nor Maria Schrallhammer, had made any attempt to conceal their loathing of the defendant.

Oral argument began October 17, 1983, at Rhode Island Supreme Court, the first time that such proceedings had been telecast. Hints from the bench suggested an antagonism towards this development; nor did they extend a wholehearted welcome to Dershowitz. Many in the deeply conservative Rhode Island judiciary seemed to regard this media-friendly attorney as a carpetbagger, someone who had usurped the status quo. At one point Judge Thomas Kelleher remarked caustically to Dershowitz, "You weren't present at the trial, and it seems to me lots of times in these cases, where somebody comes in as an appellate counsel . . . they argue a better case than might have been tried."

But there could be no second-guessing Dershowitz's logic and on April 27, 1984, the Court announced that it had reversed the conviction and ordered a new trial.

Easily the most significant outcome of this decision, evidentially, was that it now afforded Dershowitz access to notes made at the time of the investigation by the family's attorney, Richard Kuh. These had not been introduced at the first trial, and in a letter Kuh had assured Dershowitz that "there is not a scrap of paper in my files that might even arguably be viewed as exculpatory." This, as Dershowitz discovered, was very much a matter of opinion.

In defense terms the notes amounted to legal dynamite, as even the kindest interpretation of their content cast grave doubts on Maria Schrallhammer's veracity. At the trial she had described finding insulin vials in a black bag before Sunny's second attack. But as these contemporaneous notes showed, she had no idea what the vials contained because, on her own admission, *the labels had been scraped off!* Also, not once did she ever mention insulin, until hearing that Sunny's body contained traces of the drug. In a pretrial hearing on January 4, 1985, Dershowitz got his first opportunity to cross-examine Kuh. The abrasive tone he adopted there was continued in the second trial which began April 25, 1985.

Whereas first time around the defense had been circumspect, here they mounted a full-court press. With Dershowitz pulling the strings off-stage, court presentation was left in the hands of Thomas Puccio (q.v.), fresh from his triumph in the ABSCAM Trials[1], and now handling his first big case as a defender. With two such strong personalities, clashes were inevitable—most often over cross-examination techniques—but when it really mattered, Puccio and Dershowitz were able to shelve their disagreements and work together.

---

[1]*Between 1980-81 numerous politicians were arrested and tried for corruption in what became known as the 'ABSCAM Sting.'*

B. Witnesses Crumble

The trial proved to be a miserable experience for many of the prosecution witnesses. Schrallhammer reluctantly admitted that she had never mentioned insulin to Kuh, while family members confessed that they had reached a tacit agreement to offer Von Bülow a considerable sum of money if he would renounce all claims to their mother's estate.

The expert witnesses fared no better. Blood-sugar expert, Dr. George Cahill—so single-minded in the first trial that insulin and insulin alone could have induced Sunny's symptoms—was now forced to concede that certain prescription drugs might also produce a similar reaction. All of which bolstered defense claims that Claus Von Bülow was being tried for a crime that never happened.

Because Dershowitz felt that the whole trial hinged on medical testimony, he urged Von Bülow not to testify. This did not sit well with the defendant. In the first trial he had been similarly advised and bitterly regretted it. But Dershowitz's intuition was that Von Bülow, with his patrician air of haughty disdain, could only do harm to an otherwise massive case. Reluctantly, the defendant acquiesced. On June 10, 1985, he reaped the benefits of Dershowitz's instincts when the jury acquitted him on all charges.

Rarely are appeals so successful. Dershowitz's demolition of an ostensibly overwhelming prosecution case was total and complete. Of course, Claus Von Bülow was and is a very rich man, and there can be no doubt that only someone with very deep pockets could have mounted such an assault. But nothing should detract from Dershowitz and his team: without them, all the money in the world might not have saved Von Bülow.

In the years since then, Dershowitz has remained at the cutting edge of legal representation. During the O.J. Simpson trial, he stayed in constant fax contact with the courtroom defense lawyers, coaxing, chiding, advising on points of law, again employing the Harvard-team tactics that had served him so well in the Claus Von Bülow case. He has also found time to write an impressive string of best-sellers, both non-fiction and novels, explaining and illuminating the law in an enviably clear style.

But perhaps his greatest personal achievement came in 1983, when the Anti-Defamation League of the B'nai B'rith presented him with the William O. Douglas First Amendment Award for his "compassionate eloquent leadership and persistent advocacy in the struggle for civil and human rights." In presenting the award, Nobel Laureate Elie Wiesel commented, "If there had been a few people like Alan Dershowitz during the 1930s and 1940s, the history of European Jewry might have been different."

OTHER NOTABLE CASES:

Leona Helmsley (1989); Jeffrey McDonald (1991);
Mike Tyson (1994); O.J. Simpson (1995)

Thomas Dewey
(1902–1971)

I. Career

History tends to cast Thomas Dewey as the great "might have been" of American politics. Because his two abortive tilts at the White House figure so prominently in the public consciousness, it is sometimes easy to forget that for millions in the Great Depression Dewey was a genuine hero, the only law enforcement officer prepared to take on the Mob at the highest level. He became so famous that movies were made about him, as well as a popular radio show called *Gangbusters*. Short and sturdily built, he had a terrier-like tenacity, and his trademark toothbrush moustache, featured on countless front page photographs, became one of the era's most copied fashion accessories.

Unlike J. Edgar Hoover—his only serious rival in the public's adulation of crime-fighters—Dewey didn't restrict himself to soft targets; he took dead aim at the very top of the tree. Of those organized crime figures indicted by Dewey or his office, an astounding ninety-four percent were convicted; reason enough for the man from Owosso, Michigan to be considered the preeminent prosecutor of the twentieth century.

NO
SMOKING

His background was orthodox, upper middle-class, WASP. The Deweys were staunch Republicans and nothing the young Thomas ever did in his youth or teenage years gave any hint of undermining the status quo. In 1919 he entered the University of Michigan in Ann Arbor, and four years later he traveled across country to pursue his legal education at Columbia Law School. After being admitted to the bar in 1924, he spent his legal adolescence in relative obscurity in New York City, until 1928, when he acted as junior counsel to George Z. Medalie, a prominent trial attorney. It was a fortunate meeting. Three years later, Medalie was named U.S. Attorney for the Southern District of New York, and remembered the bright young lawyer. Dewey joined the office in March 1931, as Medalie's chief assistant. Not yet thirty years old, he was already in charge of lawyers much more experienced than himself. It was the beginning of an incandescent rise through both the legal and political cosmos.

First, there were the office banalities to overcome. He found day-to-day minutiae humdrum and wanted little to do with it: his heart was in the courtroom. At university he had studied voice, a talent he now put to good use as he stretched his prosecutorial muscles, all the while gaining invaluable experience in the preparation and trial of complex criminal cases.

The more he burrowed into the close links between New York's organized crime and the city politicians, the more frustrated Dewey became. The mobsters had most local politicians sewn up tight, and they just thumbed their noses at state and local charges. Where they were vulnerable, though, was at the federal level, and it didn't take Dewey long to discover organized crime's vulnerable soft underbelly—income taxes.

II. James Quinlivin (1931)

The first newsworthy case that Dewey homed-in on was by no means his most famous, but in its meticulous preparation and tenacity it set the tone for all the other investigations that he and his team would launch.

Thomas Dewey leaves court with two of his assistants, William B. Herland (left) and Milton Schilback (right). (AP Wide World)

In April 1931, James J. Quinlivin, a rotund, ruddy-faced veteran of the Vice Squad, was slapped with an indictment alleging that, for several years, he had failed to disclose to the federal tax authorities the full extent of his income. Ordinarily the salary of a lowly patrolman might be considered of minimal interest to anti-racketeering crimebusters, but Officer Quinlivin was no ordinary cop. Dewey, handed the case as a baptism of fire, devoted much of the summer to its preparation. The details shocked but did not surprise him.

It appeared that Quinlivin, who was detailed to enforce the Volstead Act which prohibited the sale and distribution of alcohol, could be found most nights propping up the bar of a 125th Street speakeasy called the Nedana Club. Closer examination of the club's activities revealed that, far from being a mere customer, Quinlivin, in partnership with another man, actually owned this illegal establishment and stocked it with booze seized from other speakeasies. Even more damning was the revelation that between 1927–29 this officer of the law had *banked* $80,000 over and above his actual salary. Neither was his an isolated case, as investigators exposed five other vice squad members whose lifestyles far outweighed their paychecks. Between them, these officers had saved in excess of $550,000 from their "salaries."

But it was Quinlivin who stood trial first, in September 1931. In his opening address Dewey warned the jury that the Quinlivin affair "goes down into the sewers of the city." As if to prove the point, he then called the chief prosecution witness, Harry B. Levey.

Levey had worked for Quinlivin between January 1928 and January 1929 as a chauffeur. His principal duty had been to collect between $50-150 a week protection money from each of 125 speakeasies and brothels in Upper Manhattan, money which Quinlivin shared with his police partner William O'Connor. Those that didn't pay were raided. If obliged by circumstances to raid a place that had already paid, Quinlivin always provided advance warning, with the result that he rarely recovered more than half a pint of liquor on these "friendly visits."

For his troubles Levey was paid $50 a week, but he managed to supplement his income by earning the same amount each day in "tips" from the club proprietors, and in kickbacks from bail bondsmen eager for leads that might produce business. In his testimony, Levey claimed that Quinlivin had tried to bribe him to leave New York for the duration of the trial. For good measure he added that Quinlivin had received $850 for perjured testimony in the trials of three women charged with morals offense.

A. Handwriting Experts Confirm Suspicions

When defense attorney James Murray told the jury that Levey "is as slimy an individual as it will ever be your misfortune to listen to," he may well have been speaking the truth, but Dewey was ready for him. To fortify Levey's shaky credibility, he introduced the incontrovertible evidence of bank records, reviewed over many weeks with the help of Sydney Burg of the Internal Revenue Bureau. These showed the disputed sums, more than $80,000, paid into the account of one S.A. Duffy at the First National Bank. Documents experts who examined the deposit slips could discern no difference between Duffy's handwriting and that of Sarah Quinlivin, the defendant's wife.

In the absence of any defense witnesses, Murray was reduced to a feeble plea that Dewey's case be thrown out on grounds that, not only had the prosecution failed to produce a single speakeasy owner to swear the payment of bribes, but that the court lacked jurisdiction to try what was a federal offense. Dewey snorted in disgust, "Did you ever hear of a speakeasy proprietor coming in and saying, 'Yes, I run a speakeasy'? The defense had the same opportunity to call proprietors of places named in this trial."

The jurisdictional dispute was similarly swept aside, and Quinlivin trudged off to begin a three-year jail term at the federal penitentiary in Atlanta. Within a week of Quinlivin's conviction, forty bootleggers, including seven of his police colleagues, miraculously materialized at the federal building to pay back taxes.

Overnight, Dewey became headline news. When Medalie left the post of U.S. Attorney in December 1932, his young deputy stepped in as a temporary replacement. He lost no time in stamping his own authority on the job. Inside a month he set in motion the prosecution of the notorious hoodlum, Waxey Gordon; followed by a long string of cases that cemented his reputation. Dewey was the archetypal crusading district attorney, relentless in his pursuit of lawbreakers, seemingly incorruptible. In 1935 he received a new post, that of a special prosecutor, charged with ridding New York's streets of crime. An apparently thankless task, under Dewey's stewardship the grand jury returned hundreds of indictments against some of the city's biggest crime bosses. The biggest of all, Lucky Luciano, listened incredulously as he was sentenced to a 30–50 year prison term on prostitution charges. So powerful was Dewey's hold on the public psyche, that when Dutch Schultz suggested killing the underworld's bete noire, his fellow mobsters shot him instead, reasoning that Dewey was too important to be assassinated!

Lucky Luciano, convicted on prostitution charges, leaves court handcuffed to detectives after being sentenced to a 30–50 year prison term. (AP Wide World)

B. The Governor of New York

In 1942, Dewey made the natural step into mainstream politics with his election to the governorship of New York, a position he held for twelve years. Controversy stalked his every move. In 1946, he stunned New Yorkers by announcing that Luciano was to be paroled and deported to Italy after serving just ten years of his prison sentence. (It later transpired that Luciano had assisted in the Allied war effort.) Dewey shrugged off the criticism and got on with his career. Twice he ran for the presidency, in 1944 and again in 1948, when he was confidently expected to win. Somehow he managed to confound the pollsters and finish a close second to Harry Truman. Never again would he figure so prominently on the national stage.

Despite all these setbacks his crime-fighting instincts remained razor sharp. In 1951, when still governor, he announced a sweeping investigation of conditions in the Port of New York. He later declared that the public hearings had disclosed "the existence of conditions on the waterfront . . . which are a disgrace and a menace." A subsequent inquiry by the Crime Commission into racetrack operations revealed similar chicanery.

In 1954 he left the governorship to resume private life. *The New York Times* had no doubts about his place in history. "Thomas E. Dewey," it wrote, "will surely be ranked high among this state's ablest governors, a fact usually conceded even by his political opponents." Private life was good to Dewey, his practice thrived, and he lost none of his influence in the upper echelons of the GOP. When he died in Miami on March 15, 1971, of a heart attack, he left behind a legacy unrivaled in American twentieth century jurisprudence.

Thomas Dewey did not, of course, consign crime to the history books, but it is sobering to ponder what life nowadays in New York might have been like without his ground-breaking efforts. Sadly, in recent years those efforts have been tainted with accusations that Dewey himself was corrupt, a well-paid pawn of the very mobsters he was supposed to be indicting.

The charge was first made by Dewey's old antagonist, Lucky Luciano. Without documentary proof—unlikely to surface after this passage of time—Luciano's claim is unverifiable and bears more than a whiff of petulant vindictiveness. After all, how else could an impotent mobster strike back at the prosecutor who had first jailed him, then tossed him out of the country?

OTHER NOTABLE CASES:

Empire Trust (1931); Waxey Gordon (1933); Lucky Luciano (1936); James Hines (1938); Richard Whitney (1938)

John Doar
(1922–)

I. Career

John Doar was not a lawyer prepared to throw in the legal towel without a struggle. On one memorable occasion he pursued a case all the way to the Wisconsin Supreme Court just to win a $50 judgment. It was tenacity of this kind that made Doar a natural candidate for high office when the Kennedy administration decided to take a stand against racial segregation in the South. Earlier, in 1960, Doar had joined the Justice Department and was immediately pitched onto the front lines of the most bitter internal dispute to hit America since the Civil War. Two years later he was on hand to shepherd black student James Meredith through his riot-torn admission to the University of Mississippi. Confronting frenzied mobs, dodging stones and bricks, and learning to stand impassively by while every kind of epithet was hurled at him became a way of life. In 1964 President Lyndon Johnson appointed him chief of the Justice Department's civil rights division, making John Doar one of the most potent figures in the fight against racial injustice.

It was all such a long way from the small town of New Richmond, Wisconsin, where he had spent his childhood.

Assistant Attorney-General John Doar waits for an elevator with a U.S. Marshall. (AP Wide World)

His father had been a lawyer, too, and it was pretty much taken for granted that the young boy would maintain the family tradition. Doar had Ivy League credentials and an intellect to match, graduating from Princeton in 1944, just as World War II was reaching its bloody climax. He served as Second Lieutenant in the Army Air Forces. After discharge he graduated from Boalt Hall, Berkeley in 1950, determined to make his way in California, but when his father became ill, he returned home to New Richmond and there he remained for a decade. Then came the summons to Washington, D.C.

His forte was civil law, and during his time at the Justice Department, he prosecuted more than thirty voting rights cases. Most never made the front pages, but they did provide the legal ammunition for the concerted assault on the fortress mentality that had preserved the antiquated status quo. Doar was determined that blacks everywhere would enjoy the same rights granted to their white fellow citizens. To this end, he rode with the Freedom Riders and also helped quell the riots that engulfed Jackson, Mississippi, after the murder of Medgar Evers.

He once said, "I'm a lawyer. I like to take on difficult cases." Brave words. But not even this most tenacious of prosecutors could have foreseen just how difficult the following case would be to tackle.

II. Price & Bowers & Others (1967)

On August 14, 1964, acting on information received, FBI agents in Neshoba County, Mississippi, dug up the bodies of Michael Schwerner, James Chayney, and Andrew Goodman, three young civil rights campaigners missing since June 21. On that day they had been arrested by Cecil Price, deputy sheriff of a small town called Philadelphia, and charged with speeding. After spending several hours in jail and paying a $25 fine, they were released.

Informants within the Ku Klux Klan later revealed that Price had detained the trio long enough for a lynch mob to organize, and that later, after rearresting the three young men, Price had delivered them to his co-conspirators. Although aware that they were dealing with willful murder, the state authorities dragged their heels over a prosecution and it was left to the federal government in 1967 to take action. As the killings had not occurred on federal property, the government could not file murder charges; instead, they invoked a ninety-seven year-old Reconstruction-era law, charging that a conspiracy had existed to violate the victims' civil rights.

Of the seventeen defendants who eventually stood trial, public attention focused mainly on Price and local KKK Imperial Wizard, Sam Bowers, Jr. Back when the bodies were discovered, Bowers had joked that "Judge Cox would probably make them take those bodies and put them back because they were found on an illegal search." This was a reference to trial judge William Harold Cox, whose past record on civil rights issues had given the defendants every reason to expect lenient treatment.

However, with the media microscope on full power, Judge Cox dealt a crushing blow to redneck justice, dismissing out of hand a whole slew of frivolous defense objections with the words, "We are not going to have a big show out of this case."

This was music to Doar's ears. He was certain that if a jury got to hear the full facts, multiple convictions would follow. The defendants, he said, had plotted to murder the young men "because they didn't like what they stood for."

Much of Doar's case was based on the word of informants and turncoats. Meridian policeman Sergeant Carlton Miller testified that he joined the KKK in March/April 1964 and became a paid FBI informer the following September. He named several of the defendants as active KKK members and recalled being told, one week after their disappearance, that Chayney, Goodman, and Schwerner were "buried fifteen feet in a dam." In chilling detail, Miller spelled out the KKK's protocols, used to determine which victims deserved "whipping, beatings" and which were earmarked for "elimination."

Another disaffected Klansman, James Jordan, described being posted as a lookout down a country lane, a short distance from where the three men were being held. "I heard car doors slam, some loud talk that I could not distinguish, and then I heard several shots." He later saw the three bodies dumped into a prepared grave, which was bulldozed over.

In some respects Doar had too much evidence. As the defendants turned viciously on each other, problems arose over whom to believe. One, Horace Burrage, claimed that Jordan, far from being a distant lookout, was actually the person who shot Chayney, saying that he arrived after the two white youths had been killed, complaining, "You didn't leave me nothing but a nigger, but at least I killed me a nigger."

A. Multi Alibis

Others stoutly maintained that it was all lies, with dozens of defense witnesses prepared to swear alibis for the accused. Skillfully, Doar threaded his way through the tangle to expose the obvious inconsistencies and prejudices. When a Mr. and Mrs. Finnis McAdory testified that at the estimated time of the killings—

around midnight—they were with Price at the police station in Philadelphia, Doar asked Mrs. McAdory her motivation for taking the stand. After considerable hesitation, she replied that she was "testifying for my county."

Which was precisely the point that Doar emphasized in his closing speech. "A thousand eyes explored every corner of Neshoba County . . . but Neshoba County closed ranks and remained silent. Rarely in the history of law enforcement was information so hard to obtain. . . . If there is to be any hope for this land of ours, the Federal Government has the duty [to oppose] evil forces that seize control of law enforcement."

The defendants, he said, had engaged in a "diabolical plot" to stage "midnight murder." Pointing at Price, Doar taunted that the defendant had used "the machinery of his office—the badge, the car, the jail, the gun . . . to further the conspiracy."

Doar's final charge to the jury was a plea for common sense. "If you find them not guilty, it would be as true to say there was no nighttime release by Cecil Price, there are no White Knights, there are no young men dead, there was no murder."

In reply, all the defense could offer were weak, often shameful attacks on the characters of the dead men.

On October 20, 1967, after two days of tense deliberation, the jury returned guilty verdicts against seven of the accused. The remainder were either acquitted or granted mistrials. Outside the courthouse the town of Meridian seemed dazed by the verdicts. The Confederate flags hung limply, and a planned parade drew less than 250 people.

For the first time a Mississippi jury had brought in guilty verdicts against white defendants charged with civil rights violations, and this in a state where a whole series of racial killings had gone unpunished since the 1955 murder of young Emmett Till. Afterwards, petulant state officials complained weakly that Justice Department maneuverings had hampered their own efforts to proceed against the defendants.

At a subsequent hearing all of the convicted defendants were sentenced to lengthy prison terms.

B. A Public Servant

For John Doar this trial was the culmination of his struggle against civil rights infractions, but he continued to crop up in the news, most noticeably when he was appointed as counsel on the House Judicial Committee that conducted impeachment proceedings against President Richard Nixon. Doar's controversial role in that body's deliberations has been the subject of heated debate to the present day.

In February 1975, he received Princeton's prestigious Woodrow Wilson Prize for long-term public service. It was a fitting reward for a remarkable career and shortly after this he returned to private practice. In June 1977, when the position of Director of the FBI came vacant, his name was one of those most often mentioned, but he remained a private citizen, content in the knowledge that few members of the legal profession have served their country better.

OTHER NOTABLE CASES:

Collie Leroy Wilkins (1965); Eastman Kodak (1977);
Alcee Hastings (1989)

Jacob W. "Jake" Ehrlich

(1900–1971)

I. Career

Jake Ehrlich always was a great talker, and like most outstanding orators, the lawyer known to generations of San Francisco court watchers as "The Master" knew the value of embellishment. He was not above warning jurors that, if found guilty, his client was surely destined for the Golden Gate Bridge. Since few people wish to be considered potential accessories to suicide, it is hardly surprising that most juries came to see things Jake's way, especially in murder cases. This flair for dramatic adornment also extended to his personal life. For most of his career, those who knew this feisty little scrapper had accepted the authorized biography—born just outside of Rockville, Maryland, at the turn of the century, hoboed his way across country to San Francisco, obtained a law degree from San Francisco Law School, then achieved fabulous success through his own efforts: a genuine rags-to-riches saga.

It turned out, in his 1965 autobiography *A Life in My Hands,* that Jake had been fooling everyone all along. He was old money, born to plantation affluence in a white porticoed mansion that overlooked the Potomac, where his grandfather's languid conversation had tinkled easily in the ear, interrupted only by the chink of ice in the mint juleps. Fired by the Civil War exploits of his garrulous grandpa—a Confederate general, by all accounts—sixteen-year-old Jake had taken off for the army and Mexico in hot pursuit of the outlaw Pancho Villa.

Since army records show that Ehrlich's military career lasted all of *eleven days,* and his recruitment papers list his father as having been born in East Prussia, much of this *Gone With The Wind* pedigree is probably best taken with a hefty pinch of salt. The more likely version has Ehrlich arriving in San Francisco in 1920, marrying that same year (he always claimed that his total cash reserves at the time were $3.70), and working as a railroad official's secretary by day and in a tire factory at night to make ends meet. He also funded his legal education by using his fists as a professional prizefighter, initiating an interest in the sport that he retained until his death. His admission to the California Bar in 1922 was not an open door to the good life. In the beginning of his career, he was happy enough to serve summonses at $1 each.

During this time, a kind landlady took pity on the struggling young attorney and deferred some unpaid rent, saying, "You look like an honest hard worker to me." Years later her kindness was repaid in full when Ehrlich defended a police inspector, without charge, only to subsequently learn that he was the landlady's son. Like many of the quoted incidents from Ehrlich's life, it sounds too good to be true, but there could be no doubting his courtroom success. An early break came in 1929 when Jerry Giesler (q.v.) added him to the defense team of accused rapist Alexander Pantages. Together they won a famous acquittal and Ehrlich was on his way. In 1930, he took his only stab at politics, an unsuccessful tilt for the Republican nomination for Attorney-General.

As a truly great murder trial defense attorney, none of Ehrlich's clients were executed. (UPI Corbis-Bettmann)

Although Ehrlich handled dozens of celebrity clients, including Howard Hughes, Errol Flynn, fan dancer Sally Rand, and jazz greats Gene Krupa and Billie Holliday, he is best remembered as a truly great murder trial defense attorney who never had a client executed.

One jury took just thirteen minutes to acquit a young woman charged with murdering her boyfriend in a hotel bedroom, despite the victim being found with three bullets in his back. Another jury required only four minutes to find another of Ehrlich's clients not guilty of murder. By 1955 he had defended fifty-five murder cases without a single first-degree conviction. A staggering forty-one were outright acquittals, with the remainder reduced to either second-degree murder or manslaughter. But not even Ehrlich, with all his vast experience, was quite ready for Gertrude Morris.

II. Gertrude Morris (1952)

On the afternoon of April 10, 1951, Gertrude Morris traded insults with her husband Milton at his office in San Francisco, unraveling the last few strands of their twenty-one year marriage. Among other things, Milton, a well-to-do executive, could not understand why Gertrude refused to drive the new Chevrolet coupe he had just bought her. Gertrude, eaten up by suspicion and overwhelmed by tears, ran off. That evening the fight continued at their luxurious Lakeside home, until 6:30 P.M., when Milton announced he was leaving for good and began packing his bags. Before he could reach the door a .32 caliber slug cut him down.

Gertrude made no attempt to deny murder and when her trial opened on January 22, 1952, she seemed indifferent to her fate, laughing as Ehrlich sat a jury where women outnumbered men 3-1. The entire prosecution lasted only two and a half hours, the briefest ever heard in a capital case at San Francisco's Superior Court. For Norman Elkington, chief assistant DA, the facts were plain: Gertrude admitted shooting her husband in the back, with premeditation; therefore, it was first-degree murder.

Inspector Al Nelder told how Gertrude, when arrested at the crime scene, had been most insistent that there was no other woman involved. Nelder, puzzled, had asked, "Do you realize what you have done?"

"Yes, sir. I do now."

"Are you sorry?"

"I certainly am, because I loved him. Maybe that was my whole trouble, I loved him too much."

Another witness, neighbor George W. Jones, testified that Gertrude had knocked on his door at 2:00 A.M. and asked him to call the police. This timing was important because, on Gertrude's own admission, she had shot her husband some seven hours earlier and in all that time she had done nothing to help him.

Ehrlich's opening speech must rank as one of the most remarkable ever made by defense counsel in a court of law. It amounted to a wholesale impeachment of his client's credibility, as he warned the jury that Gertrude would shape her story in such a way that they would send her to the gas chamber. Twice, in custody, she had attempted suicide, he said, now she was asking the state to finish the job. And contrary to what Gertrude had told the police, noted Ehrlich, she *did* suspect her husband of infidelity, in particular that he had been "intimate with his secretary." He outlined other discrepancies in her story. Originally, she had claimed it was all spur of the moment, later she said she had hidden the murder weapon in her sweater while waiting an "opportune moment" to shoot him.

Gertrude absorbed all this, just staring into a handkerchief, emotionless. Then Ehrlich called her to the stand. A plain, plump woman, she sat with a wrinkled coat draped across her shoulders, answering questions wearily. After a few minutes she leaned towards the judge and murmured, "I want to plead guilty to first-degree murder."

Judge Harry J. Neubarth blinked. "What?" When she repeated her request the judge said, "You just tell the story. We'll let the jury decide what the verdict should be."

As Ehrlich struggled to bring out details of the argument, Gertrude began to drift. Ehrlich boiled over. Striding towards her, finger extended, he shouted, "I've told you time and time again that I want you to tell how it happened, and not try to build it up so you'll be executed."

A. Wild Scenes in Court

Elkington's complaint that Ehrlich was leading the witness ignited uproar in court. Amidst the bedlam, the pugnacious defender bellowed, "It is my moral duty to protect this woman. This woman is trying to destroy herself." He claimed that her problems stemmed from an overnight train journey she and her husband, together with Milton's secretary, had taken in 1941. Using a diagram that showed sleeping arrangements on the Pullman car, Ehrlich established how Gertrude had surprised the other two in what she believed was a compromising situation. Ten years later, when questioned about this incident, Gertrude muttered, "I still think there was something wrong there."

On cross-examination she lapsed back into torpor, repeatedly answering, "Yes," to every question posed by Elkington. "That's right, keep it up," jeered Ehrlich, "She'll say 'yes' to anything you ask her." When Ehrlich complained that "no man, no lawyer living ever heard anything like this," Gertrude called him over. "Can't we plead guilty to murder now, and have it over with?"

"No," snapped Ehrlich.

When Rose Goolo, Milton Morris' attractive secretary, took the stand, Gertrude fled hysterically into the judge's chambers, the only time she ever showed any interest or emotion during the trial. Brought back sobbing into court, she heard Goolo admit that Morris drove her to work, took her out to lunch "three or four times a week," and that he drove her home each night after work.

"What was your relationship with Morris?" demanded Ehrlich.

"I was his secretary."

"Any more than that?"

"No," she said archly, though she later conceded that they were "friends" and that Morris bought her perfume.

When, in his closing speech, Elkington constantly and disparagingly referred to what he termed "Mr. Ehrlich's story," Ehrlich squared up to his much bigger opponent and shouted, "If you indicate that I make up stories, Mr. Elkington, you are a common, ordinary street liar." The crowded public gallery roared its approval.

After calm had been restored, Elkington got back on track. "She shot him," he told the court. "She saw him fall. She heard him cry, 'Get a doctor.' And she did not get a doctor. She walked away and let him bleed to death." Then came an earnest plea to the jury to exercise caution when heeding Ehrlich. "He is resourceful. He is an attorney you can count on to come up with an unexpected defense. If it succeeds, you will hear about it in the future as the clever defense in the Morris Case."

Elkington had cause for concern. Ehrlich's peroration was superb, as he told how Morris had tried to placate his wife with a diamond ring. "What good is it to give a diamond ring if, as Mrs. Morris testified, he never put his arms around her . . . She didn't want any diamond ring, she wanted her husband." More than one juror had to wipe away a tear by the time Ehrlich was through.

On February 11, 1952, Gertrude Morris was convicted of manslaughter, and later imprisoned. Upon hearing the verdict she allegedly turned to Ehrlich and said, "You are a very talented man, you missed your vocation on the stage . . . But maybe hanging [sic] would have been the best thing."

B. A Legal Scholar

Besides courtroom brilliance, Ehrlich was also a legal scholar of note. In 1959 he published *Ehrlich's Blackstone* a modern version of William Blackstone's *Commentaries on the Laws of England,* for a long time the basis of Anglo-American legal education. As his fame grew, so did media fascination. In the 1960s a TV series *Sam Benedict* billed itself as being "based on the living character of J.W. (Jake) Ehrlich," a characterization that brought Ehrlich a sharp rebuke from the State Bar which felt that this amounted to advertising.

He also found himself in hot water for what many felt was his racist defense of a San Francisco police officer accused of killing a black man. But others prefer to remember Ehrlich for his presidency of the Saints and Sinners, an organization devoted to getting free milk for schoolchildren.

After his death on December 24, 1971, dozens of those who knew Ehrlich best—lawyers, cops, judges, and just friends—gathered at San Francisco's Hall of Justice to honor "The Master." Said Melvin Belli (q.v.), "Jake loved the little guy . . . When we lift a glass, we'll always remember this great lawyer, this great San Franciscan."

For decades he had been a legend, resplendent in the expensive suits and highly polished cowboy boots that were his sartorial trademarks. He was particularly proud of his cufflink collection from around the world and valued at more than $25,000. Most had been acquired from the proceeds of his murder trials, for Jake Ehrlich had a simple method for calculating the size of his fee in capital cases—all of the defendant's worldly goods. Every single thing! "Why not?" he said, "If they go to the gas chamber it won't do them any good!"

OTHER NOTABLE CASES:

Alexander Pantages (1929–31); Laverne Borelli (1946);
Sally Rand (1946); Michael O'Brien (1969)

William J. Fallon
(1886–1927)

I. Career

Everyone called William Fallon "The Great Mouthpiece," and with good reason. Few lawyers, if any, of the twentieth century could have held their own in a verbal slugfest with this native-born New Yorker, whose mastery of emotive rhetoric could glaze the eyes of opponent and juror alike. The fact that he was wholly untroubled by the niceties of law or such trifling concerns as the truth did, of course, help his discourse, as Fallon always felt that facts tended to hamper a good story and so had little place in his marathon epics. His career was brief—a lifelong affair with the bottle insured that—and yet his place at the forefront of American advocacy is assured. He defended 126 clients accused of homicide, and got every one of them acquitted. How he achieved some of those acquittals almost defies belief.

One particular husband, accused of poisoning his wife, seemed on his way to the electric chair when the triumphant prosecutor brandished before the jury a vial of poison that had been recovered from the defendant's valise. Things only worsened as a clutch of experts testified that the poison in the vial matched poison found in the dead woman's body. Fallon didn't flinch. Timing his summation to conclude right on the lunch recess, he first informed the jury that the vial did not contain poison and then accused the prosecutor of engaging in an outrageous hoax. To prove his point, he picked up the exhibit, withdrew its cork, and slowly swallowed the "deadly" contents, while everyone watched in horror. Smiling broadly, he sat down. Amid scenes of unprecedented bedlam, the judge was barely able to make himself heard as he hastily gaveled the court to recess. Fallon, still smiling, strolled insouciantly outside, then bolted to a nearby empty courtroom where doctors were waiting to pump his stomach, which had been lined with some sort of antidote to the poison. Once again his client walked free.

Stunts like this made Fallon a legend, and lent authority to his earlier ambition to follow a career on the stage. His mother, having intended him for the priesthood, refused to countenance such rebellion, and as a compromise he suggested the law. Sorrowfully, she nodded her assent.

At Fordham University Fallon's formidable debating skills brought him to the attention of faculty member, Eugene F. McGhee, already a successful criminal lawyer. The young student's phenomenal memory and ability to think on his feet were rare and valuable commodities in the legal marketplace. McGhee recognized talent when he saw it and tried to recruit Fallon upon his graduation, but the young man opted for the Westchester County district attorney's office, where his keen handling of witnesses and forceful eloquence won many convictions.

He always claimed that his subsequent departure from the DA's office was precipitated by conscience, he had prosecuted a man whom he knew to be innocent. Given Fallon's subsequent shenanigans it is difficult to know how much credence to accord such a statement, but in 1918 he joined forces with his former mentor and the law firm of Fallon & McGhee was born. In terms of clientele and notoriety they were rivaled only by their infamous predecessors Howe & Hummell (q.v.). McGhee, with his matchless underworld contacts, was terrific at drumming up business; Fallon was well-nigh unbeatable in court. Although McGhee spent his professional life laboring in the younger man's shadow, he did not have a scrap of jealousy in him. Like most acquaintances, he was overawed by Fallon's verbal firepower, and was fully prepared to suppress personal ambition for the greater good of the firm and his own bank balance. In time the press dubbed them "The Broadway and Forty-Second Street Bar Association" because of their phenomenal success.

Fallon, a bluff handsome man, red-haired and with an unquenchable thirst for whisky and women, became one of the great Manhattan characters. He

was a close confidant of Arnold Rothstein—the gambler suspected of fixing the 1919 World Series—and through Rothstein he gained an entree into the murkiest depths of the New York underworld. Along the way he engaged in just about every debauchery going. Although married to a long-suffering wife, Fallon would swagger along Broadway with his latest conquest dangling from an arm, glorying in the attention that reverential admirers heaped upon him. His life revolved around a neatly described triangle of beds, bars, and courtrooms.

His moral standards were marvels of ambiguity. In one breath he would refuse, as a good Catholic, to handle divorce cases; and in the next declare that, "Most jurors are dumb," to rebut accusations that he routinely bribed his way to victory. "All I have to do is pick out the dumbest of the dozen, concentrate everything on him, and my client is sure of a hung jury."

But was this true? How much did Fallon really owe to his verbal dexterity? And how much was a result of graft and well-greased palms? Or was it a combination of the two? The answer, oddly enough, came in the trial that many regard as The Great Mouthpiece's finest hour. And this time the defendant was himself.

II. William Fallon (1924)

By 1924, press baron William Randolph Hearst was becoming greatly exercised by the curious number of 11-1 hung juries that seemed to crop up in trials where Fallon was the defense counsel. Sensing a good story, Hearst assigned a flock of reporters from *The American* to shadow those jurors who had thrown the verdicts into dispute. They alighted on Charles Rendigs, who had cast the dissenting vote in Fallon's defense of bucket shop operators, E.M. Fuller & Co., and was now suddenly flush with money. Eventually enough evidence was amassed to indict Fallon on charges of bribing Rendigs to the tune of $25,000.

A. The Fight of His Career

Fallon readied himself for the most bitter fight of his spectacular career. At stake was not just his professional reputation, but liberty itself: failure meant a

"The Great Mouthpiece," William Fallon.
(UPI Corbis-Bettmann)

lengthy spell behind bars. In the weeks preceding the trial Fallon even forswore alcohol as he concentrated on getting himself into the best shape possible.

The courtroom testimony seemed conclusive, with Rendigs admitting that Fallon had bribed him. But Fallon was superb. Although his partner McGhee was the official counsel of record, Fallon took over and conducted his own defense, and for once the old legal maxim that "a lawyer who defends himself has a fool for a client" failed to hold water.

After cross-examining many of the prosecution witnesses, Fallon took the stand and gave evidence on his own behalf. Next came a chain of character witnesses who all told the court what a marvelous fellow the defendant was. Then it was time for Fallon to give his summation. It is still reckoned among the greatest speeches ever heard in an American courtroom. As with all great performances, mere words fail to do it justice, for Fallon was a consummate actor, able to wring buckets of emotion out of the seemingly coldest prose.

He rose at twenty minutes before noon and spoke until one o'clock, when the court recessed for lunch. Colleagues had counseled Fallon against splitting his speech, saying its impact would be diminished, with the second half appearing anti-climactic. "Don't worry about your anti-climaxes," he purred. "I'll save the real fireworks until afternoon, when the jurors will have returned from dinner, their stomachs full."

After lunch Fallon spoke for a further two emotion-packed hours, ridiculing prosecution claims that he was cornered. "I am not with my back to the wall, as the court has said, I am right in the front line. I have faced every accuser, and when I shall have finished, I believe that you will find that there is absolutely no truth or foundation for the charges brought against me."

Referring to his earlier brash courtroom conduct, he offered this, "If you think I have been impetuous during this trial, let me say it is not easy for a man who has stood here and defended others, to defend himself . . . Who of you could stand up and face your accusers without being impetuous and overbearing? If you heard men lie, and knew they were lying, wouldn't your animosity be aroused?"

B. Secret Birth Certificate!

He thundered to a crescendo. This entire travesty had been orchestrated by the Hearst press in order to ruin him. And the reason? Fallon tapped his breast pocket knowingly, saying it contained evidence which the court would not, could not admit into testimony. He alluded to copies of birth certificates that he had unearthed in Mexico while on another case, certificates showing that a certain Hollywood actress had given birth in secret to her lover's child!

In making this statement, Fallon could have only one target in mind—Marion Davies, minor movie star and mistress of William Randolph Hearst. A gasp of amazement sizzled through the court. One Hearst editor galloped for the phone and called his boss at his Californian resort. Hearst, ever the hard-headed businessman, took the news stoically. "Well," he told the hesitant editor, "you won't have to think twice about what your lead headline will be tomorrow."

Meanwhile, back in court, Fallon had deflected all the attention away from himself and shouldered it onto Hearst, making it appear as though it was he who should have been on trial. "I say to you now, and I say it is the truth, that *The American* deliberately set out to destroy Fallon." Rendigs, too, was savaged. "Who would believe Rendigs . . . that miserable creature who faces ten years under a conviction for perjury?" His evidence, claimed Fallon, had been adduced as part of a plea-bargain. It was the same with all of the other prosecution witnesses; each received the kind of verbal mauling that only Fallon could dish out. At the end he implored the jury, "All that the whole world means to me, I now leave in your hands." Head bowed, arms at his side, Fallon stood motionless, silent. An eerie stillness hung over the court as he walked slowly back to his chair.

Neither the prosecution summation nor the judge's direction could dent the impact of Fallon's great speech, and on August 8, 1924, he was acquitted of all charges. Mobbed by well-wishers, Fallon shouldered his way over to the jury and shook everyone by the hand. A few minutes later, as he exited the court, he beckoned toward Nat Ferber, one of the Hearst reporters who had helped build the case against him. "Nat," he whispered, "so help me God, I'll never bribe another juror."

The next day when Fallon went to the Polo Grounds where the Giants were playing the Reds, he received a standing ovation from the crowd.

Although a great personal triumph, this victory marked the beginning of the end for Fallon. The firm of Fallon & McGhee went into serious decline as gangsters, certain that Hearst was still gunning for The Great Mouthpiece, took their profitable business elsewhere and cold-shouldered their former ally.

His alcoholism worsened to the point where a single glass of whisky could unhinge him. Illness interrupted his career several times. In 1926, while holed up in a cheap hotel room, he was temporarily half-blinded when a jealous woman threw acid in his face. He refused to call the police, fearing that such news would get into the papers and doom his already faltering career. The end came on April 29, 1927, when he was struck down by a heart attack. He was just forty-one years old.

OTHER NOTABLE CASES:

Jules "Nicky" Arnstein (1920); Ernest Fritz (1920); Don Collins (1922); Alvin "Cozy" Dolan (1924); Dandy Phil Kastel (1926)

Percy Foreman
(1902–1988)

I. Career

Texans prefer their heroes to be larger than life, and in Percy Foreman they had a lawyer who constantly seemed to be bursting at the seams of existence. He was a huge man, with an ego to match, and his towering physical presence dominated courtrooms around the Lone Star State for more than half a century. Like many ultra-successful attorneys he was prone to memorable bouts of self-glorification. "There is no better trial lawyer in the U.S. than me," he once trumpeted, and for once the boast that has been heard in just about every law office in America seemed to contain more than just a grain of justification.

His record was staggering. With the possible exception of Edward Reilly (q.v.), no twentieth century lawyer has handled as many capital cases, over 1,500, and of those fewer than half went to trial; the remainder were either not indicted or pleaded guilty to lesser offenses. When Foreman did go before a jury he was superb. Of the hundreds of capital cases he argued, he lost just fifty-four. In an era when the death penalty was applied with far greater frequency, only one of his clients suffered execution; and not even Foreman, an implacable foe of capital punishment, could find anything to say about Steve Mitchell, a restaurateur convicted of murdering his wife, other than "he deserved to die."

His commitment to his clients was legendary. "They may not always be right, but they are never wrong," was an oft-repeated maxim and he was ready to adopt any ploy to get this message across. When defending one woman who had killed her husband after he had flogged her with a whip, Foreman punctuated his closing argument with ear-splitting cracks from the whip that sounded like gunshots in the courtroom. Such showmanship came naturally. He dressed to be the epicenter of attention, with his black and white plaid jackets and florid bow ties, all the time consciously steering the court's attention toward himself and away from his client. Another favorite diversionary ruse was the "aw shucks" air of country-boy disorganization that he liked to affect, when nothing could have been further from the truth. At no time was he anything other than meticulously prepared.

The rural background was true enough, though. He grew up in a log cabin near the East Texas town of Coldspring. His father was the local sheriff and at age eight Foreman got his first job as a shoeshine boy. Unencumbered by false-modesty, he later claimed that he quit school at fifteen because "I knew everything they could teach me." Several years later, drawing on some correspondence courses, $6,000 in his pocket, and his mother's advice that "law would be my best bet," he entered the University of Texas Law School. After graduation he served briefly as assistant county prosecutor before plunging headlong into private practice. For years afterwards he kept the $5 bill he received as the fee for his first case: drawing up a lease on a five-acre orchard.

It wasn't long, though, before Foreman put all that behind him. As his fame soared, so did his fees. It was his allegedly prohibitive rate that scared off Jack Ruby's family in 1963, when Ruby was charged with murdering Lee Harvey Oswald. "Ruby's family was quoted four times higher than the fee I had actually asked, and they turned it down," shrugged Foreman, "I don't know how something like that happened, but it did."

Just a couple of years later came the biggest payday of his career, when he defended a young man accused of murder. The fee was guaranteed by the young man's co-defendant, a glamorous blonde socialite, who stood to receive $20 million dollars if she was acquitted, and 2,000 volts of electricity if she was not.

II. Melvin Powers (1966)

In the early hours of June 30, 1964, Houston property magnate Jacques Mossler, age 69, was battered and stabbed to death at his Key Biscayne apartment in Florida. Neighbors saw a "dark-haired man in dark clothing" flee the scene. Just

Melvin Powers (left) looks away as his attorney Percy Foreman whispers in his direction. (AP Wide World)

minutes earlier, Candace "Candy" Mossler, the dead man's forty-four-year-old wife, had loaded their four adopted children into a car and driven to a nearby hospital complaining of a migraine. Skeptical detectives soon suspected that Candy had planned the murder with her twenty-three-year-old nephew, and alleged lover, Melvin Powers, who fit the description of the fleeing man.

A. Hard at Work

Candy admitted having marital problems, blaming the fact that Jacques had undergone a personality change after a mystery illness, revealing hitherto unsuspected homosexual tendencies. Garbage, said the state: with Mossler dead, Candy would be worth millions, and she could have Melvin to herself. Despite a whole host of suspicions and doubt, it took Florida almost eighteen months to file murder charges against the couple.

Foreman had already been hard at work. When Powers was first arrested in Houston, Foreman led a cavalcade of reporters and cameramen to the Harris County jail, demanding to see his client. Told that Powers was being held elsewhere and incommunicado, the flamboyant lawyer hosted a dramatic tour of the county's various houses of detention. Foreman, who could exert a frightening presence, especially when backed up by the threat of multi-million dollar lawsuits for damages, eventually scared Harris County officials into letting him see Powers with his claim that, by denying Powers his constitutional rights, they were jeopardizing Florida's chances of pursuing a prosecution.

Although Foreman was technically acting for Powers alone, and was just one of half a dozen counsel hired by the wealthy defendants, most viewed this trial as very much a one-man show. In that respect the Texas maestro did not disappoint. Early on he laid siege to the prosecution's claim that Jacques Mossler's death had been the result of a cunning conspiracy, motivated by money and incestuous sex. Yes, there was a sexual factor, boomed Foreman, but it had been provided by the dead man, whom he accused of "every conceivable sex deviation that anybody ever had," a pervert who had been killed by a spurned homosexual lover. By the time Foreman was through, Mossler's reputation lay in tatters, stripped bare of any redeeming quality.

Foreman needed to be brutal because the prosecution had amassed a solid circumstantial case against both defendants. Its only weakness was the caliber of witnesses that they were obliged to call. Mostly ex-jailbirds, they made a bad impression on the court, and were cannon fodder for someone like Percy Foreman. Even so their testimony hurt the defense, as they testified that Powers had openly canvassed for a hit-man to kill Mossler, with one inmate even claiming that, while awaiting trial, Powers had admitted the murder.

B. Eye Witnesses

Infinitely more credible were the two airline employees who remembered Powers flying into Miami on the night of the killing, and the manager of a lounge near Mossler's home who placed Powers in his bar between 7:00 and 8:30 P.M. that same night. And then there was Candy's Chevrolet, abandoned at Miami International Airport, containing Powers' fingerprints. Foreman dismissed such irrelevancies, reminding the fingerprint expert that he couldn't say "whether Melvin Powers drove that car in June, May, or April in Miami."

More difficult to explain away was a palm-print of Powers' found in Mossler's home, on a kitchen counter-top that family handyman Roscoe Brown remembered wiping clean just hours before the killing. Brown also revealed how, after the murder, Candy telephoned him repeatedly, trying to convince him that his memory had been faulty.

Yet all of this counted for nought once Foreman rose to make his peroration. He began with a swipe at District Attorney Richard Gerstein, "It took guts and courage for him to appear personally in this case when he could have given the job to a subordinate. Few prosecutors would have chosen to appear in a case where the evidence is not overwhelming, let alone almost absent. The fact that Gerstein wasn't any better was no fault of his. It was the fault of his case."

Then Foreman cut loose, charging that the defendants had been victims of a "monetary conspiracy" hatched by corrupt police officers, and reinforced by testimony bought from the worst witnesses possible. After four hours of this high-octane oratory, Candy could stand no more and collapsed. She was assisted out of the courtroom. Fifteen minutes later she returned, and Foreman picked up where he had left off, without missing a beat. One hour later he reached a gripping climax, with the words of Jesus to the woman taken in adultery, "Neither do I condemn thee. Go and sin no more!"

Foreman's magic did the trick. On March 6, 1966, both defendants were acquitted and set free.

Still, controversy rankled. Foreman's fee, rumored to be $200,000, had been secured by Candy's jewels and land in Houston. When the promised funds were not forthcoming, he exercised his rights and sold the property, precipitating a rancorous court battle between himself and the defendants that was finally brought to an end with Candy Mossler's untimely death on October 26, 1976.

Before this, Foreman was again back on the national stage. In 1969 he had represented James Earl Ray, alleged assassin of Martin Luther King, Jr., taking over the case just thirty-six hours before it was due to go to trial. Ray, who had dismissed his previous attorney after conferring with Foreman for several hours, later complained that Foreman had pressured him into pleading an unwanted guilty plea by saying he was "ninety-nine percent certain" he would be executed if he faced a jury in Tennessee. Whatever the truth of this story, Foreman always insisted he had done right by his client. He returned to his home state to rejoice in his role as the elder statesman of the Texas bar, a position he maintained until his death on August 25, 1988.

OTHER NOTABLE CASES:

James Earl Ray (1969)

Harold Lee (Jerry) Giesler

(1886–1962)

I. CAREER

"Get me Giesler!" was a heartfelt cry uttered by just about every well-to-do California resident who found themselves in conflict with that state's statute book during the 1940s and 1950s. There was ample reason for such confidence. In a career that spanned seven decades, the diminutive Jerry Giesler proved himself to be a giant among American criminal trial lawyers; a man who, in more than seventy capital cases, never once lost a client to the gallows or the gas chamber. Rivals were baffled by his success. There was nothing of the traditional "great advocate" about him—he was short, plump, with thin hair and a reedy voice—but whatever he may have lacked in physical advantage was more than outweighed by two vital assets. First, there was his meticulous pretrial preparation; when Giesler entered the courtroom it was with the knowledge that he had anticipated and allowed for every foreseeable contingency, nothing was left to chance. This left him free to concentrate on his forte—working the jury.

A natural exhibitionist, at times his courtroom antics drove opposing counsel and judges wild, but it was all part of a craftily fashioned smokescreen, designed to place Giesler between the evidence and the jury. And when it came to

Guided by Giesler, Errol Flynn tells his story from the witness stand. (AP Wide World)

filtering evidence, nobody could touch him. Hollywood knew his worth; and it was a rare screen-mogul who did not have Giesler's phone number logged in his diary, under the section marked 'trouble.' He was discretion personified, the ideal choice to represent some errant movie star whose private peccadilloes posed an imminent threat to studio profits. In his time Giesler buried dozens of scandals, but in the courtroom he brought facts and situations to light in a way that was incomparable.

He had the best possible teacher. Earl Rogers (q.v.) knew more than most about bailiffs, and when Giesler, a scrawny young University of Southern California student who financed his studies by operating a part-time debt collection agency, came clamoring at Rogers' offices for settlement of an outstanding obligation, he so impressed the great attorney that he left with the offer of a job.

It was a just reward for tenacity. Brought up in Wilton Junction, Iowa, this banker's son had been forced to abandon his law studies at the University of Iowa in 1905 when he was struck down by an eye ailment. In the depths of despair he headed west, to the emerging city of Los Angeles, where he drove a horse drawn lumber wagon from 4:00 A.M. to darkness for $2 a day. As his health improved, he resumed his studies. Then came the chance encounter with Earl Rogers.

He served his apprenticeship well and learned many of the master's tricks. Eventually, he assumed the mantle of the premier lawyer on the West Coast, picking his clients from the famous, the infamous, and the just plain wealthy. Among them were the likes of Charlie Chaplin, Marilyn Monroe, Shelley Winters, Barbara Hutton, Mickey Cohen, and Bugsy Siegel.

Many accused him of being a better actor than most of the movie stars he represented, and there can be no denying his talent for hammy theatrics, but as the following notorious love-triangle murder trial demonstrates, when it came to conceiving brilliantly innovative points of law, Jerry Giesler could stand comparison with the very best.

II. Paul Wright (1938)

Everything Evelyn Wright wanted she got; husband, Paul, made sure of that. He was crazy about his gorgeous young wife, prepared to pander to her every whim, at no matter what financial cost to himself. Evelyn, on the other hand, entertained no such emotions about her husband; to her way of thinking, he was simply a passport to the better things in life, and she was determined to grab as much of South California's good life as possible. The first warnings signs came early in their marriage. Evelyn had her heart set on a fancy house in an exclusive part of Glendale, just north of Los Angeles. Paul blanched when he checked out local real estate prices; there was no way his modest junior executive's salary could stretch to that kind of mortgage. Rents, too, were sky-high.

But Evelyn kept needling, and eventually Paul bit the bullet and signed a lease on a red-tiled stucco building—more medieval castle than house—perched atop its own little hill in Glendale. Still Evelyn wasn't satisfied. To make the most of all the California sun, she wanted a flashy convertible; and then a whole new wardrobe of designer clothes. Paul, frantic that he might lose her, plunged ever more deeply into debt, struggling to keep pace with his wife's extravagance. And not once did he doubt that she was worth every dime. He was blinded by love.

Until the early hours of November 9, 1937.

The evening had started well enough, with Paul and best friend John Kimmel dining together at the Hollywood Athletic Club. Afterwards, Paul suggested a nightcap at his house. Evelyn joined them, and together they talked into the small hours. Around 3:00 A.M., dog-tired, Paul announced he was going to bed. John wished him good night and said that he would be leaving shortly.

Paul fell into a deep slumber, only to be awoken some time later by the sound of a single key being struck repeatedly on the living room piano. Puzzled by the noise, and also because Evelyn had not come to bed, he stumbled into the hallway. As his eyes adjusted to the light, he could see Evelyn and John sat facing each other on the piano stool. It was John who was striking the piano key with one finger, presumably to convince any casual listener that music was the order of the day, when, in truth, his penis was exposed and receiving Evelyn's undivided attention.

A. Maddened by Jealousy

So great was their mutual preoccupation, that neither partner noticed Paul dart back to the bedroom, where he snatched an automatic pistol from a nightstand drawer, then returned to the living room, spraying bullets with every step.

Evelyn Wright and John Kimmel fell to the floor in a hail of lead, their bodies entwined, and with Kimmel's left foot sticking up grotesquely on the piano keyboard. As the smoke cleared, and with it his befuddled senses, Paul began to realize the enormity of what he had done. Trance-like, he phoned the police.

Paul Wright was pacing the sidewalk when the police arrived. In between processing the crime-scene, officers overheard Paul phone his father in Milwaukee. "There has been a terrible tragedy . . . I've shot Evelyn. I caught her cheating. It's just as you said it would be."

The detectives weren't so sure. Their version of events, later amplified in court, was that this "tragedy" had been a planned execution. They reasoned that Wright, homicidally jealous of his wife's adulterous relationship with Kimmel, lured the couple into a compromising situation, and then lurked outside the living room, gun in hand, until shooting them in *flagrante delicto*. As a theory, it fitted the facts of the situation well enough for the state to file first-degree murder charges against Wright.

Despite Wright's limited financial resources, Giesler took the case immediately. Given the sensational circumstances, he knew that the upcoming trial would be plastered across every newspaper in California, and no ambitious attorney worth his salt could afford to turn down such an opportunity.

But first there was a defense to prepare. Wright's volunteered confession, made just after the killings and without any hint of coercion, was doubly damning, and Giesler realized he would have to come up with something spectacular in order to save his client's life. The route he chose was a plea of "temporary insanity", arguing that if Wright were insane at the time he pulled the trigger, legally he was not responsible for his actions; and if he were now sane, he could not be confined to a mental hospital. There was plenty of precedent in California law for such a plea, but Giesler intended adding his own special kind of spin to this traditional defense ploy.

To support a plea of temporary insanity, he relied on Wright's own words, used to describe his emotions at the moment when he saw his wife and best friend cheating on the piano bench. "A white flame exploded in my brain," Wright told the court, before going on to explain how, in a haze, he had emptied his automatic pistol at the couple in two convulsive bursts of gunfire.

Giesler set about convincing the jury that what Wright saw when he entered the room was so traumatic, so devastating, that every vestige of reason deserted him. After studying police photographs of the death scene, and after conducting a series of experiments with his own wife on the actual bench and piano, Giesler had hatched a plausible scenario of how events unfolded on the fateful night. Wheeling the piano and bench into court, and with himself in the role of the dead man, Giesler demonstrated how Kimmel had been sat with his left foot on the piano, while Evelyn, still fully dressed, fondled his penis. The first fusillade hit Evelyn in the back and threw her onto the floor. Kimmel, struck from the front by the second burst, toppled onto his dying lover.

B. Addresses Court from Floor

At this point, Giesler, a master showman, fell from the bench, and continued addressing the jury from the floor.

It was great theater, but was it what had happened? The prosecution thought not and brought in Wright's neighbor—an elderly spinster—to rebut Giesler's claim. Her testimony directly contradicted Wright's insistence that he had fired two shots from the doorway and the rest some seconds later from close range. She described hearing five shots fired "in rapid succession without a break," which dovetailed neatly with the state's claim that Wright had fired all the shots at close-range, quite coolly, and in rapid succession—just the way he had planned it.

Unable to shake her testimony and unwilling to lay himself open to accusations of bullying a senior citizen, Giesler sought to minimize the impact of the damaging testimony by ignoring it. But the state wasn't about to let him off so lightly. Barely able to suppress a gloating grin and eager to press home his advantage, the chief prosecutor approached the witness on redirect-examination and handed her a pencil, with a request that she tap out the sequence of shots.

After some considerable reflection, the woman began tapping. The first two raps came in quick succession. But there then followed a distinct pause, before three more raps.

Instantly, the mood in court altered. Those few seconds—the product of prosecutorial overkill—allowed Giesler to demolish the state's argument that Wright had fired all the shots in rapid succession, and led to his client being convicted of manslaughter rather than first-degree murder.

But it was during the penalty deliberations that Giesler dropped his legal bombshell. He reminded the judge that during the first phase of the trial, where the defendant had enjoyed the presumption of innocence and the state bore the proof of murder, custom dictated that the prosecution make the first opening argument and the last closing argument. Now, with the situation being reversed—the defendant having to prove his own insanity—Giesler argued that such a burden entitled him to the same privilege of first opening and last closing arguments.

Such an impudent motion—without precedent—brought the prosecution to its feet in fury. Hastily, the judge sought to defuse the volatile situation by inviting both sides into his chambers, where they presented arguments. After a lengthy deliberation, he decided in Giesler's favor.

Having the last word in such an emotive trial was of incalculable value to someone so skilled in jury psychology as Jerry Giesler. Again and again he returned to the theme of the innocent husband, betrayed in his own living room, and the searing "white flame" that had temporarily destroyed his powers of reason and logic. It worked. The jury decided that Wright was not guilty by reason of temporary insanity; and when, after a psychiatric examination established that he was no longer insane, Paul Wright was set free.

Others in California had used the insanity defense before in a murder trial, but never in quite so imaginative or effective a manner. Victories such as this paved the way for Giesler to become California's highest paid criminal lawyer, someone whose name alone was enough to make prosecutors tremble in their boots.

When Jerry Giesler died on January 1, 1962, of a heart attack at his Beverly Hills home, he took with him the old style ultra-flamboyant advocacy. The courtrooms he left behind might have been less heavily charged with his passing, but they were also far duller.

OTHER NOTABLE CASES:

Clarence Darrow (1912); Norman "Kid McCoy" Selby (1924); Alexander Pantages (1929-31); Walburga Osterreich (1930); Errol Flynn (1943); Robert Mitchum (1948); Cheryl Crane (1958)

Richard Haynes
(1923-)

I. Career

The high school football coach was apoplectic. Every time his running back took off with the ball he headed toward the sidelines. "What do you think you are," he bawled at the offending player, "a racehorse?" Most players ridiculed in this fashion, in front of the entire team, would have slunk away in embarrassment but not Richard Haynes. He just stood grinning. "Racehorse" sounded good to him, and so "Racehorse" Haynes he became, carrying the name to the peak of the Texas legal profession.

He grew up on Houston's tough North Side, real blue-collar territory, where a little kid like him soon learned how to use his fists if he wanted to survive. At school he turned this combativeness loose in the boxing ring and on the gridiron, and excelled at both, making up in confidence what he lacked in stature.

When he graduated from high school, World War II was reaching its bloody crescendo. In 1944 Haynes joined the Navy and the following year saw action at Iwo Jima, where he was honored for saving lives. Peacetime returned him to a humdrum civilian life that held little appeal for someone of his temperament After an aimless four years he decided to make the military his career, this time the army paratroopers.

It was here that he gained his first experience of the law. A young enlisted man was accused of stealing food from the mess and Haynes was appointed to defend him. Although he lost the case, the way that everything seemed stacked against his client infuriated Haynes and convinced him where his future lay. In 1954 he entered law school at the University of Houston on the GI Bill, which he supplemented with an assortment of jobs that included lifeguarding and shooting pool.

From school he went straight into criminal practice. The first felony case he ever tried involved a poor black man charged with theft. The fee was $300 and Haynes won. He never forgot the feeling of elation he felt watching his client being embraced by ecstatic and surprised family members. With a wife and family to feed, Haynes needed fast money, and this put him off civil practice where the awards, and the concomitant fees, sometimes took years to filter through. His specialty was defending people on drunk driving charges. Nobody around Houston did it better. In the early 1960s he won 163 straight DWI cases.

Defense attorney Richard "Racehorse" Haynes. (AP Wide World)

His most significant DWI victory never came to court; in fact, the driver never even got a ticket. It was Haynes himself, pulled over by the police and asked to account for his erratic driving. In his most strident and persuasive fashion, Haynes insisted he was sober and even performed a back flip off the bumper of his Porsche in order to prove the point. Case won, right there at the roadside.

He brings a lot of that flamboyance into court with him. And in the bar afterwards, reporters can always rely on Haynes for good quotable copy. But in between the homespun aphorisms and licks on the guitar, Haynes also delivers genuine legal brilliance. His trademark is the multi-faceted defense, a complex plan in which he offers the jury a number of simultaneous scenarios, all designed to impugn the prosecution's case.

A classic example came in his defense of two Houston cops accused of violating the civil rights of a black prisoner by kicking him to death. (They had previously been acquitted in a criminal trial.) First, Haynes succeeded in moving the trial from Houston to New Braunfels, a deeply conservative town in the Texas hill country. "I knew we had the case won when we seated the last bigot on that jury," he later declared. At various times during the trial, he contended: a) that the beaten prisoner suffered severe internal injuries while trying to escape; b) that he actually died of a morphine overdose; c) that his lacerated liver had been caused by a careless pathologist during the autopsy. In the face of such bewildering obfuscation, the jury was only too pleased to acquit. Shortly thereafter came the trial—one of those high-rolling extravaganzas that only ever seem to happen in Texas—that made Racehorse Haynes a lawyer of national repute.

II. John Hill (1971)

When thirty-eight-year-old Joan Hill died in a Houston hospital in March 1969, attending physicians were unable to agree on the cause of death; some blamed pancreatitis, others opted for hepatitis. Only one person seemed in no doubt—Joan's father, Ash Robinson, a bellicose and extremely wealthy oilman. He told anybody who would listen that his daughter had been murdered—poisoned by her scheming husband, Dr. John Hill.

Had Hill said or done nothing, it is likely that Robinson's accusations would have been dismissed as the grief-induced ravings of an overly protective father, but when, just three months later, Hill married long-time lover, Ann Kurth, the old man had just the ammunition he needed. Eventually, Robinson bullied the DA's office into filing charges against his son-in-law; a bizarre indictment that read "murder by omission," in effect, killing someone by deliberate neglect.

A. The "Perfect Murder"

Haynes, hired by Hill, knew this case had everything: sex, glamour, money, drugs, and rumors of a "perfect murder." It even had a woman scorned, for after just nine months of marriage, Hill ditched Ann Kurth. Temperamentally disinclined to turning the other cheek, the most recent ex-Mrs. Hill went straight to the authorities; and what she said was pure dynamite.

Jury selection began on February 15, 1971. Haynes is fond of likening a jury to a computer, saying, "The thing has an average IQ of 1200, and 400 years or more of living experience. It's scanning all the time, observing all the time, sworn to pay attention. A formidable machine." Ordinarily, he is a master of *voir dire* (the questioning of potential jurors by attorneys from both sides), but on this occasion he came off second best as assistant District Attorney, I. D. McMaster, managed to sit a jury of eleven men and just one woman. (Haynes, mindful of his client's undeniably handsome appearance, had hoped for more women.) Even so, he was still confident: to his way of thinking, the state had been browbeaten into an unwise prosecution. Earlier, he had shown his contempt for the rare indictment by holding it upside down in front of a reporter and saying, "It reads just as intelligently this way as it does right side up."

Opening for the prosecution, McMaster first detailed Joan's sudden and violent illness, then claimed Hill had deliberately failed "to provide timely hospitalization for her in order that she would die."

Haynes listened to all of this, expressionless. Without Ann Kurth, the state didn't have a prayer, and he was going to fight tooth and nail to keep Hill's ex-wife off the stand. Under Texas law, he argued, she was barred from testifying against her former husband. However, when the prosecution unearthed some obscure precedent that said otherwise, Judge Fred Hooey ruled uneasily that Ann Kurth could take the stand, with the proviso that he might stop her testimony at any time.

After describing her relationship with Hill, Ann Kurth told of entering Hill's bathroom and finding three petri dishes—the kind used in laboratories—with "something red in them." Hill came in and angrily shooed her from the room, saying that it was " . . . just an experiment." The next day she noticed some unusual pastries in the refrigerator. Hill, again annoyed, told her not to eat them.

B. Startling Evidence

She next provided a vivid account of an incident just weeks into their marriage, when she claimed Hill tried to kill her, first in a car crash, and then immediately after with a syringe. When asked how she knew that the syringe was harmful—after all, might it not have been a sedative following the traumatic incident?—Ann replied triumphantly, "Because he told me how he had killed Joan with a needle."

Haynes rocketed off his chair, hollering "Mistrial!" at the top of his lungs. After considerable deliberation, Judge Hooey ended the trial on grounds that the defense had not had an opportunity to prepare themselves against this direct accusation of murder.

In trying to avenge herself against Hill, Ann Kurth badly overplayed her hand. If, as she alleged, the murder attempt took place just four weeks into a nine-month marriage, why had she stayed with a man who had tried to kill her? Ann claimed to have been frightened into immobility, but anyone who knew the lady found this hard to swallow. Grim-faced, the prosecutors went back to the drawing board.

Mistrials usually favor the defendant, they sour the prosecution and quite often lead to a dismissal of all charges. Certainly, Haynes thought this was the likeliest scenario; all the same he still prepared for the possible retrial with his customary diligence. Then came disaster. Hill got married again.

Just four months after the mistrial, Dr. John Hill took his third bride to the altar. For once in his life Haynes was dumbstruck. Arrogance, stupidity, call it what you will, Hill's actions were probably instrumental in deciding the state to try him again.

But before that second trial could take place, John Hill was dead, shot down at his River Oaks mansion by an unknown assailant, in what had all the hallmarks of a contract killing. Eventually police would arrest three people in connection with the shooting, two of whom were later imprisoned. Rumors that Ash Robinson had ordered the killing were nullified when the old man was acquitted of all charges.

As Haynes suspected, the Hill saga did indeed establish his reputation on the national stage. The big cases rolled in and with them the kind of fees that led to a lavish home in the same exclusive Houston suburb where John Hill had been gunned down. In the process Racehorse Haynes has become one of America's most visible and successful lawyers.

C. Attention to Details

From his early success defending DWIs, Haynes understands that lawsuits are not won by courtroom showboating, but by careful attention to detail and hard scientific analysis. Even so, he's prepared to use pure effrontery if necessary. He explained his philosophy at an American Bar Association seminar: "Say you sue me because you say my dog bit you. Well now, this is my defense: my dog doesn't bite. And second, in the alternative, my dog was tied up that night. And third, I don't believe you really got bit. And fourth . . ." here he grinned slyly, "I don't have a dog!"

OTHER NOTABLE CASES:

Cullen Davis (1977 & 1978)

William Howe
(c.1828–1902)
Abraham Hummell
(1850–1926)

I. Career

During a 1884 vice clean-up campaign, New York City police officers arrested seventy-four brothel operators. When asked to name their legal counsel, all of them replied, "Howe and Hummell." It was a similar tale some years earlier; a survey of those Tombs prison inmates then awaiting trial for murder—some twenty-five in total—recorded no less than twenty-three as clients of what is arguably the most successful criminal law firm in history. Such domination, unprecedented at the time and unmatched to this day, has guaranteed William Howe and Abraham Hummell their place among the greats of American advocacy.

But that only tells half the story: Howe and Hummell were also two of the most crooked lawyers ever to set foot in any courtroom anywhere. Ethics flew out the window with this pair. They bribed judges, suborned perjury, blackmailed at will, and engaged in just about every other form of chicanery going, although they did manage to sidestep any accusations of jury-fixing; probably because Howe, with his monumental powers of verbal persuasion, considered such precautions unnecessary.

So why include them here?

A. The Father of the Criminal Bar

In the first place, the numbers are fantastic. Between 1869 and 1907, when it was put out of business by District Attorney William Travers Jerome, the firm of Howe & Hummell defended more than 1,000 people indicted on charges of either murder or manslaughter. Howe himself appeared in more than 650 homicide cases, enough for famed jurist and 1904 presidential candidate Judge Alton B. Porter to call him "the father of the criminal bar in America."

Secondly, they operated in a frenetic, freewheeling age, when standards were low and justice could be bought and sold like any other commodity. They just happened to be the best.

From their offices directly across from the Tombs, William Howe and Abraham Hummell ran a legal empire that included most of New York's very worst inhabitants. Their cable address read LENIENT, and that was the name of the game. Except when it came to money. Howe once said, "We always look ahead. When we take a case, we secure fees covering even an appeal to the Court of Appeals. If our client dies before the appeal is granted, he will never need the money and we might as well have it."

Their backgrounds were widely diverse. Howe was born in either Boston or England—nobody is certain which—but he definitely grew up in London. When he arrived in America in 1858 it was as a parolee, though the nature of his offense in England remains lost to history. Because of his skill in medical cases some suspected a physician's background, but Howe was always tightlipped about his antecedents and liked to keep people guessing. There is no record of his receiving any legal training in America but by 1861 he was practicing in New York City, defending Civil War deserters, and earning for himself the nickname *Habeas Corpus Howe.* A flashy dresser, he was renowned for wearing diamonds that he had bought for just ten percent down. When the bills came in, Howe would instruct his underlings to ignore them, saying it provided good practice in fighting claims.

In 1863 he hired a thirteen-year-old office boy, Boston-born and blessed with quicksilver intelligence. Abraham Hummell's astounding ability to absorb intricate legal detail led to him being made a full partner by age twenty. Howe was immensely proud of Hummell's superior mental acuity. "You'll have to talk to my little Abie about that," he would coo when confronted by some arcane legal matter. "He's so smart."

They made an odd couple. Howe, built like a battleship, and sporting a huge walrus mustache and a mane of wavy gray hair, would sweep imperiously into court, light glinting on the diamonds that hung off him like Christmas illuminations. At his side trotted Hummell, barely five feet tall, with a huge bald head and spindly legs, always in funeral black, with jet-like eyes that never stayed still and an expression that never moved.

Curiously, their private lives were in complete contrast to their courtroom demeanor. Whereas Hummell was a fixture on the New York social scene, a bon vivant who rarely missed a first night in the theater, Howe preferred to stay home with his wife.

B. Split Duties

Their legal roles were just as delineated. Howe handled the big trials; Hummell dealt with obscure points of law. Under Howe's tutelage, Hummell did become a competent trial lawyer, but his specialty was civil litigation, particularly "seduction under promise of marriage suits." Thinly disguised blackmail, this was a lucrative field that regularly harvested sums between $5,000–10,000 from wealthy men desperate to pay off young ladies whom they had bedded.

Once the dupe had paid, all relevant affidavits and blackmail papers disappeared into a pot-bellied stove that stood in the middle of Howe & Hummell's sparsely furnished office; the delighted young lady would leave with her fifty percent of the haul; and Hummell would head for nearby Pontins Restaurant to meet his partner and divide that day's take.

A sizable portion of this cash found its way into the pockets of newspaper reporters as an inducement to write flattering accounts of their trials, copies of which were then circulated among underworld types who might be in need of representation. In 1888 the duo went one better, writing a book, *In Danger,* that, under the guise of offering cautionary advice to the innocent and the unwary in New York, was little more than a how-to manual of malfeasance, solely designed to drum up new business by telling readers just how easy it was to commit crime.

When the delinquents did come calling they received the full benefit of Howe's unique talents. He never worried about juries, and always tried to pick the first twelve men offered. Invariably his clients were "more sinned against than sinning," or else "poor wretched souls passed in this world of tears by fortune and providence alike," and it was a mood caught in the public gallery, where relatives of the defendant were encouraged to shed copious tears on their behalf. If, by chance, the client lacked actual familial sympathy, Howe could always rustle up a lachrymose "relative" or two from the stable of professional spectators that he maintained for just such a contingency. He was a great believer in tears, and richly deserved his title of "The Great Weeper" for his ability to sob at will.

With his stentorian voice and the ability to work himself up into the most frightful lather, Howe cut an intimidating figure. One summation, hours long, was actually delivered from a kneeling position. But it wasn't all bombast. He was a forerunner in the use of the insanity defense, even if on one occasion he did spend an inordinate amount of time pointing out to the jury the physical defects in his client's head, assuring them that "he is Nature's madman!"

During their prime—1875–1900—Howe and Hummell reigned supreme. Not until the late nineteenth century did the first signs of a crack appear in their aura of invincibility.

II. Martin Thorn (1897)

On June 26, 1897, a headless torso was recovered from the East River off Lower Manhattan. An odd-shaped strip of skin had been cut from the chest, as though some distinctive feature, a tattoo, maybe, had been excised. Over the next days, as other body parts were recovered from the river—only the head was never found—tabloid reporters ran riot over what they termed the *Jigsaw Murder.*

A check of missing persons turned up the name of a tattooed masseur named Willie Guldensuppe. His landlady, Augusta Nack, vaguely remembered the masseur, but when taken to the mortuary she declined to identify the body parts as those of her former tenant. Other residents of the boarding house were more forthcoming. According to them, Nack and Guldensuppe had been lovers until the brawny masseur came home unexpectedly one day and found Augusta sharing her favors with a young barber, Martin Thorn. Despite being pummeled senseless by Guldensuppe, Thorn continued to meet the statuesque Augusta, and together they planned their future. It was about this time that Guldensuppe vanished.

New York's yellow press kept their hungry readers well fed on a diet of lurid copy. One avid follower of events was a Long Island farmer who, just before Guldensuppe's disappearance, had rented out a cottage on his Woodside farm to a couple who strongly resembled newspaper descriptions of Thorn and Nack. His suspicions about the couple had been aroused when, one afternoon, some ducks splashing in water beneath the cottage's disconnected waste disposal pipe, had all turned bright pink. A closer look convinced him the water contained blood.

Detectives summoned to the cottage not only confirmed the presence of blood, they also found a gun, some rope, a carving knife, carbolic acid, and a saw; enough to charge Thorn and Nack with murder.

For someone with the publicity instincts of William Howe, who handled this case solo, the *Jigsaw Murder* provided a prime opportunity for some serious self-aggrandizement, and a better than even chance that he would get his client off. He took the court by storm. Typically he would start every trial smothered in diamonds, and then subtract a few each day, so that by the final summation he was clad in somber black. But all that was a long way off; for the time being, he needed to mount a credible defense. Accordingly, he opted to represent Thorn alone. This allowed him to claim that, not only did his client not know the victim, but he was unacquainted with Mrs. Nack as well. Such brazenness endured until the testimony of the Long Island farmer who identified Thorn and Nack as the couple that had rented the cottage.

A. Mystery Dead Man?

Howe swiftly altered tack. Now it became a full-frontal assault on the identity of the dead man, ridiculing prosecution claims that these assorted limbs belonged to Willie Guldensuppe. Clearly, he roared, *corpus delicti* had not been proved. What evidence was there that Guldensuppe had ever existed? In order to sell the jury on this notion of a fictional character, Howe littered his argument with references to Goldylocks, or Golden Soup or Guildedsoap, anything but Guldensuppe.

He further stirred the pot by arguing that if such a person as Willie Guldensuppe did exist, then there was no proof that he was not still alive. Read in cold print many of his claims now sound ludicrous, but it should be remembered that Howe could work up an awesome head of verbal steam when in full flow, and he was the king of jury manipulation. Once again, in the view of most observers, the old master was cruising to yet another famous victory, when calamity struck—Augusta Nack confessed.

She had been visited in her cell by a priest, who had been accompanied by his four-year-old son. Apparently this precocious lad had clambered onto Mrs. Nack's lap and implored her, in the name of all that was holy, to confess her guilt, if indeed she was culpable. In the face of such supplications, Augusta Nack buckled. Many claimed her confession resulted from divine intervention; others suspected the hand of press magnate William Randolph Hearst, whose papers miraculously scooped the competition with news of the confession.

Nack admitted that she and Thorn had rented the place with the sole purpose of murdering her violent former lover. Guldensuppe had been lured to the cottage with promises of a renewal in their liaison, then killed and dismembered by Thorn.

B. A Woman in Distress

Such a betrayal forced Thorn into a corner. Predictably he off-loaded all the blame onto his mistress's broad shoulders. It was she, he said, who had shot Guldensuppe. His dismemberment of the body had been solely occasioned by a desire to aid a woman in distress.

Howe, preparing what should have been his valedictory summation, was shattered. He wrote to Hummell, who was in Paris at the time: "Dear Abe: I had the prettiest case, and here is all my work shattered. I can still prove they could not identify Willie's body, and that it wasn't cut up in the Woodside cottage. Now all my roses are frosted in a night and my grapes withered on the vine."

In the event, Thorn went to the electric chair, while Nack plea-bargained her way to a twenty-year jail term.

Howe never quite recovered from this setback. He tried a few more cases, but the spark was gone, and the heavy drinking that had dogged him all his life began to worsen. A succession of heart attacks ended his life on September 2, 1902, when "The Great Weeper" died at his home in the Bronx.

Abraham Hummell tried manfully to maintain his partner's scurrilous traditions. Many claimed that it was he, not the distinguished attorney Joseph Choate, who coined the epigram: "There are two kinds of lawyers, those who know the law, and those who know the judge." It certainly sounds like Hummell. But in 1907 his legendary luck finally ran out, and a one-year sentence for perverting the course of justice (soliciting perjury) led to his disbarment and dissolution of the firm. One week after his release from prison he sailed for Europe, where he spent the remainder of his life, until dying in London on January 21, 1926.

OTHER NOTABLE CASES:

William Griffin (1863); Dr. Jakob Rosenzweig (1871); William Blakely (1873); Richard Croker (1874); Jack Hahn (1886); Henry Carlton (1888); Burton Webster (1888); Ella Nelson (1891)

William M. Kunstler
(1919–1995)

I. Career

History is divided on William Kunstler. Some idolized this cantankerous firebrand as the quintessential radical lawyer, the spiritual ancestor of Clarence Darrow (q.v.), a champion of the oppressed who would take on any case, no matter how forlorn. Others held a less charitable view, despising what they saw as an opportunistic blowhard more concerned with massaging his own ego than in pursuing the course of justice. As usually happens, the true essence of the man lay somewhere between these polar extremes. He could be mercurial, of course, and he was often an unnecessary and frivolous thorn in the side of courts all across America, but he was also a constant reminder that without guaranteed individual rights—and without lawyers prepared to battle for those rights—the statute book is just a hollow volume. If on occasion overzealousness got the better of him . . . well, that was just Bill Kunstler.

In light of his later left-wing activism, it came as a shock to many to learn that Kunstler's roots were solid Ivy League. He had majored in French at Yale until World War II got in the way, then he served in the Pacific at a time when the fighting was at its bloodiest. Critics of his subsequent anti-Vietnam War rhetoric often failed to appreciate that this was a battle-hardened veteran speaking, someone who had risen to the rank of major and won the Bronze Star. After demobilization he resumed his studies at Columbia Law School until graduating in 1949. His career in civil litigation got off to a flying start. Then came a pivotal moment in his life. In the mid-1950s he represented a State Department employee whose passport had been confiscated to stop him traveling to China as a freelance journalist. The basic injustice dealt out to this innocent citizen left an indelible mark on the young attorney and changed him forever. Turning his back on a lucrative civil practice, Kunstler went after the establishment.

There was plenty to outrage a young left-wing attorney in the 1950s. With McCarthyism still an insidious force in the land, Kunstler found himself forging ever closer ties with the ACLU. Simultaneously he joined forces with Martin Luther King, Jr. and the Civil Rights struggle. Despite all these diversions he still found time to author several books, including *The Minister and the Choir Singer* (1964), which remains the definitive account of the sensational 1922 Hall-Mills murder case. All through the 1960s, Kunstler operated at the heart of the radical movement, filing motions, arguing appeals, sometimes just being plain obtuse. In 1966, together with other like-minded lawyers, he co-founded the Center for Constitutional Rights (CCR), with the aim of finding creative uses of the law as a tool for social change.

His own highwater mark regards personal involvement with the radical left came in 1969 when he represented the notorious Chicago Seven. For a few months William Kunstler was the most famous lawyer in America, garnering almost as many headlines as the recalcitrant defendants. At one point the courtroom chaos reached such a pitch that Kunstler was himself sentenced to four years imprisonment for contempt (later overturned).

Thereafter he became a fixture on the radical circuit, representing Native-American activists, prisoners after the Attica rebellion of 1971, anti-war protesters, and flag-burners, anyone, it seemed, who couldn't find good legal counsel anywhere else turned to Kunstler.

One such person was El Sayyid Nosair.

II. El Sayyid Nosair (1991)

Just minutes after delivering a speech at a New York City hotel in November 1990, Rabbi Meir Kahane, militant conservative and former head of the Jew-

William Kunstler (right) confers with fellow attorney Michael W. Warren at a press conference held during Nosair trial.

ish Defense League, was shot down by a gunman. In making his escape the assassin wounded another Kahane aide, then ran outside, where he was tackled by an armed Postal Service officer. A fierce gun battle erupted and both men were hit. After receiving treatment for his wounds, El Sayyid Nosair, a thirty-six-year-old Arab, was charged with murder.

It appeared to be an open-and-shut case: Nosair had been caught fleeing the crime scene, in possession of the murder weapon, and numerous eyewitnesses were prepared to swear that his was the hand on the gun that killed Kahane. For the mob of furious Jews who thronged the courthouse steps on the trial's opening day, November 4, 1991, there could only be one outcome. Just yards away, beyond a barricade of harassed police officers, a cabal of equally incensed

Arabs traded insults and worse with their traditional enemies. Death threats, too, had been issued, including several aimed at trial judge Alvin Schlesinger.

Kunstler knew that in such a volatile case, jury composition would be critical. Early on, chief prosecutor William Greenbaum gave anguished voice to his suspicion that Kunstler was deliberately keeping whites off the jury. Kunstler, an old hand at media manipulation, preferred to fight his battles at his daily news conferences. "It's true that Mr Greenbaum has been objecting to the exclusion," he said, shaking a sorrowful head. "And that's because he wants an all-white middle-class jury to hear this case. But the truth is, he excluded two whites, one of whom I believe was Jewish, who we were willing to accept." Significantly, the prosecution declined to comment on this observation and Kunstler got the representative jury he was after: five black, one Hispanic, six white. He also succeeded in seating nine women on the panel.

When the prosecution in its opening statement failed to attribute any motive to Nosair—presumably in the belief that the sheer weight of other evidence made such a submission redundant—Kunstler pounced. The reason for this omission, he told the jury, was simple: his client was innocent. Then, he unfolded an extraordinary story. Far from being a fanatical assassin, Nosair was actually a fall guy, someone lured to the meeting by an unidentified aide of Kahane with the express purpose of being framed for the killing. The real gunman, according to Kunstler, was a disgruntled member of the Jewish Defense League, who shot Kahane in a dispute over "missing funds," and gasps of astonishment greeted his claim that Nosair and Kahane once met on the very friendliest of terms in Kahane's car!

A. Victim of Circumstance!

When the rabbi was shot, Kunstler said, Nosair was right at the back of the room. He fled from the room by choice, he was chased, because he was the only Arab present. "You'll have to decide who shot Meir Kahane," Kunstler warned the jury solemnly. "This case is not cut and dried." Although unable to produce a single witness to corroborate this wild theory, Kunstler stuck to it resolutely for the duration of the trial.

Much of his time was spent in discrediting the prosecution witnesses. He was particularly tough on Dr. Steven Stowe, a Bellevue Hospital anesthesiologist resident who moonlighted for a Jewish ambulance service, and who had attended Kahane just after he was shot.

"Didn't you do everything in your power that night to see that Meir Kahane never reached Bellevue alive?" demanded Kunstler.

"No, sir," replied the baffled doctor, although later Kunstler was able to draw vague testimony from other witnesses which implied that Stowe had appeared to hamper treatment at the hospital.

Like all great lawyers, Kunstler was an arch exponent of psychological warfare. At one point the prosecution complained bitterly because Kunstler kept a copy of Meir Kahane's book *False Prophet* on his desk in full view of the jury, feeling it could send the wrong message. Kunstler willingly removed the offending volume, only to replace it with a reprint of an article he himself had written for a legal journal, entitled *The Bill of Rights—Can it Survive?*

It wasn't all mind games; Kunstler did have some evidentiary points to argue. Because a full autopsy had not been performed (Kahane's widow had requested this in accordance with Jewish law), he claimed it was impossible to determine the exact path of the bullet that entered the victim's neck and exited his right cheek. More precise information about the trajectory, he said, would have proved that his client was not physically in a position to fire the shot.

This was a moot point. More concrete was the revolver found next to Nosair and identified by ballistics expert, Detective Robert Cotter, as the murder weapon. Kunstler simply glided over this inconvenience by claiming it had been "planted" by the real killers of Kahane.

B. Acquitted of Murder

In exercising his right to silence, Nosair put his entire fate in Kunstler's hands. He was amply rewarded for his trust. Kunstler favored the jury with a vivid account of a man trapped by circumstances, and on December 21, 1991, they rewarded his eloquence by acquitting Nosair of murder or attempted murder, and convicted him only on assault and weapons charges. When queried by the press later, jury members said they felt that the prosecution failed to prove Nosair actually fired the gun.

Kunstler had nothing but praise for the jurors, saying he had aimed for a jury of "third world people" and "people who were not yuppies or establishment types . . . these jurors understand life as it is lived." Interestingly, he also revealed his own doubts about the case. At first he had considered the prosecution evidence so overwhelming that he advised Nosair to plead insane, because this would likely lead to a lesser sentence. But Nosair had refused, insisting, "I didn't do it. I am innocent."

Asked how the jury could acquit Nosair of being the assassin, yet convict him of possessing and firing the murder weapon in the assault of the post office worker and a spectator at the meeting, Kunstler just shrugged. "The logic cuts both ways," he said, though he did later characterize the split verdict as "strange, irrational, inconsistent, and repugnant."

Nosair had no doubt where the credit lay. "All praise is due to Allah," he said. He was later sentenced to 7-22 years imprisonment on the lesser charges.[1]

Any impartial viewing of the evidence would have to conclude that this was one of the most astounding verdicts in the history of American jurisprudence. Achieved in the face of an apparently watertight prosecution and massive intimidation, it remains a brilliant tribute to Kunstler's shrewd insight into human nature and unique adversarial skills. The price he paid on a personal level was brutal. Fellow Jews vilified him publicly for daring to defend an Arab, and each day the seventy-two-year-old Kunstler ran a gauntlet of squalid abuse as he entered the courthouse building. Needless to say the invective bounced off his shoulders, in much the same way as it had for the previous four decades. He had become very used to upsetting people.

On September 5, 1995, the famous gruff voice was silenced forever. Kuntsler's death left an unfillable void in the American judicial system. A couple of months later more than 3,000 mourners, friends, relatives, clients and admirers gathered at the Cathedral of St. John the Divine in New York for a memorial dedicated to the life of this courageous and crusading lawyer. The eulogies were eloquent and heartfelt, though none was more appropriate than an earlier tribute to Kunstler paid by longtime friend Alan Dershowitz (q.v.), "I have great compassion for God now, because I think Bill is going to start filing lawsuits as soon as he gets to heaven."

OTHER NOTABLE CASES:

The Berrigans (1968); Chicago Seven (1969); Joanne Chesimard (1977); Gregory Lee Johnson (1989); Qubilah Shabazz (1995)

[1] *In January 1996, at a federal court trial which included participants in the World Trade Center Bombing, Nosair was convicted of conspiracy to murder Meir Kahane and was sentenced to life imprisonment. William Kunstler played no part in this trial.*

Samuel J. Leibowitz
(1893–1978)

I. Career

Samuel Leibowitz always knew how to create an effect. An early demonstration of this came while he was studying at Cornell College of Law, with his announcement that, after graduation, he intended specializing in criminal practice. When the College Dean, Professor Edwin Hamlin Woodruff, expressed surprise—at that time Cornell's traditions were strongly rooted in corporate law—Leibowitz explained it simply, "I have no business connections in New York, my parents are poor. I'd never get a chance to represent big corporations or railroads or real estate holders. Criminal law is the only way for a man to get a foothold in a large city. Once I am well-known, then maybe I can attract worthwhile clients."

Woodruff smiled, "You've got it all figured out."

"I've got it all figured out," the young graduate nodded.

He had no other choice, really. Right from the cradle, Leibowitz had been brought up knowing that life wasn't going to grant him any favors. He was still only four years old when his parents, weary from the epidemics of anti-Semitism

Samuel Leibowitz rolls up his sleeves before he re-enters the courtroom. (AP Wide World)

that regularly scourged Eastern Europe, fled their native Romania and joined the migration west. Like millions of others, Sam Leibowitz got his first glimpse of the New World from the deck of an immigrant ship as it steamed slowly towards Ellis Island. His family liked what they saw and settled in Manhattan's Lower East Side. Life was tough but the youngster thrived. He was smart, too. Urged on by his ambitious father, he studied law at Cornell University, moving easily through his classes, though it was in the debating and dramatic clubs where his true talents prospered. There, he learned how to marshal his thoughts, how to advance both sides of an argument, how to modulate his voice, when to make the most effective use of body language. In short, he acquired all the skills inherent in good advocacy, and in doing so, found his true niche in life—public speaking. Come graduation time, Leibowitz decided that his silver tongue would pave the path to a golden future.

After a couple of years clerking in the New York law offices of Michael F. McGoldrick, the young man's itch for courtroom action became irresistible. In early 1919 he approached Judge Howard P. Nash in his chambers, offering his services to any indigent defendant who might be appearing before him. A few days later Nash assigned Leibowitz to defend a man accused of breaking into a saloon and stealing $7 from the cash register. Since the defendant was found drunk on the premises, in possession of a skeleton key, and had confessed to the arresting officers, the case appeared to be a formality. Somehow Leibowitz managed to convince the jury otherwise. The manner of his remarkable success drew appreciative comments from other lawyers in the courthouse corridors, though Leibowitz did not much care for the appellation"'kid" that generally accompanied their praise. To combat his still youthful appearance the lanky young attorney took to wearing pince-nez, an affectation that he felt gave him greater gravitas.

Soon afterwards, in May 1919, lured by the prospect of independence, Leibowitz struck out on his own. It was the genesis of a truly remarkable career. In quick order his almost supernatural gifts of persuasion came to the attention of those who needed him most—gangland mobsters. During the Roaring Twenties Leibowitz's client list read like a Who's Who of organized crime: Al Capone, Harry "Pittsburgh Phil" Strauss, Benjamin "Bugsy" Siegel, Abe Reles, Harry Stein, Vincent Coll, all of these and more had good reason to appreciate his talents. In the process they made him a very rich man.

But he was more than just a slick-talking mouthpiece for the mob. Although never as committed as, say, Clarence Darrow to righting the wrongs of society, Leibowitz still responded angrily to situations where he felt that some "little guy" had been steamrollered by the system. Curiously enough, it was just such a case that put the name of Samuel Leibowitz on the national map.

II. Harry Hoffman (1929)

An occupational hazard for any successful defense attorney is the daily stream of letters from prison inmates, all proclaiming total innocence and all begging for representation. By 1929, after a decade of virtually unrelieved triumph,

Sam Leibowitz's mailbox was regularly stuffed with such requests. Why New York's premier defense lawyer happened to single out Harry Hoffman's letter from among all the others was a mystery that Leibowitz was never able to explain, least of all to himself. But something inspired him to visit the Sing Sing convict who swore that he had been framed. It was a momentous decision for both men.

Five years earlier Harry Hoffman, a movie house projectionist, had been convicted of murdering an attractive Staten Island housewife named Maude Bauer. The circumstances of her death were bizarre. She had been at the wheel of her mother's car, when the vehicle skidded out of control and crashed. Leaving her three-year-old daughter in the car with her mother, Maude went in search of a wrecker. As she reached an intersection, just 150 feet away, a Model T Ford drew to a halt. Maude explained her situation to the driver, then shouted back to her mother that the stranger had offered to give her a ride to a nearby garage.

Later that afternoon Maude Bauer was found shot dead by a bullet from a .25 caliber Colt automatic. Witnesses described the driver of the car as dark complexioned, overweight, and wearing tortoise-shell glasses, a brown hat and overcoat. One month later Harry Hoffman was arrested. Not only did he fit the description of the mysterious driver, drive a Ford sedan, and offer an alibi that was palpably false, but he also owned a .25 Colt that a police ballistics expert declared to be the murder weapon. Just about the only surprising outcome at Hoffman's trial was that the jury brought in a verdict of guilty to second-degree murder only, thus sparing him the electric chair.

Most prisoners in similar circumstances might consider themselves fortunate, do their time quietly, and wait for a chance to impress the parole board. Not Harry Hoffman. He never once stopped protesting his innocence. A legal technicality led to him being granted a retrial that resulted in deadlock. A third hearing ended the same way. By the time Hoffman wrote his letter to Sam Leibowitz, the once plump movie projectionist had worried off about one hundred pounds and was desperate for another trial.

A brief review of the evidence convinced Leibowitz that the case was hopeless: so bad, in fact, that he advised Hoffman to withdraw his appeal and serve the time, particularly in light of the district attorney's office hardball announcement that, in the event of another trial, they would be going all out for the death penalty. Hoffman just shook his head. He would take his chances, he told Leibowitz.

A. Phony Alibi

So, what about the false alibi? Hoffman frankly admitted concocting a false story, but blamed it on panic caused by having no alibi. Leibowitz winced. While juries might accept the absence of an alibi—after all, who can account for every hour of every day?—proven liars never look good. Hoffman, a Jew, protested that he had lied because he had feared a repetition of the Leo Frank tragedy. (In 1913, Leo Frank, a Jewish factory manager in Atlanta, had been sentenced to death for murdering a young girl. When doubts surfaced about his guilt, the sentence was commuted to life imprisonment. On August 16, 1915, a mob, inflamed by anti-Semitism, stormed the prison farm where Frank was being held and lynched him. Later it became clear that Frank was entirely innocent.)

Leibowitz, no stranger to discrimination himself, empathized with Hoffman, and, despite some reservations, agreed to take the case. Later, after studying the facts more closely, he became convinced that Sing Sing Convict 75990 was an innocent man.

His chance to test this belief came on May 6, 1929, when Hoffman faced a jury for the fourth time. Leibowitz came to court armed with the strand of reasoning that he believed would free his client. Some surreptitious digging had uncovered rumors of a prosecutorial cover-up; now, Leibowitz intended fine-tuning those rumors to his own advantage. Like every great advocate, he was a master of allusion and innuendo; during the impanelment process he let both run rampant. Each prospective juror came under Leibowitz's penetrating gaze, and each was asked the same question: "Do you know Horatio J. Sharrett?" When puzzled jurors shook their heads, Leibowitz would enlighten them. "He is the brother of Clinton J. Sharrett, political leader on Staten Island." Over state objections, Leibowitz kept insinuating Sharrett's name into the proceedings, to the point where prosecutor, Albert C. Fach, protested, "We will produce Horatio J. Sharrett and show that he was not the slayer of Mrs. Bauer, as defense counsel has intimated."

Leibowitz affected his best air of outraged innocence. "I intimated no such thing," he chimed sweetly, "However, Sharrett was seen in the neighborhood of the murder just after Mrs. Bauer was killed, he answers the description of the man who drove Mrs. Bauer away, and he certainly acted in an extraordinary manner." By this subterfuge Leibowitz managed to sow a seed of suspicion—any suspicion—in every juror's mind.

Piece by piece, Leibowitz dismantled the prosecution's case. Under his gentle but firm prodding, one of the eyewitnesses, a dull-witted girl of eighteen, admitted that five years earlier she had been coerced by the police into identifying Hoffman. Another eyewitness, this time a police officer, admitted only coming forward to identify Hoffman one month after the crime and after the issuance of a $8,500 reward notice. A further witness admitted that his evidence, at first helpful to Hoffman, had been radically altered after he was beaten by a police officer.

B. Science Reveals the Truth

Finally, there was the evidence of the bullet. At the earlier trials Sergeant Harry F. Butts, a police firearms expert, had positively identified Hoffman's gun as the murder weapon. Now science made a liar of him. Using the recently invented comparison microscope, which enabled two bullets to be viewed simultaneously, four independent ballistics experts stated unequivocally that Hoffman's gun had not fired the fatal bullet.

For most of the trial Leibowitz had presented a hard-headed appraisal of the facts, bereft of emotion, but in his peroration he allowed the oratorical talents to flow full-bore. As a tearful Hoffman looked on, Leibowitz proclaimed, "I do not believe any jury would convict a dog on the evidence presented here!"

The jury agreed. Later that day Hoffman walked out of the court a free man, and back into the welcome obscurity from whence he had surfaced. No proceedings were ever taken against Horatio J. Sharrett, who resumed his real estate business in Staten Island.

Leibowitz's scintillating performance in this trial drew lavish praise far beyond the hardboiled New York legal profession that knew him so well, and throughout the 1930s his star continued to shine as he featured in a string of sensational cases. Just about the only blot on an otherwise impeccable copy book came in the overheated aftermath of the Lindbergh tragedy, when a German immigrant named Bruno Hauptmann found himself facing charges of kidnap and murder. Not only did Leibowitz pointedly and publicly decline to represent Hauptmann, but before the trial he took to the airwaves to inform radio listeners all across America of his belief that Hauptmann was guilty. For someone who had railed so long and so hard about the difficulties of ensuring a fair trial, it was a strange lapse in judgment.

Nevertheless, Leibowitz rode out the storm and went back to winning cases. His only significant setback came in 1938, when, after 139 straight capital cases, he finally lost a client to the electric chair. Like most who knew the thuggish Salvatore Gatti, Leibowitz was unconcerned by the killer's fate; what he did resent was the behind-the-hands gloating engaged in by so many of his envious contemporaries.

C. Taking the Bench

Such backbiting and the constant strain of capital cases began to wear on Leibowitz, turning his ambitions more and more towards the bench. When, in 1940 the Democratic Party nominated him for the judgeship of the King's County Court, political enemies gleefully seized on this decision, howling that "Leibowitz would empty out the jails," a reference to the hundreds of shady characters he had defended in his time. How many of those former clients came out to vote is unknown, but what is certain is that the "gangland lawyer" won in a canter and took his place on the bench on January 6, 1941.

Anyone expecting a "revolving door" court was in for a grievous shock. Leibowitz, the judge, was hard-nosed and nobody's pushover. Ironically, the advocate who had fought so hard to keep Sing Sing's electric chair empty harbored no such ambitions when it came time to pass sentence. He was tough but fair; and always his primary concern was the rehabilitation of first-time offenders. The majority of such defendants who came before him were given a second chance: recidivists could look forward to a long spell behind bars. After serving as the presiding judge on a Brooklyn grand jury inquiry into police corruption and waterfront racketeering, Leibowitz reached the pinnacle of his career with his 1961 appointment to the New York Supreme Court, where he served with distinction until his retirement in 1969.

But it is as an advocate that Leibowitz will be remembered best: a marvelous orator, unabashed ham, and a meticulous preparer on matters of law. The priceless asset for a trial attorney of being able to think on his feet came easily to him. When it did not, then there were always a few precious seconds of respite to be gained by removing the pince-nez and giving them a ruminative polish. He has been called "the greatest actor-lawyer of his time." It is doubtful if Samuel Leibowitz ever saw any distinction between two such closely related professions.

OTHER NOTABLE CASES:

Vincent Coll (1931); Scottsboro Boys (1934); Vera Stretz (1936);
Robert Irwin (1938); Joseph Scutellaro (1939); Alvin Dooley (1940)

Martin Littleton
(1872–1934)

I. Career

Almost every time an attorney rises in court it is for the purpose of persuasion. Facts are shaded, testimony is obscured, witnesses are nudged in the desired direction, laws are interpreted according to need; always there is a conscious attempt to influence either a jury or a judge. The great advocates achieve their design more often than not. A very select few—like Martin Littleton—pull off feats of legal legerdemain that seem to defy belief. He was a colossus. In both the legal and the political arena, Littleton, with "his unrivaled collection of trained adjectives and awe-inspiring nouns," was regarded as an awesome opponent.

He came from a long line of Tennessee mountain men, and it was from them that he inherited the strong streak of independence that marked his career. When he was age eleven, his family left their Knoxville roots and migrated to North Texas. An undistinguished academic record gave few clues to the spectacular career to come. He first found work on the railroads, then came a job in a printing office where he learned to set type. Toughest of all was a backbreaking stretch spent toiling on the hot, dusty roads in Parker County, just west of Dallas. By night he studied law, attracting the attention of a local attorney who, impressed by the young man's formidable mental acuity, offered him a clerical position in his office. In those less stringent times, Littleton obtained his law degree and was admitted to the bar in just two years, becoming an assistant prosecutor. Soon though, Dallas was too small to hold the ambitious young lawyer and he set out for the biggest prize of all—New York.

Again, times were hard, and at first he was forced to take a job as a clerk, but gradually he managed to build his own, mainly civil, practice in Brooklyn, until being offered the post of assistant District Attorney of Kings County. Concomitant with public office came an interest in politics and, in 1910, Littleton was elected to Congress as the Democrat Representative for the First New York District. His subsequent return to private practice in 1915 continued his inexorable climb into the upper echelon of New York trial lawyers.

He played a significant role in the notorious Teapot Dome Scandal, when he secured the acquittal of Harry Sinclair on a charge of bribing Albert Fall, the Secretary of the Interior. At each stage Littleton outmaneuvered the prosecution as he kept them from introducing evidence it had heavily relied upon. Not even he, though, could prevent Sinclair from going to jail for contempt of the Senate.

In court Littleton cut a majestic figure, his massive head covered with thick gray, almost white hair. And there was his voice, once described as having the timbre of a cello. Such attributes were rarely squandered in a losing cause and neither were they used to better effect than in Littleton's last great courtroom triumph.

II. James Maxon, Jr. (1931)

As head of the Episcopalian Church in Chattanooga, Tennessee, Bishop James Maxon was one of the most respected and renowned religious leaders in America, a preacher whose writings and sermons were published widely, a thinker who sowed his philosophical seed on the national stage. Sadly for the bishop, however, the stoniest ground was around his own feet. His twenty-one-year-old son, James, Jr., wanted nothing to do with him. From the sanctuary of a New York flop house, Maxon ignored his father's letters with their dire warnings against "living riotously and inadvisedly," preferring, instead, to guzzle Prohibition-era gin while he worked on his ambition of becoming a murder mystery novelist.

One of his earliest efforts was a thriller tentatively entitled "The Deadline." In its opening chapter the manuscript described the discovery of a dead body, which was exactly what greeted police officers in the early hours of April 18, 1930, when they were summoned to quell a brawl at the boarding house where Maxon lived. In the basement they found David Paynter, a seventy-three-year-old handyman, beaten to death. There could be no doubt about his killer's identity; three other elderly tenants and the landlady had all suffered bruises and abrasions during James Maxon's drunken nocturnal rampage. For detectives the half-finished manuscript found in Maxon's room provided convincing evidence that here was a tragic case of life imitating art.

The next morning, Littleton—a lifelong friend of the Maxon family—was hired to defend the prodigal son. He immediately set about salvaging Maxon's tarnished credibility (if police press briefings were to be believed, the young man's callousness during interrogation was something wondrous to behold). After declaring that Maxon had blacked out and could recall nothing of the incident, Littleton diverted media attention by organizing a well-publicized family visit. When Bishop Maxon emerged from the jailhouse meeting he professed complete belief in the innocence of his son, though he did add sagely, "Any man is a fool who will drink this liquor nowadays, and I'm not preaching prohibition."

After considerable delay and dispute, which saw the charge amended to second-degree murder, James Maxon's trial began on February 2, 1931. Assistant District Attorney William D. Moore told how witnesses had seen Maxon batter and kick Paynter to death. Then, when arrested, he had refused to talk, waving officers away with the words "I'm drunk now and I was drunk then . . . It would be more sportsmanlike to question me later." Although he admitted that there had been a general brawl and he had "got into it," he blamed the numerous cuts and bruises that covered his own body on having been run over by a steamroller!

A. Basement Brawl

The fight started, claimed Moore, after Maxon went to his landlady's bedroom in the basement around 3:00 A.M., intent on having sex. When Rose Hickney, fifty-three, resisted his advances, Maxon lost all control and began attacking her. The sound of Mrs. Hickney's screams brought other lodgers, including David Paynter, running to her assistance. Paynter's attempts to calm Maxon were fruitless and a full-scale brawl broke out, which led to Paynter's death.

In his opening statement Littleton coolly defused the volatile atmosphere. The entire incident had been a giant misunderstanding, he explained, Maxon had merely been acting out of public mindedness. A gas fitting had broken in the second floor bathroom and, fearful of a fire or worse, the young man had gone to report the problem to Mrs. Hickney. Unfortunately, she had misinterpreted his intentions and the incident had escalated from there. Littleton claimed that his young client had acted in self-defense when attacked by a group of older men in a darkened basement. "There was no reason for Maxon to hit Paynter . . . there was no quarrel . . . between them . . . the boy was terror-stricken at being unjustly accused."

B. Cracks in the Story

Mrs. Hickney would have none of it. She testified that Paynter tried to placate the maniacal Maxon, saying, "Get upstairs, my boy," only for the young man to go berserk. It was a well-told story—until Littleton rose to cross-examine. All at once, cracks began to appear. Mrs. Hickney's earlier forthrightness faltered as Littleton listed numerous discrepancies between her evidence given earlier at court and now; particularly as to whether Maxon had made any reference to a broken gas fitting. He again scored heavily when lodger James McGarry reluctantly conceded that, before the fight broke out, Maxon *had* mentioned the faulty fitting.

Littleton was less successful with another lodger, Samuel Ecclesine. He was adamant that Maxon picked up a chair and hit Paynter without provocation, and then kicked him repeatedly.

Despite this, Littleton was able to successfully paint a picture of a seedy boarding house where tenants and landlady alike drank themselves into a stupor on the fateful night, and had no real idea of what had happened.

This was a theme echoed by Maxon on the stand. Looking haggard and worn, he answered questions quickly and without any noticeable guile. Yes, he had consumed several gins that night. And yes, after breaking the bathroom fitting, he had gone to Mrs. Hickney's room and tried to rouse her. Unable to get an answer, he entered her bedroom and began shaking her in bed. She immediately screamed, "Let me go!" Thereafter it was all a blank.

"To the best of your knowledge, did you strike Paynter at any time?" asked Littleton.

"I did not."

Maxon's obvious remorse and an impressive array of defense character witnesses, all supremely orchestrated by Littleton's dexterous touch, clearly had their effect on the jury. On February 5, 1931, they found Maxon not guilty of all charges. Maxon appeared dumbfounded by the verdict and could not stop shaking Littleton's hand. Outside the court, the great defender modestly told reporters, "The verdict speaks for itself."

As mentioned earlier, this was Martin Littleton's courtroom valedictory. Just a few years later, on December 19, 1934, he succumbed to a heart attack. His premature death robbed the legal profession of one of its finest practitioners, a hero to many, including the young Samuel Leibowitz (q.v.), who, as a boy, used to devour newspaper accounts of Littleton's victories, while dreaming of his own triumphs to come. One thing is certain, even the great Sam Leibowitz would have struggled to better Martin Littleton's amazing performance in this remarkable trial.

OTHER NOTABLE CASES:

Harry Thaw (1908); Charles Morse (1909); Oresto Shillitoni (1915); Michael Rofrano (1916); Harry Sinclair (1927–28)

Ephraim London
(1912–1990)

I. Career

If it's the criminal lawyer who makes the headlines, then it's the constitutional lawyer who makes the difference. Through their constant examination of the 7,000 or so words that make up the Constitution of the United States, these legal scholars have shaped and formed a nation. Their impact on the day-to-day life of America is enormous, and few have created quite so much impact as New York attorney Ephraim London. His specialty was censorship, a thorny issue that he felt was best left to the individual.

In the early 1950s, when London came to prominence, he had already been practicing law for close to two decades, since earning his degree at New York University in 1934. As he was born into a family of Brooklyn lawyers, it was inevitable that he would join the firm founded by his father, Horace, and his uncle, Meyer, who was a member of the House of Representatives. For his efforts London received the magnificent sum of $12 a week, but the education he received at the hands of his relatives was invaluable. When war broke out in 1941, he saw active service in North Africa as the captain of an anti-aircraft artillery unit. After the cessation of hostilities he put his multi-faceted legal talents to work as special investigator for the War Crimes Commission in Germany. When he returned to New York, the struggle against bigotry and narrow-mindedness began.

II. J. Burstyn Inc. v. New York State Board of Regents (1951)

On December 11, 1950, a movie opened at the Paris Theater in New York City that would forever change the face of American filmgoing. Called *The Miracle,* it was directed by Roberto Rosellini, husband of Ingrid Bergman, and starred Anna Magnani as a feeble-minded Italian peasant girl who is seduced by a stranger whom she believes to be St. Joseph. Finding herself pregnant and believing the child to have been immaculately conceived, she takes to calling the infant "my Holy Son." For many Roman Catholics of the time, this amounted to a grotesque parody of the birth of Jesus, and furious crowds picketed the theater, determined to get the film banned. More extreme opponents even made bomb threats.

Showings were halted on December 23, 1950, after Edward T. McCaffrey, City Licensing Commissioner, viewed the film and found it "officially and personally blasphemous." Advised that such an arbitrary decision was likely to be set aside by court injunction, Cardinal Spellman of New York urged Catholics across America to boycott the movie and any theater showing it. The film was, he declared, sacrilegious. Despite the fact that the writer, director and cast of *The Miracle* were all devout Catholics, antipathy grew and in February 1951 the State Board of Regents revoked the film's license, thus prohibiting public exhibition. Taking their cue from New York, dozens of cities around the nation also banned the controversial movie.

When the film's distributor, Joseph Burstyn, appealed this decision to the New York Court of Appeals in October 1951, the court, by a 5-2 majority, sustained the unanimous finding of the State Board of Regents that *The Miracle* was sacrilegious.

At Burstyn's behest, London filed a petition with the Supreme Court, asking that it review the constitutionality of the New York State Laws which banned the film. In February 1952, the Court agreed to hear arguments.

London realized the importance of this case. This would be the first time that the Supreme Court had dealt directly with the subject of film censorship since the celebrated *Ohio* case in 1915. At that time the Court ruled that movies were in the same category as carnivals and spectacles and thus not entitled to the protection of constitutional guarantees of freedom of speech and press. By 1952 the mood of the Court was shifting. In recent years it had indicated a willingness to regard motion pictures in a class with newspapers and radio. Arguments were heard on April 24, 1952. As laid out in his brief, London fought the case on four fronts:

a) Was the statute under which the petitioner's film was banned so vague and indefinite and its meanings so uncertain that its enforcement violated the due process clause of the Fourteenth Amendment?

b) Did the statute as construed violate the constitutional warranty of separate church and state?

c) Did the statute infringe the free exercise of religion?

d) Did the statute impose an unconstitutional restraint on freedom of expression and communication?

At issue were four sections of New York State Education Law that barred the exhibition of a motion picture without a license granted by the Motion Picture Division, or its director. Reasons for refusing a license were many; it could be denied if a film was considered to be "obscene, indecent, immoral, inhuman, sacrilegious."

Yet nowhere, argued London, did the New York Statute define the term "sacrilegious," and no reported opinion of any U.S. court "prior to that rendered in the instant case, has been found in which the term is construed."

Ephraim London addresses a press conference held in the offices of Brennan, London, & Buttenwieser in New York City. (AP Wide World)

A. Sectarian Divide

Reaction to the film had divided on sectarian lines, said London: a small Catholic minority had decided that it was sacrilegious, "while all Protestant ministers who expressed themselves publicly" found nothing objectionable in its content. He went on to argue that movies should not be censored in advance for any reason.

"Not even for obscenity?" asked Justice Sherman Minton.

"No, your Honor," London replied. "Obscenity should be punished by prosecution after the film has been shown. The same rules should apply to movies that apply for magazines and newspapers." London urged the court not to confine its decision to the question of sacrilege, but to kill off censorship entirely.

An early indicator of the eventual outcome was given when New York State Solicitor-General Wendell Brown for the State Board of Regents argued that the 1915 Ohio movie censorship law was still valid, only for Chief Justice Fred M. Vinson to remind him of a 1948 anti-trust case in which the Court ruled that movies *were* protected by the free speech guarantee of the Constitution.

On May 26, 1952, the Court decided unanimously that pictures were entitled to Constitutional protection. Justice Tom Clark wrote the opinion: "We conclude that expression by means of motion pictures is included within the free speech and free press guaranty of the First and Fourteenth Amendments. To the extent that the language in the opinion [in the *Ohio* case] is out of harmony with the views here set forth, we no longer adhere to it."

London's victory was not absolute, however, as Clark pointed out that only the term "sacrilegious" was at issue here, not the censorship of obscene films. "That is a very different question from the one now before us. We hold only that under the First and Fourteenth Amendments a state may not ban a film on the basis of a censor's conclusions that it is sacrilegious."

London was triumphant. At a celebratory dinner in New York a month after the Supreme Court decision luminaries from the East Coast arts community presented he and Burstyn with congratulatory scrolls. London graciously described the victory as not the work of "one or two men, but the work of many."

B. *Lady Chatterley's Lover*

In 1956 London was again back before the Supreme Court, this time on behalf of Kingsley-International, distributors of the film, *Lady Chatterley's Lover.* This time his pleas caused the Court to strike down an important part of New

York's thirty-six-year-old film censorship rules. All nine judges agreed that the ban was improper, with a majority of five ruling that it was improper for New York to prohibit showing a film deemed obscene simply because it depicted conduct that was deemed immoral.

London didn't just restrict himself to the arts. He was equally as concerned about individual liberties, and for that reason remained active in the New York Civil Liberties Union (CLU). In 1956 he won reinstatement for Dr. Harry Slochower, a Brooklyn College professor, who had been dismissed for pleading the Fifth Amendment when questioned by a Senate sub-committee about prior membership of the Communist Party. Again London was victorious in the Supreme Court as they voted 5-4 in Slochower's favor.

London's biggest setback came in 1962, when he handled the appeal of convicted Soviet spy, Dr. Robert Soblen. With bail bondsmen refusing to have anything to do with Soblen, London's law partner, Helen Lehman Buttenwieser, with whom he was associated for more than forty years, raised the necessary $60,000 surety. On the eve of his scheduled surrender to begin serving a life term, Soblen fled to Israel, and bail was forfeited. London and Buttenwieser were devastated. Three months later, after having been deported from Israel, Soblen stabbed himself to death at a British airport to avoid returning to the U.S.

For many years London taught courses on constitutional law, and on the relationship between literature and the law, at the New York University Law School. He also found time to write *The World of Law* a two-volume work widely used as a law school textbook. The struggle for the preservation of individual liberties was always at the heart of his work. When he died on June 12, 1990, the bare bones of his record showed that he had argued nine cases before the Supreme Court, without a single defeat. What could not be tallied in numbers was the fact that Ephraim London was a lawyer who helped change America.

OTHER NOTABLE CASES:

Lady Chatterley's Lover (1956); *The Lovers* (1964); Lennie Bruce (1964); Robert Soblen (1962); *The Language of Love* (1971)

Thurgood Marshall (1908–1993)

I. Career

Charting the course of Thurgood Marshall's life is like holding a mirror up to the path of civil rights in mid-twentieth century America. The two are inextricably linked. At the time of his birth—1908—the lynching of blacks was still relatively commonplace, not just in the South, but across the country, and Marshall himself understood what it was like to dodge the rope of mob rule. But never once did this lumbering, crusty man with the explosive temper lose sight of the rightness of his cause. If Martin Luther King, Jr. was the most potent visible sign of the civil rights struggle, then Marshall was its backroom driving force. Where King fostered change in public attitude, Marshall changed the law. He was there at every major turn in the civil rights road between 1935 and the momentous year of 1967 when he became the first black appointee to the Supreme Court.

His father, a Pullman-car porter in Baltimore, could scarcely have dared dream of such advancement on those days when he would sit in the public gallery at his local courthouse and marvel at the legal discourse. He knew his own career aspirations had been stymied by history, but he refused to countenance such limitations for his son. Education, that was the answer, and he resolved that Thurgood was going to receive the best available.

It wasn't easy. Denied entrance to the University of Maryland because of his color, Marshall went to a small private school for blacks, Lincoln University in Oxford, Pennsylvania. Because his family could not meet the tuition costs of $300 per year, the young student worked a series of campus jobs to pay his way. He also indulged in some formidable socializing, refusing to kowtow to the notion that high academic achievement was solely the prerogative of the hermit. His mother, a kindergarten teacher, still entertained notions of Marshall being a dentist, but his mind was made up. In 1933 he graduated magna cum laude from Howard University Law School in Washington, D.C., and went straight into private practice in Baltimore.

His career began in the depths of the Great Depression, and with sixteen million people unemployed there was little call for a fledgling lawyer. He persevered though, and was rewarded for his efforts the following year when he became a lawyer for the Baltimore chapter of the National Association for the Advancement of Colored People (NAACP). It was no coincidence that one of his first lawsuits was against the very institution that had barred him, the University of Maryland. Gradually he worked his way up through the NAACP hierarchy and on October 6, 1936, he was hired as chief legal officer on a six-month contract. A quarter of a century later, he was still in the same job. At times he was given the roughest of rides. J. Edgar Hoover, Director of the FBI and a lifelong foe, tried repeatedly to impugn Marshall's character. All to no avail. Despite Marshall's undisguised fondness for the good life, there was never a breath of scandal attached to his name.

In those early years Marshall was worked off his feet, often traveling over 30,000 miles a year to all corners of the nation, and at great personal peril. He was always searching out cases that would hit the headlines and test the legitimacy of the "Jim Crow" laws that had grown and festered since the early nineteenth century.

Marshall, along with his mentor Charles Hamilton (the first black lawyer to win a case before the Supreme Court), developed a long-term strategy for eradicating segregation in schools. First, they targeted graduate and professional schools, believing that white judges would be more likely to sympathize with the ambitious young blacks in those settings. Then, as the team's confidence and success rate grew, they turned toward elementary and high schools.

Even before Marshall tackled segregation in schools, he had already made his name, in one of the most significant civil rights cases to be argued before the Supreme Court.

II. Smith v. Allwright (1941)

In 1940, Dr. Lonnie E. Smith, a black dentist, presented himself at the Texas primary and asked to be allowed to vote. Despite holding the required qualification—a valid poll tax receipt—Smith was denied because of his race and color. With the backing of local NAACP leaders, Smith sued two Harris County election officials, asking for a declaration of judgment upholding the rights of Negroes to vote in the primaries. The litigation had already entered its initial phase when Marshall joined the case, and he found evidence of mismanagement at a local level. This was nothing new. During his travels he frequently uncovered examples of NAACP legal incompetence—something he found intolerable—and his very vocal criticism in the wake of such findings often antagonized local lawyers.

Here, Smith's legal team had been unable to obtain the names of the election officials who should have been named as defendants. When Marshall turned up at the county courthouse in an effort to remedy this neglect, he, too, was rebuffed. But he was made of wilier stuff, and, donning the guise of a newspaper reporter, he returned and obtained all of the missing names.

The following year, on November 7, 1941, Marshall and his fellow lawyers went back to the state court in Houston, challenging the "white primary." By this time, Marshall had already argued and won before the United States Supreme Court, the first of twenty-nine such victories in his long career, so this particular body held few terrors for him. However, there was plenty of well-organized opposition on tap. For most Texans, Thurgood Marshall and others like him, represented a fundamental threat to their way of life, one that they were determined to crush before it gained steam.

Marshall presented his case in what would become his hallmark style: straightforward and plain-spoken. He argued that because the Texas primary was an integral part of the election machinery of the state and that the Democratic Party determined the final election, access to both should be available to all citizens. Then, to show how skewed the situation was in Texas, Marshall reminded the court that *all* white citizens—regardless of political affiliation—were permitted to vote in the Democratic primary. The only barrier was color.

Judge T. M. Kennerly remained unconvinced, and he dismissed the case on May 11, 1942, a decision later upheld by the United States Court of Appeals for the Fifth Circuit.

Jim Crow still held sway.

Then, unexpectedly, in June 1943, the NAACP was granted a petition for writ of certiorari, clearing the way for the case to be heard in the Supreme Court.

It was argued on January 12, 1944. In preparation, Marshall contacted Herbert Wechsler, an attorney in the U.S. solicitor-general's office, to see if the government would support the NAACP. Wechsler's lukewarm response left Marshall on his own. Earlier he had been assisted by William Hastie, chairman of the NAACP's legal committee, but animosity had surfaced within the Texas NAACP from homegrown lawyers resentful of the fact that "outside" attorneys had poached their glory. Marshall, who always found such pettiness tiresome and on this occasion dismissed it as "running off at the mouth," assuaged local sensibilities by arranging for Texan lawyer W.J. Durham to travel to Washington, D.C. so that he might be in court.

After hearing both sides, the justices discussed the case for three days, then announced they would reveal their decision later.

History was made on April 3, 1944, when, by an 8–1 majority decision, the Supreme Court decided that blacks could vote in the Texas primary. The opinion, which overturned decades of discriminatory precedent, was written by Justice Stanley F. Reed, a Southerner from Kentucky. "The right to vote in such a primary . . . without discrimination by the state . . . is secured by the constitution."

A. Hostile Reaction

Dixie exploded in anger.

Texas governor Coke Stevenson, in particular, took the news badly and conspired with other officials to find ways to keep blacks from voting. When rumors spread that white citizens might take it upon themselves to keep blacks from voting, Marshall issued a warning, "If citizens try to keep Negroes from primary polls, we are going to take them to federal court. Such persons will be violating the Supreme Court decision just the same as election judges."

Somewhat naively, Marshall now believed the way was clear for full-blown black enfranchisement, but a chilling editorial in the *Jackson Daily News* spelled out the reality. "The United States Supreme Court rules that the Negroes can vote in party primaries, including Democratic party primaries. They can't in Mississippi. The Supreme Court may think so, but it is quite wrong insofar as Democratic primaries in Mississippi are concerned. If anyone doubts that, let 'em try."

The menace was there for all to see, and for many blacks in the South, full participation in the democratic process was still decades away. But the seeds had been sown.

Many years later, when asked to select the most significant of his numerous court triumphs, Marshall could never decide between *Smith v. Allwright* and *Brown v. Board of Education of Topeka* (1954). The latter case, which struck down the practice of segregation in public schools, has achieved greater legal eminence, but *Smith v. Allwright* was no less important: for as Marshall was quick to point out, without access to the ballot box, all the education in the world isn't going to help you.

After the Second World War, Marshall's star climbed steadily. In 1951 he visited South Korea and Japan to investigate charges of racism in U.S. armed forces. His report revealed a deliberate policy of "rigid segregation" and further enhanced his reputation as a champion for civil rights. That led to his 1961 appointment to the Second Circuit Court of Appeals, and then four years later, he became solicitor-general.

B. Appointed to the U.S. Supreme Court

The greatest accolade of all came in 1967 when President Lyndon Johnson appointed Marshall to the Supreme Court, the first black man ever to achieve such a position. Johnson commented, "I believe this is the right thing to do, the right time to do it, the right man and the right place."

On the Court, Marshall said little during argument sessions, but he could be sarcastic if he felt the occasion demanded it. When, during a 1981 death penal-

Thurgood Marshall was the first African-American United States Supreme Court Associate Justice. (UPI Corbis-Bettmann)

ty argument, Justice William Rehnquist suggested that an inmate's repeated appeals had cost the state too much money, Marshall interrupted, "It would have been cheaper to shoot him right after he was arrested, wouldn't it?"

Such testiness brought brickbats, and he was not universally popular with all factions of the civil rights struggle. A stickler for the law, he had no time for extremism, adamant that change should only be achieved within the legal framework.

In his later years he watched, with dismay, the Court's inexorable drift to the right, and his last opinion was a dissent in a death penalty case, which opened with the biting sentence, "Power, not reason, is the new currency of this court's decision-making."

On June 29, 1991, he announced his retirement from the court after twenty-four years of service. As a mob of reporters crowded round him at the press conference, one hollered, "What's wrong with you?"

Marshall's jowly face wreathed in that familiar scowl as he fiddled with his hearing aid. "What's wrong with me?" he snorted at last. " I'm old, coming apart."

Eighteen months later, on January 24, 1993, he died.

OTHER NOTABLE CASES:

Murray v. Pearson (1935); Seaborne v. University of Maryland (1935); Chambers v. Florida (1940); William Pillow & Lloyd Kennedy (1946); Shelley v. Kraemer (1948); Sweatt v. Painter (1950); McLaurin v. Oklahoma State Regents (1950); Briggs v. Elliott (1951); Brown v. Board of Education (1954); Garner v. Louisiana (1961)

Marvin Mitchelson

(1928-)

I. CAREER

In the high-stakes world of celebrity divorce litigation, Marvin Mitchelson is a lawyer apart. Others have won greater settlements, some might even drive harder bargains than this eloquent magician, but none comes within hailing distance of topping his flair for self-promotion. This relentless drive for publicity has kept Mitchelson's name at the forefront of public consciousness for more than three decades. His speciality is the estranged wife of a rich husband; and to see Mitchelson squiring his latest icon of outraged womanhood before the world's media is to witness one of the great sights of modern American jurisprudence. No lawyer in recent memory has so readily and so publicly identified with his clients. And, if some of the clients are to be believed, it is a kinship that has, on occasion, been reciprocated in the most intimate of terms.

Because divorce litigation is an area of law where emotions run especially high, the cases that Mitchelson routinely handles are media blockbusters. Titillation and prurience go hand-in-hand with a client roster that reads like a Who's Who of the Hollywood disaffected, but it is how Mitchelson finesses each case that makes him so special. He is the axis around which everything revolves.

Given enough time, even the most forthright client can find themselves relegated to a secondary role, as Mitchelson takes center stage, orchestrating every step with a magician's touch. It is a talent that has brought massive reward. Over the years he has made and spent several fortunes on the kind of sybaritic lifestyle that others can only envy. But it wasn't always that way; before the glitz and glamour, before the green Rolls Royces and the multi-million dollar settlements, there was a struggling son of immigrants, a young kid eager to carve off his own sizable chunk of the American Dream.

He was born in Detroit on May 7, 1928. One year later his family got a head-start on the Depression and moved to Los Angeles. Through sheer hard work they clawed their way up the economic ladder, until they were able to afford their own home in Atwater Village, between the Los Angeles River and Glendale. Being Jewish in a predominantly Gentile school at the outbreak of World War II brought its own set of problems, and early on Mitchelson suffered the sting of anti-Semitism. By dint of personality and a devastating tongue he was able to overcome the taunts, but channeling these obvious talents wasn't always easy. After graduating from Los Angeles High, he joined the Navy, and in February 1946, at age seventeen, he shipped out aboard the *USS Columbus*, en route for Shanghai.

Two years later he enrolled at the University of Oregon, with high hopes of becoming a gridiron hero. A series of nagging injuries restricted him to just one game on the freshman football team, and disillusioned, he returned to L.A. Shortly afterward, a badly broken wrist sidelined all of his sporting aspirations for good, leaving him with no choice other than to pursue an academic career. Without much enthusiasm he gained a degree in history; then came the problem of how best to utilize that qualification. After a few false starts—he toyed with the possibilities of journalism, medicine, and movie management—he opted for the law.

In order to finance his tuition at the Southwestern Law School, he took up work as a part-time process server, working on commission. His massive self-confidence made him a natural, and sometimes earned him as much as $2,000 a month. One of his early successes came with a twenty-two-year-old Joan Collins, bursting in on the set and handing the startled actress a sheaf of divorce papers while she was shooting a bubble bath scene. Collins didn't think much of the intrusion and told him so. Thirty years later, in rather different circumstances, she would have good reason to favorably revise her opinion of the impudent process server.

School, though, was a different matter. Mitchelson always found the books hard going, and after graduating from Southwestern in 1956, he failed the bar exam. After another year—his fifth—at law school, he was finally admitted to the California Bar in June 1957. It was an inauspicious start but the rookie lawyer would only have eighteen months to wait until he began making the kind of legal waves that would follow him throughout his career.

II. William Douglas (1959)

If there has been a constant in Mitchelson's tempestuous career, it is his uncanny ability to gauge the mood of the times. In *Marvin v. Marvin (1979)*, the famous "palimony" suit that revolutionized the rights of live-in lovers, he sensed that the California judiciary was casting round for just such a case in order to effect a change in the law. He got it spectacularly right on that occasion, but this was far from an isolated triumph. Two decades earlier, Mitchelson's legal antennae twitched again and told him that history was about to be made. It began in the most banal of circumstances, a routine search and arrest procedure in Los Angeles that spiraled into tragedy, and ultimately led Mitchelson all the way to the Supreme Court.

On the evening of October 20, 1958, two Los Angeles police officers, Walter Bitterolf and Gene Nash, acting on a tip, called at an apartment in the Watts district. This was rumored to be the hideout of Bennie Meyes and William Douglas, two men suspected of carrying out a spate of recent local robberies. After gaining access to the apartment, Bitterolf remained in the living room while Nash went to check out a back bedroom. A sudden fusillade of shots rang out from the bedroom. When Bitterolf ran to investigate he found his partner mortally wounded and the window open. As he lay dying, Nash gasped that he had shot both suspects. Only now did Bitterolf realize that one of the men, Douglas, was slumped in the bedroom closet, nursing five serious bullet wounds. A trail of blood from the bedroom window led other officers to Meyes, lying unconscious on the floor of the intended getaway vehicle.

Under the impression that Douglas was already dead, Meyes, a career criminal with multiple arrests and jail terms behind him, began heaping blame for the killing on his erstwhile partner. Douglas, who had no previous conviction, was equally resolute that it was Meyes who had shot Nash. All he had done, he claimed, was to crouch down for self-preservation in the closet. This was consistent with his wounds; one of the bullets had pierced his rectum, then traveled up through his body and into the chest. Had it not been for a series of operations Douglas would have died before reaching court, but as it was, on February 24,

1959, when the case came to trial, he found himself, with Meyes, facing charges of first-degree murder.

When Mitchelson took Douglas' case, things could not have looked worse: Douglas was poor, black, and he'd been branded a cop-killer. Even though Meyes had by this time admitted shooting Nash, albeit in self-defense, under California law Douglas would be regarded as equally culpable if found guilty, and therefore a certainty for the gas chamber at San Quentin. Won over by Douglas' mother's insistence that her son was innocent and her offer to pay him $40 a month—all she could afford—he agreed to take the case.

His first task was to save Douglas from death row, and in this respect, first time around, he succeeded admirably. After thirteen days of testimony, the jury took another four to declare themselves hopelessly deadlocked. The resulting mistrial allowed Mitchelson precious time to review his case and tighten up the weak points.

A. New Trial

The second trial got underway on May 18, 1959, and Mitchelson was ready. This time, instead of merely pleading for his client's life and portraying him as a hapless victim of circumstances, he went on the offensive, quizzing Bitterolf about his treatment of Douglas while the latter was in custody.

"[Do] you also recall telling him 'I ought to kill you.'?"

"No, I do not."

"Are you sure you didn't kick him in the thigh?"

"I am positive, I didn't kick him any place."

"In the back?"

"No place."

"Did you say, 'Go ahead and die, you black bastard.'?"

"No, I did not."

And so it went; Mitchelson desperately trying to impugn the witness's credibility, Bitterolf not buckling one inch. Mitchelson pursued much the same line of attack with the other prosecution witnesses, with much the same result, but gradually over the six-week trial he managed to convey an image of Douglas as an innocent bystander, cowering on the floor and being shot when he was unarmed.

When he took the stand Douglas was impressive, calmly asserting that it was Nash who had fired first, without reason, and that he himself had been struck by the first bullet and played no further part in the drama. Only an intervention by the bench prevented Mitchelson from yanking Douglas' shirt up so that the jury might better view the dreadful injuries he had sustained.

Mitchelson's final speech to the jury, supercharged with passion, was typical of hundreds he delivered in his long and eventful career. At one point he even summoned up the possibility of divine intervention. "I can't help but think that God must have had His hand on this boy. He has seen him through three or four operations and He has seen him on death's door." It was emotive stuff. Effective, too: on June 23, 1959, Douglas was acquitted of all charges. Meyes, rather more fortuitously, was convicted of second-degree murder, which automatically excluded the death penalty.

Mitchelson pulled off a miracle. During this time in American history, it was remarkable enough for a black man accused of murdering a police officer to avoid the death penalty: what Mitchelson achieved almost transcended belief.

Marvin Mitchelson. (AP Wide World)

Furious at this setback, the Los Angeles DA's office immediately slapped multiple fresh robbery charges on both men, rushed the trial through in double-quick time, and sat back gloating as this time both men were convicted. Given that neither defendant had been properly represented during the trial, the whole business smacked of official vindictiveness. Douglas, with considerable justification, felt that being tried alongside a convicted murderer had jeopardized his rights, and filed an appeal. But because there was no automatic right to counsel during appeal, Douglas had to draft all his own motions unaided.

Enter Marvin Mitchelson. Conventional wisdom of the day suggested that the Supreme Court was ready to strike down *Betts v. Brady* (1942), which stated that there was no universal assurance of lawyer assistance in a criminal trial. Although most states at that time *did* provide representation during trials, few extended the privilege to appeals, and this was the point that Mitchelson seized upon in his petition to the Supreme Court. To great general surprise the Court agreed to hear oral argument on the matter.

Appellate pleading, with its strong reliance on precedent and exhaustive knowledge of the law, requires a special kind of advocate. Mitchelson, smart enough to realize that he was not that person, hired Burton Marks, a noted legal scholar, to draft the petition. However, when it came time to argue before the Supreme Court, Mitchelson refused to play second fiddle to anyone and jumped right in. In this most august and arduous of settings, he sallied forth into a typically impassioned plea on behalf of his client. "Your Honors, there isn't any doubt in my mind that this whole proceeding is a result of the bias of the Los Angeles Police Department. . . . They want the taint of Bennie Meyes to rub off on Douglas." Hardly the dry, reasoned argument of most appeals, Mitchelson's case was still very compelling.

B. Momentous Decision

The Supreme Court's ruling was issued on March 18, 1963, coincidentally the same day it handed down the landmark *Gideon* decision, guaranteeing legal representation to all defendants charged with a crime. Though less known Douglas actually came first: 6-3 in favor of the appellant.[1] It was Mitchelson's finest hour. Other cases would grab bigger headlines but this was a legal milestone.

Throughout the 1970s and 1980s, Marvin Mitchelson became the undisputed champion of women's rights in divorce actions, winning huge settlements. Some of the gloss went off that reputation when a woman brought charges, later refuted, that he had raped her. Suddenly the attacks came from all directions. *60 Minutes* broadcasted damaging allegations about Mitchelson's private life, and this was followed, in 1990, by the biggest blow of all.

According to the IRS, Mitchelson had been underreporting income for years and they finally filed charges for tax evasion. The case meandered for three

---

[1]*In real terms the decision did Douglas little good. At a retrial both he and Meyes were convicted of several robberies and sentenced to long jail terms.*

years through the courts and ended with Mitchelson's conviction on February 9, 1993, for failing to report $2 million in income. A long appellate process ended on May 27, 1996, when the Supreme Court turned down his appeal. At this writing Mitchelson is still fighting the case, claiming that medical problems make his incarceration unfeasible. He faces a thirty-month jail term.

All his life Marvin Mitchelson has played a kind of high-stakes poker with life. "I have to tell you this," he once boasted. "The best press agent I ever had was Marvin Mitchelson! . . . I know how to do this!" Only time will tell if he still retains the magic touch.

OTHER NOTABLE CASES:

Mason v. Mason (1964); The Beatles (1964); Khashoggi v. Khashoggi (1979); Marvin v. Marvin (1979); Morgan v. Bloomingdale (1982); Collins v. Holm (1987)

Louis Nizer
(1902–1994)

I. Career

When Louis Nizer was still in diapers, his father left the family home in the East End of London to join the transatlantic migration to America. One year later Nizer Sr. saved enough money to send for his wife and only son. They made the long journey in steerage class and right to the end of his long life, Louis Nizer insisted that he could remember, with crystal clarity, his arrival as a three-year-old at Ellis Island. At first life was hard, but his father worked every available hour and soon scraped together the wherewithal to buy his own cleaning and dyeing store in Brooklyn. Nizer received a traditional Jewish upbringing, absorbed the ethos of hard work and self-sufficiency, and studied like a demon. It paid off. After high school, he was accepted at Columbia University Law School.

He set out to make himself stand out on campus. A tiny man, he turned his lack of inches to great advantage by coxing the college eight at rowing. That got him noticed, but it was elsewhere that he flourished. He could talk. Twice, his beautiful speaking voice won him the Curtis Oratorical Prize at college, and after graduation in 1924 and admittance to the bar one year later, he used that same mellifluousness to conjure up some very favorable press coverage of a case in

which he championed the interests of a group of Brooklyn merchants.

Louis Nizer (right) at work in the courtroom. (AP Wide World)

He was already something of a novelty, mainly because of his employer. In 1925 female lawyers like Emily Janoer were a rare item, and as her law clerk Nizer bathed in the reflected attention. Soon, though, he was making news on his own account. He began by taking every case that came his way, no matter how small. Most he won, and with that success came an enhanced profile in the New York legal community and the offer of a job in the successful law firm run by Louis Phillips. Within two years Nizer produced so much business for the company that he was made an equal partner, and thus began the illustrious firm of Phillips and Nizer. Founded in 1928, Phillips and Nizer built an empire covering every aspect of litigation and legal work.

It was through Phillips' professional association with the New York Film Board of Trade, that Nizer gained his entree into the movie industry and access to many wealthy clients. Over the years he represented clients as varied as Johnny Carson, Salvador, Eddie Fisher, Alan J. Lerner, and Mae West, all the way to basketball great, Julius Erving. But one of his greatest triumphs involved no household names, just an ordinary housewife who had suffered an extraordinary tragedy.

II. Donelon v. Long Island Railroad Company (1951)

On Wednesday, November 22, 1950, two trains packed with vacationers leaving New York for the Thanksgiving holiday, departed from Pennsylvania Station during the evening rush hour. Just minutes apart they raced eastbound on the same track. At approximately 6:30 P.M. the first train made an unscheduled stop on a fifteen-feet high embankment at Richmond Hill, on the outskirts of the city. Four minutes later the second locomotive, traveling at sixty mph, smashed into the stationary train, killing seventy-seven passengers and injuring 300 more. Governor Thomas Dewey (q.v.), attributing the disaster to "human failure," promised a full inquiry.

Among those killed was John Joseph Donelon, a thirty-year-old homeward-bound commuter, and it was his widow who instructed Louis Nizer to file suit against the train operators, Long Island Railroad Company (LIRC). Since anyone entering a train has a right to expect the carrier to provide safe passage, and because LIRC conceded negligence, there was no real dispute about liability. At issue was the amount of damages payable.

The law has always struggled with the impossibility of assessing the loss of human life in financial terms. In New York at the time a rough rule of thumb existed whereby, if the deceased was a married man, the guilty party was obliged to pay the widow what she might have reasonably expected to receive from the deceased had he lived. Because a jury may award damages for pain and suffering to the living, but only loss of income to the family of the dead, this explains why a person severely injured often recovers larger damages than his estate would if he had been killed.

So the question was: what would Donelon have contributed financially to his wife had he lived his normal span of years? The raw data for such an equation came from all manner of subjective assessments. What was the state of his health? How long could his wife be expected to live? Did he have a higher than average earning potential? Was he industrious or indolent, ambitious or indifferent? All of these variables and more had to be factored into the equation and reduced to a quantifiable figure.

Nizer's task—and it was far from easy—was to map out for the jury the anticipated career of a man whose life had been snuffed out by tragedy. He began by going back. In his previous job, Donelon had started right at the bottom, just $35 a week, and had, over five years, increased this to $80. In October 1950 came a definite step-up when he was hired by the Weintraub Agency, an advertising firm, at $100 a week. Barely a month later he was dead. With these figures Nizer showed the jury an ambitious man, someone with his eye fixed clearly on promotion.

This was borne out by testimony from Mrs. Donelon. After first providing domestic details of her husband—good around the home and garden, great with their son, intelligent and well-read—she confirmed that he had attended classes on advertising and had completed a public speaking course at the Dale Carnegie Institute, all designed to advance his career. When Nizer attempted to introduce various diplomas earned by the deceased, opposing counsel objected. After considerable reflection, Judge Frances G. Hooley did admit them, though he indicated to both sides his belief that he was providing possible grounds for reversible error.

A. Puzzling Papers

Before submitting Mrs. Donelon to cross-examination, Nizer handed her a sheaf of documents and asked if she recognized them. She said they were a box of miscellaneous papers left by her husband. Although Nizer was barred at this stage from entering the papers into evidence—their relevance had not been established—instinct told him that they were important. Only later would their true significance and their profound impact on the outcome of the case be realized.

One item of evidence that Nizer did manage to get introduced, again over strident defense objections, was a congratulatory memo from a Weintraub executive to the man who had employed Donelon. "This is just to let you know that your boy, Jack Donelon, is doing a real fine job. Thanks for bringing him in . . . he is going to be a pretty important guy around here before too long." Other testimony made it clear that, despite his short tenure at the company, Donelon had already made several telling contributions to various Weintraub advertising campaigns.

In the face of such revelations, LIRC told its attorneys to offer $25,000 in settlement. Nizer, believing that the jury was warming to his plea, advised his client to turn them down; especially since he had now deciphered the meaning of those arcane papers.

They were the work of Myron E. Berrick, a former neighbor of Donelon's, a student at the time but now a clinical psychologist, and someone who had used Donelon as a volunteer guinea pig in a series of intelligence tests. Besides rating intelligence, the tests were also designed to measure one's capacity for learning and, critically, for personal growth. On each test Donelon scored well above average, but when assessed on the likelihood for personal growth he ranked in the highest ten percent.

Obviously, this was pure speculation, and the judge admitted the tests only with the gravest of misgivings, but Nizer felt the mood in court change. He also began to notice a certain unease on the opposing bench. Step by step the settlement was increased—$30,000, $40,000, all the way up to $50,000—and still Nizer kept advising his client to refuse. When the offer reached $75,000 he finally became edgy: this was, after all, the client's money he was gambling with. But he still had one final ace to play.

It concerned the way in which courts dealt with life expectancy. They relied on the Life Experience Tables of Mortality, which dated back to 1868, and were, according to Nizer, obsolete. Under these tables both Donelon and his wife were each assessed as having another thirty-five years' life expectancy. Yet when Richard Fondiller, an actuary, took the stand, he testified that nowadays insurance companies preferred to use the more up-to-date United States Life Tables. At first the judge refused to admit this evidence, saying that there was no precedent, but overnight Nizer's clerk scoured the law books and uncovered cases where other courts had found the Life Experience Tables wanting. Recalled to the stand, Fondiller explained that under the U.S. Life Tables, Donelon's expectancy was increased from 35–39 years, and his wife from 35–42.

This dealt a massive blow to the defense. In the wake of the disaster LIRC was facing hundreds of lawsuits and now saw their liabilities rising exponentially. They immediately offered $90,000. Nizer, sensing he had them on the run, still said no. The next day the attorneys for both sides huddled in a meeting. Nizer was asked what he wanted, within reason. Back came the answer—$150,000. At this stage the judge called all parties, including Mrs. Donelon, into his chambers. Judge Hooley warned Mrs. Donelon that because many of his decisions were open to dispute and might later be reversed, and bearing in mind possible costs and the risk of defeat, she might want to consider a compromise offer. The sum agreed upon was $112,500, more than four times what had originally been offered. Mrs.

Donelon did have one more request. She asked Nizer for a complete copy of the trial transcript, a present for her son, just so he would know what kind of father he had.

B. Rewriting Record Books

With verdicts like this, Nizer helped rewrite the record books on damages awards and made himself one of the best known and most feared attorneys in America. More than most of his colleagues, he has documented his legal experiences; with mixed results. His book *My Life in Court* (1961) topped the *New York Times* bestseller list and stayed on the list for seventy-two weeks. Another, *The Implosion Conspiracy* (1972) a study of the Rosenberg case, led to members of the Rosenberg family suing him for alleged defamation of character and invasion of privacy, charges that were eventually dismissed in 1977 by the U.S. Court of Appeals in Manhattan. An additional copyright dispute was later settled out of court.

In later life Nizer's caseload ranged from a high-profile libel action involving a California resort, which was settled in the early 1980s, to a price control violation claim by the U.S. Government against a unit of Occidental Petroleum. He remained in harness almost until his death on November 10, 1994, from kidney failure. Just ten days earlier, at the age of ninety-two, he had been at his office desk, still working.

Louis Nizer loved the law. He once wrote, "The excitement has never diminished. Indeed it has grown. The challenge is ever new. The contest is ever intense. Surprise is ever present." When writing these words he may well have been reminded of one particular divorce case, in which, while undergoing a rigorous cross-examination from Nizer, the frantic wife cried out defiantly, "What you say isn't true. I have been faithful to my husband dozens of times!"

OTHER NOTABLE CASES:

Bercovici v. Chaplin (1947); Reynolds v. Westbrook (1955); John Henry Falk (1962)

Thomas P. Puccio
(1944–)

I. Career

Thomas Puccio didn't get to be one of New York's top criminal trial attorneys by being laid-back. Everything he does is conducted at whirlwind pace. He talks fast, he walks the same way, he astonishes others by the amount of energy he puts into every case. "He was always so busy I had to book time with him," recalls David G. Trager, formerly Puccio's boss at the U.S. Attorney's Office in the 1970s. In his thirteen years as a federal prosecutor, Puccio handled some of the most notorious cases of the day, including the $70 million "French Connection" heroin theft, and the ABSCAM investigation and trials which ran from 1978–82, exhibiting a tough, no-nonsense approach in court that made him one of the most feared prosecutors around.

Such dynamism has its defenders and its detractors. He has been called a "fresh-mouthed . . . glory hog," while others accuse him of always looking out for "number one." It is the kind of criticism that outstanding lawyers have endured since Hammurabi first drew up his Code around 1750 B.C.

Puccio grew up in the Boro Park neighborhood of Brooklyn, the only child of a government worker and his secretary wife. In 1969, after Fordham College and

Defense attorney Thomas Puccio holds the so-called "black bag" during the cross-examination of Edwin F. Lambert, a private investigator, at the re-trial of Claus Von Bülow. (AP Wide World/Norm Sylvia)

Fordham Law School, he became an assistant U.S. Attorney in Brooklyn, where he soon gained the reputation of being a tough street-fighter with a razor-sharp brain to match. When, in December 1975, he was appointed head of the Justice Department's (JD) Organized Crime Strike Force for the Eastern District of New York, his capacity for absorbing complex detail proved invaluable, and it was a trait that continued to serve him well when he finally left the JD in 1982 to set up in private practice.

His first major triumph came when he defended Claus Von Bülow in the second of his two trials for attempted murder. Although most of the kudos for this memorable case have gone to the Harvard team headed by Alan Dershowitz (q.v.), the part played by Puccio should not be undervalued. His was the voice in court that had to convince the jury, and in this he succeeded brilliantly. He also managed to upset the bench more often than he should, though this was only to be expected when someone of his temperament crosses swords with the blue bloods of Rhode Island.

In the years since then Puccio has repeatedly demonstrated his excellence in a wide variety of litigation, but he is particularly strong in cases of suspected business fraud. By their very nature such cases are often intricate and difficult to defend, as guilt may hinge on the interpretation of a contract, or even, as one of Puccio's clients found out at his own expense, a single spoken sentence.

II. John Mulheren, Jr. (1990)

John Mulheren, a Wall Street trader, turns around in his seat during his arraignment at Monmouth Superior Court . (AP Wide World)

In 1986 Ivan Boesky, one of Wall Street's most powerful figures and an operator previously thought to be beyond the law, was jailed for insider trading. As part of his deal with the government, the so-called "King of the Arbitragers" agreed to pay $100 million in fines and penalties, and blow the whistle on dozens of ex-colleagues. Most of those named by Boesky reached hasty settlements with the government. Only one, John Mulheren, former head of Jamie Securities, elected to go to trial, adamant that he was innocent.

His trial began May 17, 1990, with assistant U.S. Attorney, E. Scott Gilbert, claiming that Mulheren had aided Boesky in manipulating the price of one stock and concealing the ownership of others so that Boesky might evade taxes. It all hinged around Boesky's attempted leveraged-buy-out of Gulf & Western with company chairman, Martin Davis. When that deal collapsed Davis agreed to repurchase Boesky's stock in G&W at $45 a share, but only if the market reached that level. According to Gilbert, Boesky asked Mulheren to buy 75,000 shares of G&W towards the end of the trading day, when the transaction was most likely to affect the stock's value. Sure enough, after Mulheren's order went in, the price rose twenty-five cents to $45, and Boesky unloaded his 3.5 million shares, at a profit of $800,000.

What sounded highly suspicious was made considerably less so by Puccio's announcement to the court that G&W had actually traded at $45 *the day before* Mulheren talked to Boesky. After establishing this fact, Puccio unleashed a furious attack on Boesky, slamming him as the "king of greed."

This was the first time that Boesky testified since being paroled, and the courtroom was packed to hear him describe how Mulheren agreed to "park" stock and thus help Boesky avoid tax liabilities. ("Parking" is where one party sells securities to another on the understanding that they will be repurchased at a later time. The purpose of the strategy is to disguise the ownership.)

Boesky further described a conversation about G&W, in which he told Mulheren, "It would be great if it traded at $45." Mulheren, he alleged, replied, "I understand." With those two words, the government contended that an agreement had been reached to manipulate the stock.

Puccio's cross-examination pulled no punches. Was it not true, he asked Boesky, that he had deducted half of the massive fine on his taxes,[1] kept millions in ill-gotten gains, and engaged in corruption while behind bars? Forced to concede every point, Boesky began to buckle, frequently mumbling "I don't recall" whenever the questions became too probing. There was no love lost between the protagonists. Once, when Puccio casually tossed a sheaf of notes to the witness, Boesky growled, "Would you mind not throwing it, sir."

"I'll try to restrain myself," Puccio sneered back, to which Boesky said silkily, "Please do."

Puccio stepped-up the attack, demanding to know if Boesky had bribed any other prison officials (apparently he paid prisoners to do his laundry while incarcerated). Angrily, Boesky refuted the insinuation. Then came another bar-

[1]*IRS officials later said that the deductions would be disallowed.*

rage from Puccio, ending with Boesky conceding that he had lied several times under oath.

In his own defense Mulheren admitted buying shares from Boesky but said he sold them on the open market, not back to Boesky as the prosecution claimed.

A. The Finger of Blame

As for Puccio, he was in no doubt where culpability lay. Describing Boesky as "a pile of human garbage who had lied repeatedly on the stand about his dealings," he turned incredulously to the jury, "and that is what the Government of the United States . . . put up to testify against John Mulheren."

Despite a whole barrage of character witnesses and Puccio's fiercely argued assertion that no crime had taken place, on July 10, 1990, Mulheren was convicted of stock manipulation. He was later sentenced to one year in prison, fined $1.68 million, and banned from securities trading.

Puccio immediately filed an appeal.

In May 1991, he appeared before the United States Court of Appeals for the Second Circuit in Manhattan, and it was soon apparent what the bench thought of the earlier verdict. "This is awfully thin proof for a criminal conviction and a $1 million fine," said Judge Ellsworth A. Van-Graafeil. E. Scott Gilbert, defending the verdict as a "classic case" of what Congress intended when it adopted securities fraud legislation in 1934, insisted that "it is a crime to go into the marketplace when the sole purpose is to manipulate stock."

Mulheren's purchase of stock—an otherwise legitimate act—was criminal, said Gilbert, because Mulheren knew that the transaction was part of an effort to help Boesky manipulate the market, an assertion that led Judge Joseph M. McLaughlin to remark that he was aware of no other case in which a physical act became a crime "solely on the state of mind of the actor."

B. Convictions Dismissed

On July 10, 1991, as expected, all of the convictions were thrown out. In a blistering critique of the prosecution's case, the court ruled that none of Mulheren's convictions could stand because the Government did not have conclusive proof that a crime had been committed. In writing the court's opinion, Judge McLaughlin said, "We are convinced that no rational trier of fact could have found the elements of crime charged here beyond a reasonable doubt." Because the convictions were dismissed, it meant that Mulheren could not be retried.

Puccio had no doubts that the Government had been overzealous in its pursuit of Mulheren. "The case should never have been sent to the jury," he said. "The Government, in my view, put multiple charges on a very, very weak case."

It was later announced that all outstanding charges against Mulheren had been dropped. Final vindication came in December 1991 when the securities ban on Mulheren was lifted. That same month he was back trading on Wall Street.

In May 1992, Puccio's talent for unraveling complex issues led to his appointment to investigate allegations of corruption among the Teamsters union, a job that would tax to the utmost his renowned tenacity. At the same time he continued his heavy criminal caseload. At the time of writing he is preparing for a retrial of the Alex Kelly rape case. Predictably, his abrasive cross-examination of the alleged victim in the first trial brought forth a ton of complaints from feminist and other assorted pressure groups. But for all those who complain about his prickly, hard-hitting manner, Puccio has this response: being a defense lawyer, he says, "is white collar warfare. Go for the jugular!"

OTHER NOTABLE CASES:

ABSCAM Trials (1980–81); Claus Von Bülow (1985); Stanley Friedman (1986); Nick Rudi (1996); Alex Kelly (1996–97)

Edward J. Reilly
(1882–1946)

I. Career

At the height of Edward Reilly's career, hordes of urchins, bootblacks, and hero-worshipers would mob this courtroom wizard as he strolled the streets of Brooklyn, pumping his hands and pounding his back. Broad-shouldered and florid-faced, Reilly beamed his approval. Flipping coins and the occasional note to the clamoring throng, he cut a splendid figure in his striped pants, cutaway coat, fawn spats, and omnipresent flower in his buttonhole.

The crowd adored him as "one of them." He attended James Parochial School as a lad and then the Boys High School. While working as a clerk with the Metropolitan Life Insurance Company, he studied law at night at Heffley's Institute. When Heffley's Institute became part of St. Lawrence University, he continued studying law and gained his admittance to the bar in 1904.

He zoomed to legal superstardom, interrupted only by a brief spell as a captain in military intelligence in World War I. Local legend insisted that anyone could "beat the rap" merely by hiring him. This wasn't true, of course, but for a quarter of a century Reilly reigned supreme as undisputed king of Brooklyn criminal trial lawyers.

He was a magnificent performer. On days when Reilly was in action, other courtrooms would fall silent as youthful lawyers obtained delays and adjournments to watch "Big Ed" wield his famed talents at selecting jurors, cross-examining witnesses, and summing up with the flowery eloquence in the tradition of Daniel Webster. He knew all the tricks: the quizzical glance over his gold-rimmed pince-nez; a knowing wink to the sympathetic juror; a sorrowful shake of his head at just the right time; a raised, skeptical eyebrow.

When it came to defending a client, Reilly would pull out all the stops, larding his speeches with mawkish references to home and mother, depicting life as a constant struggle for the chaste, inveighing against the cruelties of fate and the barbarism of society. Even a murderous bootlegger like Frankie Yale, who until his spectacular assassination in 1928 was known as the "Father of the Rackets," could be portrayed to the jury as a well-intentioned entrepreneur unfortunate in his choice of business partners.

If Reilly was ever troubled by ethics, it didn't show. When Anna Lonergan, whose husband Wild Bill Lovett and brother Peg-Leg Lonergan ruled the Brooklyn waterfront, found herself charged with murder, she learned from Reilly that an integral part of her defense would be that two of her front teeth had been knocked out. Puzzled because her teeth were perfect, sure enough, by trial time, the requisite gaps were on display for all to see.

Such connections brought Reilly a staggering volume of work. One estimate puts the number of homicide cases that he handled at over 2,000. Most never made it to court. Those that did attracted acres of newspaper coverage. And nothing guaranteed sold-out editions more than a female killer. During his career Reilly represented all but three of the women accused of murder in Brooklyn. One was so thankful for her acquittal that she publicly declared, "Brooklyn should erect its own Statue of Civic Virtue in Borough Hall Park, with Edward J. Reilly as Virtue." Someone else who felt strongly about virtue was Olivia Stone; so strongly, in fact, she was prepared to kill for it.

II. Olivia Stone (1922)

On August 5, 1921, a patrolling police officer watched in impotent disbelief as a woman emptied a revolver into fifty-four-year-old lawyer Ellis Kinkhead outside the latter's Brooklyn apartment. The woman, Olivia Stone, offered no resistance when the officer disarmed her, other than to say that she had only meant to cripple "the dog who ruined my life."

She claimed to be the victim's common-law wife. They met in Atlantic City in 1918, when she nursed Kinkhead through an illness, and during that time they went through a form of marriage ceremony. The "marriage" obviously meant more to Stone than it did to Kinkhead. After six weeks he abandoned his former nurse when he met and married, this time legitimately, a woman named Marie Gormley. In a fury Olivia Stone tracked down and killed the man who deceived her.

Ordinarily cases such as this were meat and drink for Reilly. This time, though, he had problems. Olivia Stone was impossible as a client; so bad, that when her trial began on March 28, 1922, Reilly asked to be dismissed from the case. "No man in the world can tell me that I am no longer wanted in this case," he announced. "I have given this woman the benefit of seventeen years experience at the bar and I owe it to my self-respect to ask the court to relieve me at this instant."

After Justice Joseph A. Aspinall warned the defendant to heed counsel, Reilly quickly recovered the initiative. Kinkhead was, he roared, a drug-addict and cad who had inveigled Stone into a form of marriage and then dumped her. "It is the sad case of an honorable woman whose mind could stand the strain no longer." Reilly expanded on his client's plight; believing herself to be married, she had attempted to obtain a divorce, citing Marie Gormley as co-respondent, but because of Kinkhead's legal connections, the action was dismissed on June 9, 1921.

With so much uncontested evidence the prosecution case was a formality, and all interest hinged on Stone's own testimony. She alleged that Kinkhead had introduced her to people as his wife, and had forced her to undergo an abortion. Only later did she learn that Kinkhead married another woman in Cincinnati. She told how, on the day of the shooting, she begged Kinkhead for a divorce, saying, "You are making a common, ordinary woman of me." Kinkhead, she claimed, swore at her and jeered, "That's what you are, and that is what you always have been!"

Reilly asked her to continue.

"Then everything went from me."

"What happened next?"

"I remember being awakened in jail by a matron, who told me I had slept three days and three nights."

Prosecutor Herbert Warbasse wasn't convinced. He had already portrayed the defendant as a scheming manipulator, and now he wanted to know about some letters she had allegedly written the deceased.

C. Lloyd Fisher (right) and Egbert Rosecrans (center) congratulate Edward J. Reilly (left) chief of defense counsel, for the summation he rendered in the Bruno Hauptmann case.

A. Courtroom Collapse

"Miss Stone," he asked. "Would you tell a falsehood to save your life?"

"No, sir, I would not," she replied stoutly. Then she keeled over. This was just the first of numerous fainting fits. At other times she was racked with uncontrollable sobbing. Veteran court reporters soon noticed, however, that all of these crying bouts occurred whenever Reilly cupped his right knee in his hand. Eventually she did admit writing the threatening letters, adding, "Yes, there are teardrops on the letter, which fell as I wrote." Then came another swoon, and she had to be carried unconscious from the courtroom. Upon her return she denied prosecution claims that she had tried to institute white slavery charges against the deceased under the Mann Act.

Rebuttal of this claim came from U.S. Attorney James R. Clark of Cincinnati who testified that Stone had, indeed, made Mann Act allegations against Kinkhead; charges that were found to be groundless.

Reilly's summation was a demented masterpiece. After reinventing his client as a slighted southern belle, he lambasted everyone set against her. Clark became "the most crooked liar and monumental perjurer that ever sat in this witness chair," someone that Reilly intended reporting to the Ohio Bar Association, so that they might "get rid of [him]."

Pointing at the deceased's wife, Marie Gormley, Reilly branded her "a woman of the underworld" who had forced Kinkhead into a reluctant marriage. "I'll stop this trial right now," he growled, "if Marie Gormley will take the stand and deny the accusations that have been made against her." At this, the unfortunate Mrs. Kinkhead burst into tears and fled from the court. Reilly lumped all the witnesses who testified against his client together as "dirty rats." Some from the South had taken advantage of a free trip to New York to swear away his client's life, he sneered.

After this onslaught the only surprise was that the jury needed as long as ten hours to find Olivia Stone not guilty. On April 6, 1922, she stood in triumph outside the Brooklyn Supreme Court. Five hundred people roared their approval as she kissed her gallant defender. Then it was three cheers for Reilly and off to the nearest bar.

B. Too Many Celebrations

Sadly for Reilly, there were too many celebrations, too much time spent in saloons. By 1935, when he defended Bruno Hauptmann[1], the twin torments of alcoholism and syphilis had reduced him to a shell. After the Hauptmann trial, fatigued by the stress of the ordeal and the failure of his three marriages, he was committed to the Kings Park State Hospital, suffering from paresis. Fourteen months later, longtime friend Samuel Leibowitz (q.v.) helped effect his release, and while Reilly returned to his practice, he only made occasional appearances in court before drifting into obscurity.

---

[1]*Convicted of kidnapping and murdering Charles Lindbergh, Jr.*

At the end, the man they called "The Bull of Brooklyn" was living with his mother when he died on Christmas Day 1946 from a cerebral thrombosis.

OTHER NOTABLE CASES:

Anna Lonergan (1922); Bruno Hauptmann (1935)

Earl Rogers
(1869-1922)

I. Career

Depending on the point of view, Earl Rogers was either an unprincipled rogue ready to employ any underhanded trick on behalf of his client, or he was, as Clarence Darrow so memorably stated, "The greatest trial lawyer in America." Since the former opinion was largely voiced by those whom Rogers had bested in open court, any objective appraisal of this remarkable advocate's career has to lead to the inexorable conclusion that Darrow got it right—when it came to mastering all aspects of criminal trial advocacy, Earl Rogers was untouchable.

He was the prototype modern-day attorney: skilled enough in medicine to unsettle any doctor, an expert anatomist, dauntingly knowledgeable about the still mistrusted science of psychology, and a pioneer in juror profiling. In this last area he wanted to know everything: their politics, religion, business, sexual proclivities. Witnesses, too, received the same scrutiny, as Rogers became the first top lawyer to use private investigators on background checks. Preparation of this caliber meant that he had never had to go fishing for answers on cross-examination; he already knew what was coming. So much so, that noted legal scholar, Francis

P. Wellman, declared, "Earl Rogers invented the art of cross-examination as it is now practiced."

In a later era he might have been a movie star. He was tall and slim, with matinee idol looks and a rich, baritone voice, but all of Earl Rogers' roles were played for an audience of twelve. Juries were mesmerized by him. They watched entranced as he picked hostile testimony clean of unwanted facts, until all that was left was the version that portrayed his client in the best possible light. He could be merciless on witnesses, often accentuating his disdain of their testimony by peering at them through a lorgnette, a tactic that prompted one cringing victim to seek relief from the bench. "Your Honor," he cried, "make this man stop looking at me as if I were—an insect!"

His father was a preacher in Perry, a small rural town east of Buffalo, and it was intended that Rogers should follow his father into the clergy. Two years pursuing this goal at Syracuse University, where he soaked up knowledge like a sponge, studying classics and learning fluent Greek, came to an abrupt halt when, at the end of his second college year his parents migrated to California. Rogers joined his family in Los Angeles and became a freelance reporter. While he was drinking one day with some legal cronies, one of them remarked, "You know, Earl, you'd make a pretty good lawyer yourself."

Rogers, who covered the courtroom beat, had been thinking pretty much the same himself and switched careers. In 1897 he was admitted to the California bar. Success came early to this flamboyant master showman who was to rewrite the rules of trial advocacy, but although he was to achieve many glittering courtroom triumphs, none ever surpassed the victory he gained in his first major trial.

II. William Alford (1899)

By 1898 Jay E. Hunter, a transplanted Southern aristocrat,was one of Los Angeles' wealthiest and most powerful citizens. He was also a bullying cheapskate. In the latter part of that year he engaged local handyman William Alford to repair some plumbing, then typically refused to pay the $102 bill. Alford kept submitting demands and saw every one rejected. Not even a court judgment could loosen Hunter's pursestrings.

Frustrated beyond endurance, Alford had some flyers printed that said, "JAY E. HUNTER DOES NOT PAY HIS DEBTS," and explaining the repairs, the court judgment and Hunter's refusal to pay. Then, on February 19, 1899, he called at Hunter's downtown office.

The two men met in a fourth-floor corridor. Alford thrust a handbill into Hunter's face and threatened to start plastering the flyers all over town unless the obligation was met immediately. Hunter, brandishing a heavy ornate cane, told him to go to hell. Other tenants in the building heard the sounds of men fighting. And then a shot.

Those first at the scene saw Hunter, blood pumping from a stomach wound, prostrate on the floor, fingers still clutching the cane which had shattered during the scuffle. Above him, gun in hand, stood a trembling Alford. Two days later when Hunter died in hospital, Alford was charged with first-degree murder.

The case seemed ironclad. Although there were no witnesses to the shooting, Alford's antipathy toward Hunter was well-known, and several people had overheard their quarrel in the corridor. Because of the deceased's importance, a special prosecutor was appointed to handle the case. Former Senator Stephen M. White was California's premier attorney, massively experienced in criminal trial work. With him at the helm, upper-class Los Angelenos could rest easy about the outcome.

Alford, by contrast, had trouble even finding a lawyer. Not only was he almost broke, but his case looked forlorn and the public was baying for blood. Only one person, Earl Rogers, saw any glimmer of hope. He grabbed the case with both hands. His fee was a paltry $100, and it was typical of the man that he spent $40 of that on a new suit. There was another twist: Rogers was a former pupil of Stephen White's. Now, in his first big case, the newcomer was set to do battle with the lawyer whom everyone called the "little giant."

In court Rogers listened attentively as the coroner offered his opinion of how Hunter had been shot. Since the bullet had traveled downward through the body and intestines, he thought that Alford was standing over his victim when he fired, a view shared by the surgeon who had operated on Hunter, Dr. C.W. Pierce.

A. Bullying Thug

Rogers chose not to delve too deeply into this matter at the moment, and turned instead to Hunter's dubious character. F. A. Stephenson, an attorney in the same building as Hunter and the first man on the crime scene, conceded that Hunter frequently beat people about the head with his heavy cane; just as he had beaten Alford, thus enabling Rogers to plant the suggestion that Hunter's cane had been wielded offensively, not defensively.

But Rogers knew he needed more than this. White, brilliant on cross-examination, would make Alford jump through hoops if allowed. Rogers had to find a way to neutralize this threat. After several days he found it.

White's legal prowess was a matter of record, so was his fondness for the bottle; and with each passing trial day his lunch hour grew longer and more liquid. At first, out of courtesy, the judge delayed each afternoon session a few minutes, until White arrived. But after a week, with White showing up almost half an hour late, the judge began afternoon proceedings without him. This threw the burden for much of the prosecution on to deputy District Attorney Johnstone Jones, a pompous, self-important fellow, slow-witted and short of courtroom experience. Known sarcastically as "General," Jones was completely out of his depth and took a fearful lashing from Rogers' acid-tongue.

After several days of testimony the prosecution rested. As this conclusion coincided with the luncheon interval, Rogers, after a few words with Alford, rushed to a nearby saloon favored by local attorneys and particularly Senator White. White, already glowing from the effects of a highly liquid lunch, called Rogers over and, together, mentor and acolyte enjoyed a drink, with Rogers hinting that he would put Alford on the stand later that day when everyone was tired. White chuckled into his glass and predicted that he would tear his testimony to pieces. He was still guzzling lunch when Rogers, suddenly recalling an important office appointment, announced that he had to leave.

That afternoon at two o'clock, when the trial resumed, White was missing as usual. Rogers, in his chair and ready to go, called his first witness—William Alford.

Quickly and without ornamentation, just as Rogers had instructed, Alford told how Hunter attacked him with the cane, knocked him down, and continued beating him until he feared for his life. Then—and only then—he drew his gun from its holster, pointed it up at Hunter, who was bent almost double above him, and pulled the trigger.

After just fifteen minutes Rogers spun suddenly towards the prosecution table and barked, "Take the witness!" Jones swallowed hard. The intention had been for White to cross-examine Alford: Jones, unprepared for the task, rose miserably to his feet.

Haltingly and with one eye fixed on the doorway, desperate for White to appear, he blundered into his cross-examination. Alford fielded every question firmly and well, until, urged on by an impatient judge, Jones ran out of steam after just a few minutes and mumbled, "No further questions."

Just seconds later White strolled into the courtroom. He instantly took in the situation, but before he could say a word, Rogers was on his feet, yelling, "No redirect examination." As Alford hurried from the stand, White, beside himself with rage, growled *sotto voce,* "That was a damn dirty trick, Earl." Rogers, smiling sweetly, resumed his case.

He turned to the judge and made an unprecedented request—asking that the intestines of the late Jay Hunter be admitted into evidence. A gasp rattled the old courtroom's rafters. White rose unsteadily to his feet, objecting that there was no basis for presenting such unusual evidence.

Rogers countered that White himself had provided the basis, by bringing the coroner to the stand and eliciting testimony that Alford's bullet "had ranged downward through the intestines." Rogers intended to prove that the shot had been fired up—but he needed the intestines to do it.

After much deliberation the judge ruled in Rogers' favor, and for the first time in a California homicide trial, the bowels of the deceased were brought into court. Using a colored chart of the intestines, and backed up by the testimony of Dr. Edward Pallete, Rogers presented an alternative and imaginative account of how the bullet came to travel downward through the intestines. It had been caused by Hunter's fury. After shattering his cane on Alford's head, he then used the splintered fragment as a short club, bending almost double to deliver the blows. Alford, lying on the ground, shot up at his assailant, only for the bullet to travel down through Hunter's body while his shoulders were below hip-level, and while his intestines were folded over upon themselves.

B. Fantastic Victory

It was only a theory, of course, but the jury, dazzled by Rogers' revolutionary charts and technical jargon, gobbled it up and acquitted Alford on grounds of self-defense. Stephen White, the "little giant," limped from court, a broken man, beaten for the first time and by his own pupil. His reputation never recovered.

For Rogers this was just the first in an amazing series of victories that stretched well into the twentieth century. During this time he became the finest lawyer west of the Mississippi. By instinct a defender, only once did he prosecute a capital case. He won, of course, and the accused was hanged, but witnessing the execution turned Rogers into a lifelong foe of capital punishment. Even so, he found some profit in the experience. According to San Francisco newspapers, he spent that night in the prison mortuary, assisting the surgeon in his autopsy of the condemned felon.

But it was as a defender that Rogers shone. Before him lawyers mainly directed their arguments to the judge; Rogers changed all that, zeroing in on the jury, making them his primary target. He once appeared in five successive murder trials without a day off in between; and at his peak, in almost 100 capital trials, he never lost a client to the gallows. He seemed impregnable. And in the courts he was. It was the world outside that gave Earl Rogers problems.

C. Life Outside the Courtroom

By his mid-thirties he was already a heavy drinker and gambler, and a regular in the redlight districts. Women threw themselves at the handsome free-spending lawyer and he rarely turned them away. Often he would disappear for days on drunken binges. Several times he tried to dry-out, but it was hopeless. He would stagger from sanatorium to court, perform some legal miracle, and then it was straight back on the bottle. How he managed to keep on winning is a mystery. But when Clarence Darrow (q.v.) found himself facing charges of jury-rigging after the McNamara Brothers' trial in 1911, there was no doubt in his mind as to who should represent him: Earl Rogers.

Much controversy surrounds this trial. Rose-tinted memories have Darrow, believing Rogers to be too drunk to perform, taking over his own defense and winning yet another sensational verdict. But the record tells a different story. Most of the telling cross-examination was carried out by Rogers, who, according to his daughter and biographer, Adele Rogers St. Johns, thought little of Darrow's legal skills (she also claimed that Darrow privately admitted bribing a juror). Rogers was astute enough to know that in one area—that of emotional appeals to juries—Darrow was unbeatable, which is why he stood aside at summation time and gave Darrow his head.

His own efforts on Darrow's behalf were no less effective. "Will you tell me," Rogers asked the jury, "how any sane, sensible man who knows anything about the law business—and this defendant has been at it for thirty-five years—could make himself go to a detective and say to him: 'Just buy all the jurors you want. I put my whole life, my reputation, I put everything I have into your hands. I trust you absolutely. I never knew you until two or three months ago and I don't know much about you now. But there you are. Go to it.'"

Darrow walked free, and Rogers went back to the bottle. His first wife left him because of his alcoholism, and his second, Teddy, whom he adored, died of influenza in 1919. Through every adversity he continued to win verdicts, all of them adding to the myth of invincibility that surrounded his name.

Then came Charles Bundy.

Although Rogers had entered the Bundy case late, for the first time he lost a client to the hangman's rope. He was crushed. His drinking assumed a pitiful urgency. Then Harold Denman also died on the gallows. Suddenly, Earl Rogers, like Stephen White all those years before, was a busted flush. His decline, as dramatic as it was quick, ended with him being thrown out of his offices for non-payment of rent.

Some still believed in him. In 1921, movie moguls begged him to defend silent screen star Roscoe "Fatty" Arbuckle against charges of murdering starlet Virginia Rappe. Rogers, still drinking heavily, replied, "Not a chance. I'm through." Even so, the shrewdness and knowledge of psychology was as sharp as ever, as he forecast that Arbuckle's size would be exploited by prosecutors to cast him as an obese monster. And so it proved. It took three trials to exonerate Arbuckle, but his career was ruined.

Six weeks earlier, on February 22, 1922, Earl Rogers died alone in a cheap rooming house. He was just fifty-two years old. Of all the millions of words written or spoken about this phenomenal lawyer, William Fallon (q.v.) came closer than anyone to getting it right, "Even when he's drunk, Earl Rogers is better than any other stone-cold sober lawyer in the whole damned country!"

OTHER NOTABLE CASES:

Charles Mootry (1899); Alfred Boyd (1902); Griffith J. Griffith (1903); Morrison Buck (1906); Patrick Calhoun (1908); Guy Eddy (1911); Clarence Darrow (1912); Charles Sebastian (1915); Gabrielle Darley (1915); Benton Barrett (1916)

Barry Scheck
(1949–)

I. Career

Only recently has the general public come to realize what students at Benjamin N. Cardoza School of Law at Yeshiva University have known for almost two decades: Barry Scheck has one of the great innovative legal minds in America.

In the O.J. Simpson case, it was Scheck's incisive probing of the forensic evidence that opened up the seams of an imperfectly prepared prosecution; and while it might have been Johnnie Cochran's (q.v.) impassioned advocacy which won over the jury's heart, few can doubt that it was Barry Scheck who claimed the collective mind. Set among the sleek Armani suits and Rolex timepieces, his rumpled, boyish appearance, unkempt hair and rough-hewn Queens accent seemed strangely out of place, and there was nothing particularly polished about his cross-examination technique, relying as it did on bludgeoning repetition, but he did reveal significant procedural errors, enough to provide the jury with grounds for reasonable doubt.

His pugnacious, confrontational style is not to everyone's taste—as O.J. trial judge Lance Ito made plain more than once—but there can be no doubting

Attorney Barry Scheck speaks at the Quinnipiac College Conference on Forensic Evidence and Legal Medicine, October 26, 1995, at the Quinnipiac College School of Law. (AP Wide World/Bob Child)

its effectiveness. He comes from an unusual background: his father was a show business manager, handling pop singers Connie Francis and Bobby Darin. Scheck eschewed the attractions of show business in favor of the law, and his prodigious intellect carried him through Yale first, and then Berkeley Law School. After graduation in 1974, his strong political convictions found expression in a project designed to root out abuses in federal grand juries. Then came a three-year stint as a public defender in the South Bronx, handling every kind of case and every kind of client. In 1978 he was hired by Cardoza to teach a clinic on criminal law.

For the most part his career has been scholastically inclined—he is a full professor of law—but like his fellow academics, Alan Dershowitz (q.v.) and Michael Tigar (q.v.), Scheck finds the lure of the courtroom powerfully compelling. He knows all the tricks, how the public relations game is played, and how best to play it on behalf of a client.

An outstanding example of this came in 1988. Sometimes the hallmark of a great advocate is not so much what they say in court, as what they do not. When Barry Scheck took on the case of Hedda Nussbaum, the omens were not good. Only a miracle, it seemed, could keep her from a lengthy jail term. By the time Barry Scheck was through, he had rewritten the ground-rules of defensive strategy, and reinvented a woman whom many had branded an ogress.

II. Hedda Nussbaum (1988)

When paramedics were summoned by a 911 call to a filthy Greenwich Village apartment in the early hours of November 2, 1987, they found six-year-old Lisa Steinberg unconscious, starved, and close to death. From the discolored bruising it was obvious that the child had been subjected to long-term abuse. When Lisa died three days later, the couple who had passed themselves off as her adoptive parents, lawyer Joel Steinberg, forty-seven, and his partner, Hedda Nussbaum, a forty-six-year-old book editor, were charged with murder.

Lurid details of the couple's sado-masochistic, drug-abusing relationship fueled a media feeding frenzy. At first, public opinion lumped the two defendants together; it was undeniable that they waited twelve hours to summon help for an unconscious child, and spent much of that time freebasing cocaine. When the court appointed Scheck to defend Nussbaum, he worked to reshape that view, desperate to put as much clear water as possible between his client and her unbalanced lover.

Scheck portrayed Hedda Nussbaum as hapless victim. The fact that Steinberg had beaten her so severely that she left home on five occasions, only for her to return each time, was exhibited as evidence of just how dependent Nussbaum was on her tormentor, and a vivid example of the Svengali-like hold that he exerted over every aspect of her life.

Initially, Nussbaum was a reluctant accomplice to this ploy. Steinberg might be a baby-batterer and drug-crazed psychotic, but he was still the man she loved. Clearly, Scheck had his work cut out for him.

The media was more amenable. They lapped up Scheck's supercharged soundbites, including his description of Nussbaum after Lisa's funeral as being "literally a wreck—mentally and physically. It's beyond ordinary imagination or understanding." Gradually, as the public digested these emotive opinions in their newspapers or watched them on TV, the mood began to change. Scheck's strategy was plain: take the moral high ground and ignore any critics.

His most important convert to this view was Hedda Nussbaum, herself. Gradually she began to listen. When Scheck advised her not to appear in family court, she reluctantly agreed, even though this would deny her a much-wanted opportunity to see Steinberg.

Next, Scheck arranged for her transfer to the psychiatric wing of a private New York hospital, where she was shielded from public and, more importantly, grand jury scrutiny for almost five months. She also underwent plastic surgery to repair the facial injuries that Steinberg had inflicted upon her. (A videotape of Nussbaum, filmed by police on the night of her arrest, showed the appalling extent of Steinberg's domestic violence.)

Simultaneously, a team of students from the Cardoza Law School, under Scheck's stewardship, examined every aspect of the case, conducted interviews, even sifted through several garbage bags filled with drawings, tapes, photos, and writings that Scheck had removed from the apartment two weeks after Lisa's death. Some students were assigned to monitor Nussbaum's mail. Others—the self-styled Hedda Psychological Task Force—worked with Nussbaum directly, bolstering her self-esteem, encouraging her to testify against her former lover. For although Scheck kept Nussbaum away from the grand jury, he badly wanted her on the stand against Steinberg.

Without her testimony, Scheck sensed problems. The prosecution, too, needed Nussbaum as their witness. Only she could provide the jury with the details of how Joel Steinberg lived his daily life, and how commonplace domestic violence had become to him.

A. Reluctant Witness

Still Nussbaum resisted. Not until reading a magazine article that was deeply critical of her, did she change her mind and agree to testify against Steinberg, which prompted the state to drop all charges against Nussbaum. When this decision was announced in court, one reporter sitting close to Nussbaum overheard her expel a long, heartfelt sigh of relief.

By the time Hedda Nussbaum took the stand, she had received over 200 hours of rehearsal, from both the prosecution and Barry Scheck, and she had

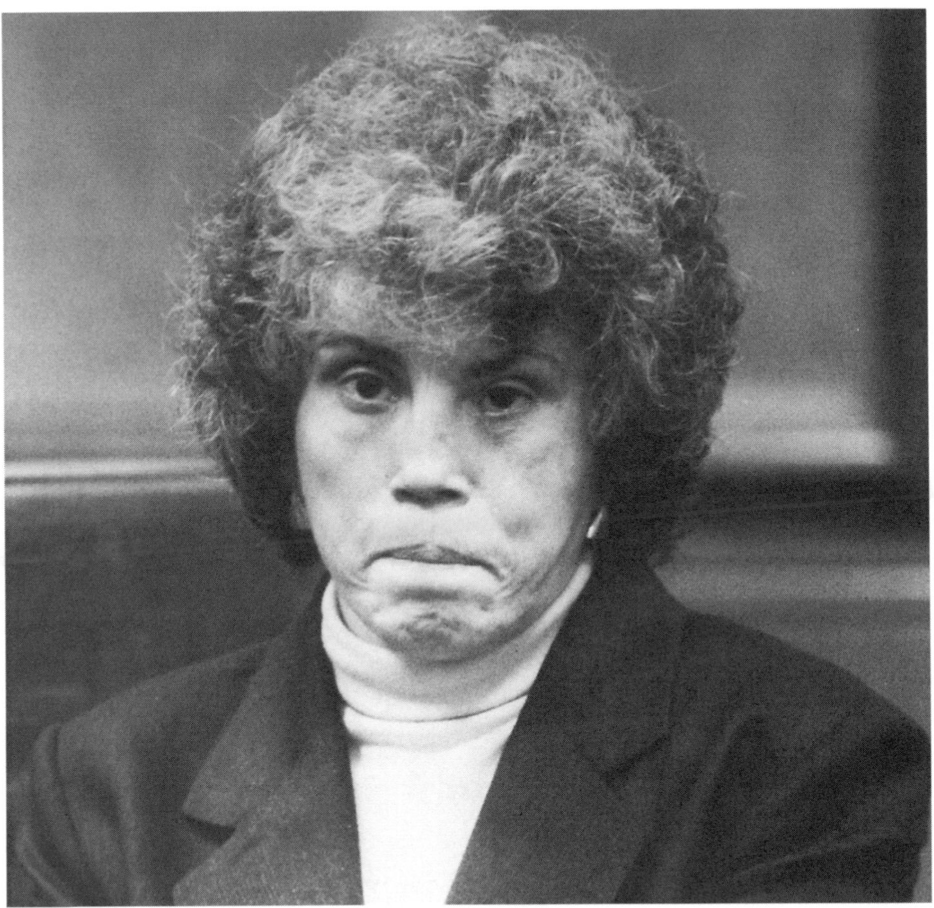

Hedda Nussbaum on the stand.
(AP Wide World/Richard Drew)

memorized the script. In a robotic monotone, she recounted how Steinberg brought the unconscious Lisa into the bathroom, and how the two of them tried for an hour to revive the little girl. Then Steinberg left to attend a business meeting. When he returned later that night, and with Lisa still unconscious, the couple freebased some cocaine and went to bed. At six o'clock the next morning, Nussbaum awoke Steinberg with the news that Lisa wasn't breathing. Minutes later she dialed 911.

For eight days Nussbaum remained on the stand. At Scheck's urging she refused to make eye contact with Steinberg. As an added safeguard, in a courtroom packed with spectators and members of the media, Scheck positioned himself in a seat that directly faced the witness, instructing Nussbaum that, while on the stand, she should focus on him as much as possible. One juror later claimed that Scheck consistently made hand signals to Nussbaum at strategic moments during her testimony.

Because Steinberg chose not to testify, the jury only heard Hedda Nussbaum's version of what happened on the night that Lisa was beaten. It was sufficient for them to convict the disgraced lawyer of first-degree manslaughter. He was later imprisoned for 8–25 years.

All across America and beyond, lawyers marveled at Scheck's adroit handling of every aspect of Hedda Nussbaum's defense. His skillful manipulation of the media, the way he kept her from the rigors of trial by jury, and his subsequent portrayal of a woman so undermined by her domineering lover as to not be responsible for her actions was a wonderfully skilled package. Admirers have labeled it the *Hedda Nussbaum Defense*. Others, more skeptical, prefer the *Abuse Excuse*. All ethical considerations aside, its efficacy in this case is undisputed.

Overnight, Barry Scheck gained admittance to that exclusive club of top-flight trial lawyers whose names are synonymous with a cause. It didn't take him long, though, to find out just how ephemeral public adulation can be. Many of those same women who lauded his efforts during the Nussbaum case turned on him savagely when he became involved in the defense of acknowledged wife-beater, O.J. Simpson. It's a reaction he takes philosophically, remarking, "You're a hero one day and a bum the next."

B. The Innocence Project

Another criticism leveled at him during the Simpson trial was the manner in which he attacked the DNA evidence, when, in other trials, he had been an almost messianic supporter of the technology. This was a reference to what is perhaps Scheck's finest achievement, the Innocence Project, an organization designed to free inmates that have been wrongly convicted. With his partner and fellow O.J. lawyer, Peter Neufeld, Scheck has employed genetic testing to exonerate more than fifteen prisoners by showing how DNA samples gathered at the crime scene differed from those taken from defendants.

In fairness to Scheck it should be stressed that much of his scathing sarcasm during the Simpson trial was directed not so much at DNA technology, as the less than exemplary manner in which crime-scene evidence had been harvested.

Meanwhile, Scheck continues to extend his interests and reap the benefits of his new-found media celebrity. He is being courted by network TV companies with a view to prepare a series of programs dealing with cases of wrongful conviction. Already he and Neufeld are rumored to have written several screenplays together. Neither man is under any illusions about their mission. As they quite rightly point out, the overwhelming majority of prisoners are guilty, but an infinitesimal number are not, and it is for these all-too-often overlooked and ignored victims of the judicial system, that the Innocence Project exists.

OTHER NOTABLE CASES:

Barry Piszczek (1994); Edward Honaker (1994); Terry Chalmers (1994); O.J. Simpson (1995); Louise Woodward (1997)

Robert Shapiro
(1942–)

I. Career

Until he was catapulted to international prominence by the O.J. Simpson trial, Robert Shapiro had long been regarded by South California's mega-rich as *the* attorney to call whenever they had a minor scrape with the law. Although he has acted as lead lawyer with considerable success in almost a dozen homicide cases, Shapiro's main claim to legal fame was his preternatural ability to paper over those little cracks that the notable would rather keep unnoticed. Characters as diverse as Jose Canseco, Johnny Carson, and Linda Lovelace all had good reason to be thankful for Shapiro's silky smooth skills.

Everyone agrees that Shapiro is slick. Too slick, say some. William Kunstler (q.v.) denounced him as "a notorious fixer, a plea-bargainer," a harsh criticism predicated more on personal disappointment than rational objectivity, and one that totally ignored the fact that a lawyer's primary duty is to his client. After all, while glorious failures might light up an attorney's resume, they are of little comfort to the person doing the time.

In 1982 when entertainer Johnny Carson found himself facing drunk-driving charges, he heeded Shapiro's advice, pleaded no contest, and spared himself the public embarrassment of a trial. That same year fellow lawyer F. Lee Bailey (q.v.), also accused of DWI, had no doubt in his mind about whom to call. By the time Shapiro finished calling more than 300 witnesses, Bailey's acquittal was a formality.

Talent of this order does not come cheap. Shapiro is expensive and effective, and the gratitude shown to him by satisfied clients has afforded this sharpest of courtroom performers a rarefied lifestyle. He wears all the trappings of the millionaire attorney, and he wears them well. It is a far cry from the young boy who grew up in Plainfield, New Jersey, where his father, a shirt factory worker, scrimped and scraped to salt fifty cents away each week for his son's bar mitzvah. His mother worked as a department store clerk. When Shapiro was still a child his family moved to Los Angeles. There his father drove a lunch wagon for forty years and moonlighted as a bandleader. Shapiro graduated from Hamilton High School, then it was on to UCLA. He gained his bachelor's degree in 1965, before, at the second time of asking, graduating from Loyola Law School. After a three-year tenure at the prosecutor's office, he began working at veteran Sunset Boulevard defense attorney Harry Weiss' office in 1972. This was a high volume practice, which often required Shapiro to work late into the night on everything from drunk driving to child molestation.

It wasn't a glamorous caseload, but it did provide the ideal training ground for a young attorney intent on making his way in criminal law, and it did eventually lead to bigger, more high-profile cases; so that when the mega-case came, Shapiro was ready.

II. Christian Brando (1990)

On May 16, 1990, the police were called to the Mulholland Drive estate owned by movie-superstar Marlon Brando, high in the Santa Monica Mountains overlooking Beverly Hills. In the den of the twelve-room house lay the body of Dag Drollet, the twenty-six-year-old boyfriend of Brando's daughter, Cheyenne. He had been shot to death. Cheyenne's half-brother, Christian Brando, was arrested at the scene after he admitted killing Drollet in a rage upon learning that Drollet had beaten his pregnant sister. Marlon Brando, who was in another room at the time of the shooting, said he tried to revive Drollet with mouth-to-mouth resuscitation, then dialed 911.

With a confession and the .45 caliber weapon used in the killing, the police did not hesitate to file murder charges against Brando. Originally he was represented by William Kunstler, who, with typical chutzpah, announced that his client would plead not guilty. Just days later Kunstler was dumped in favor of Shapiro. He responded with a very one-sided war of words against his replacement, waged with all of his customary vigor.

A. Damage Control

As for Shapiro, he was too busy working on damage control. In June 1990, shortly after telling the authorities that she thought the killing was murder, Cheyenne flew to Tahiti, reportedly on Shapiro's advice. There, she twice attempted suicide, prompting French authorities to declare her mentally incompetent and thus scuppering California's efforts to persuade her to return. Christian told prosecutors that he had struggled with Drollet and the gun went off, but they believed that he deliberately executed Drollet, after discussing his alleged brutality over dinner with Cheyenne at a Hollywood restaurant.

Hamstrung because their star witness was in Tahiti, on January 4, 1991, county prosecutors had no alternative but to grudgingly accept a plea of guilty to voluntary manslaughter. Deputy District Attorney Steven Barshop made no secret of his frustration. "Without her we cannot legally prove malice, and without being able to prove malice, this case is a provable manslaughter," he said, adding that he intended seeking the maximum sixteen-year sentence.

Shapiro sought to mitigate public hostility against his client by revealing the depth of Brando's remorse. "He is not just walking away from this case," said Shapiro, "this is a case, when all the facts are known, that will cry out for leniency . . . He wants to take responsibility for what he did . . . He did have a gun. He did confront Dag with a gun . . . he is responsible for what happened, even though it was an accident." According to Shapiro, "Christian approached Dag with a gun to emphasize the point that he did not want Dag, who is 6-foot-7 and weighs over 200 pounds, beating his pregnant sister."

At the sentencing hearing, which opened on February 21, 1991, the prosecution brief to the court pulled no punches, describing Brando as "vicious, callous and a serious danger to society," a man who "solves his problems by firing a gun at people's heads . . . [He] has engaged in a pattern of ever-escalating violence. Perhaps he thought that his famous father would get him out of any trouble he might get into."

Shapiro found their request for a maximum sentence risible. "In asking for sixteen years, the district attorney is making as ludicrous a request as we would be if we asked for a fine in this case." Then came a stinging attack on the DA's office for relying on "tabloid journalists" for information on Brando's background.

B. Earlier Shooting Incident

To support their claims that Christian Brando had a history of violence, the state produced William Smith, a felon and former fugitive, who recounted how Brando, in February 1989, fired a pistol in the driveway of his father's house, grazing the cheek of a passenger who sat in the car. He described another incident in which Christian "grabbed something—I think it was a hammer and smashed the headlights of a man's car."

Which all sounded fine for the prosecution until Shapiro got to work. He wasted no time in forcing Smith to admit that he had asked prosecutors for "a deal," because he was facing sentencing for parole violations on alcohol and drug-related charges.

Criminal Defense Attorney of the Year for 1993 and 1994, Robert Shapiro. (UPI Corbis-Bettmann)

On February 28, 1991, came the moment everyone had been awaiting. Marlon Brando took the witness stand. Brando described Christian's mother, actress Anna Kashfi, as one of the most "unhappy and cruel" people he had ever met. Christian's father also berated his own lack of parenting skills. "You always tend to blame the other parent, but I know I should have done better. But I did the best I could."

Having been coached by Brando on "how to stand, how to look, how to face a camera," Shapiro asked the actor about the public's perception that Christian was the spoiled son of a rich and famous father. Brando exploded. "Either they're a lying son of a bitch, or they don't know what they are talking about!" Gesturing towards the jury-box which was packed with photographers, he yelled, "This is the MARLON Brando case! If Christian were black, Mexican or poor, he wouldn't be in this courtroom. Everybody wants a piece of the pie."

Then came a strange interlude. Sobbing profusely, Brando first addressed individual members of the court by name, then delivered a long apology in French to Drollet's family who sat in court. Drollet's father, stony-faced, said later that he thought Brando had been acting.

At the end of it all, Judge Robert W. Thomas sentenced the defendant to ten years imprisonment, of which he served less than half.

In lesser hands Christian Brando might have been looking at life imprisonment, and it was advice of this caliber that in 1993 and 1994 led the Century City Bar Association to name Shapiro "Criminal Defense Attorney of the Year." In June 1994, he was hired to defend O.J. Simpson. At first Shapiro held the lead brief, but gradually he was shunted into the background. His post-trial comments aroused anger, particularly from fellow attorney Johnnie Cochran (q.v.), but Shapiro is unrepentant and has explained his views in his book *The Search For Justice* (1996). The race issue, he felt, was unnecessarily overused, enough reasonable doubt existed for there to have been no need for such inflammatory tactics. Asked whether he regrets his involvement with the O.J. defense team, he replied ruefully, "Well, it's not an experience I would want to duplicate, but it's not a case I would have missed."

OTHER NOTABLE CASES:

Linda Lovelace (1975); Jerry Blackmon (1980); Johnny Carson (1982); F. Lee Bailey (1982); O.J. Simpson (1994–95)

Barry Slotnick
(1939–)

I. Career

How close should lawyers get to their clients? It's an ethical dilemma that has troubled the legal profession for centuries. Top New York attorney Barry Slotnick was figuratively and literally very close to Joseph A. Colombo on the day in 1971 when the reputed Mafia crime boss was gunned down at a rally in Washington Circle. Slotnick was standing only a yard away when the attack happened. Colombo, paralyzed by the bullet, survived another seven years, and every week Slotnick would travel to visit the man he described as "a dynamic, interesting, well-read, and very cordial person."

Slotnick makes no bones about his affection for Colombo. "I never saw the side that the media described," he said. "It was an important relationship to me because he was a major figure in the world of criminal and constitutional law, and I was a beginning lawyer." By age thirty, Slotnick had argued appeals on behalf of Colombo before the United States Supreme Court, but despite having built his reputation by representing some of New York's more infamous citizens, he bristles at being termed a "mob lawyer."

"I represent people who are accused of crimes, some of them unjustifiably," he says, quick to point out that countless other well-known lawyers represent "so-called organized crime figures." Despite his proximity to such dubious characters, Slotnick's integrity remains intact. As harsh a critic as New York mayor and ex-Attorney General Rudolph Giuliani, has gone on record, describing him as "a professional, honest guy." His own partner, Mark M. Baker, once characterized Slotnick as "a very crafty, highly ethical lawyer . . . Considering some of the clients he has had, it's important to know where the line is drawn between professional involvement and personal involvement. He clearly charts where the line is, and doesn't cross it."

Slotnick's father, Meyer, was a Russian emigre and caterer who rose through the ranks of the Democratic political machine in the Bronx to a position of some authority. At age sixteen, his son enrolled at City College, earning himself a bachelor's degree in pre-law in 1959. These were important times for the young Slotnick. He later described the 1950s as his "formative years . . . when the government was blacklisting people and there was a terror running through our community. I realized what could happen with any unpopular group of people and that a strong government could become very coercive."

In 1961 Slotnick received a law degree from New York University and through his father's connections was soon able to make headway in what was a very congested field. When his own caseload allowed, he spent every spare hour in court, studying the great lawyers of the times, men like Maurice Edelbaum, Joseph E. Brill, Henry G. Singer, and Abraham H. Brodsky. Their style and their acquittal rate made a big impression on the young rookie attorney, and he absorbed every nuance, every maneuver.

It was a post-graduate course that no university could rival, and it served the ambitious young man well. Within five years he had been retained by Colombo, cementing the relationship that would endure until Colombo's death in 1978, and launching his climb into the highest paid ranks of New York criminal lawyers.

Occasionally, though, a case comes along that renders all notions of hourly rates meaningless. One such case fell into Slotnick's lap in the mid–1980s, and ended up being one of the most closely watched trials of the decade.

Barry Slotnick speaks during a news conference in New York. (AP Wide World/Richard Drew)

II. Bernhard Goetz (1987)

When New York electrical engineer Bernhard Goetz opened fire on a gang of black youths whom he believed to be muggers, he divided a nation. America was split into two camps: those who believed that Goetz had acted within his legal rights, and those who felt he was not safe to be on the streets.

The incident occurred on December 22, 1984, while Goetz was riding the subway. Ordered by four would-be robbers to hand over $5, he pulled a revolver and began shooting. As the gang members fled, one, Darrell Cabey, fell. Eyewitness accounts described Goetz walking over, carefully taking aim and firing an open-nosed bullet that severed the youth's spinal cord. After hiding out for nine days, Goetz surrendered to the authorities and was charged with thirteen offenses, ranging from attempted murder to criminal possession of a gun.

For Slotnick there was no great mystery about what kind of defense to mount: Bernhard Goetz was "Mr. Everyman," just an ordinary guy who twice before suffered at the hands of muggers, a victim so fed up that when four "savages" approached him, he pulled out a .38 caliber revolver and shot them. Foregoing his usual $350 per hour fee" because of the public interest involved here," Slotnick took the case because it raised a fundamental social issue: does the citizen have the right to defend himself or does the law mandate submission?

When the trial finally got underway in April 1987, after two years of delay, Slotnick went all out on offense. He wasn't just Bernhard Goetz's attorney, he was the self-appointed prosecutor of the four men who had formed "a criminal conspiracy" to rob his client. The only problem with this theory was that if only two of the men approached Goetz, as the prosecution alleged, then proving a conspiracy would be much harder. Legal experts did agree, though, that Slotnick's burden of proof as "prosecutor" was much lower than that of the state.

Leaving his partner Mark Baker to deal with the legal technicalities, Slotnick dictated courtroom strategy. Together the two men worked twenty-hour days on the Goetz case. Desperate to divert attention from his client's undeniably odd character and toward those of the alleged assailants, Slotnick attacked each gang member in turn. James Ramseur, subsequently arrested for participation in a savage gang-rape, was portrayed as a monster after the pregnant victim was, said Slotnick, "left . . . bleeding on the rooftop landing." Ramseur's cockiness on the stand made Slotnick's task that much easier.

Another of the alleged assailants, Troy Canty, provided much stiffer resistance. Slotnick warned the jury against being fooled by Canty, who came into court nattily attired in suit and tie. Instead, he harped on about "four menacing foes," holding up for the jury poster-sized enlargements of photos of each in their "street clothes."

A. Testimony Shaken

For two days Canty frustrated Slotnick, repeatedly answering "I don't recall" when asked if he had ever mugged "an old lady" and then threatened a younger woman who had witnessed the attack, or did he know the names Elizabeth Mays and Tanya Hays? On the third day Slotnick again asked the same questions and received the same answers; whereupon he produced a middle-aged woman, wearing a New York Housing Authority Tenants Patrol jacket, who stood in front of the courtroom, glaring at Canty. She was succeeded by a younger woman. Although neither woman was identified, their appearance clearly unnerved the witness and had the effect of driving a stake through his continued denials.

Slowly and inexorably, and despite the testimony of several witnesses that the shootings, far from being random as Slotnick had maintained, were willfully conducted, Bernhard Goetz was recast as victim, not vigilante. It was a massive feat of reconstruction. And successful, too. On June 16, 1987, Goetz was acquitted of all but one offense, that of criminal possession of a weapon in the third degree. He was later sentenced to six months in jail, plus a $5,075 fine, and four years probation. A subsequent review increased the jail sentence to one year.[1]

When Slotnick left this case his reputation was sky-high, as befits the man who regards himself as "the best criminal defense lawyer in America." Known for thorough preparation, tenacity, and ingenious legal ploys that have won acquittals in most of his criminal trials, he has carved out for himself an impressive legal empire and dresses accordingly in $2,500 suits. He also has a fondness for chauffeur-driven Cadillacs. And it was just as he was about to enter one such limousine outside his Manhattan office on July 9, 1987, that he was attacked by an unidentified man who fled on a motor scooter. The apparently motiveless assault left Slotnick nursing a broken arm.

---

[1]*On April 23, 1996, a civil court decided that Bernhard Goetz had acted recklessly and awarded Darrell Cabey $43 million in damages. Goetz, dumbfounded by the decision, declared his intention of filing for bankruptcy.*

B. Attracted to Politics

Like many lawyers he is attracted to politics and once sought the Republican nomination for State Attorney General on a platform of reclaiming the streets from the criminal and heeding their victims more. But in May 1990, he rejected the Republican nomination for Congress (Westchester) saying that he preferred to help solve the "terrible turmoil" in New York City.

Tall, lean, fit, and bearded, Slotnick continues to do what he does best, representing people in trouble with the law. At the same time his deeply conservative Republican views find expression in the numerous essays he pens for various bar journals and magazines. As for his assertion that he is the best criminal lawyer in America—a title that just about every top attorney has laid claim to at one time or another— Slotnick smiles coyly, "I am only repeating what others say about me."

OTHER NOTABLE CASES:

Meir Kahane (1975); Carmine Persico (1981); Mario Biaggi (1987)

Gerry Spence

(1929-)

I. Career

There is no more colorful character in modern-day American law than Gerry Spence. To see this monolithic champion of individual rights and freedoms stride into a courtroom is to be instantly transported back to a bygone age. At six-feet-two inches, with craggy features, buckskin-fringed jacket, longish silver-blonde hair peeking out from beneath a wide-brimmed stetson, and fancy cowboy boots, he might have stepped straight off a Hollywood set; and on a superficial level it would be easy to dismiss him as a vaunting poseur were it not for the fact that Spence wins, and wins big. His record is amazing. He claims to have never lost a criminal jury trial and no civil jury trial since 1969.

There is considerably more to this complex man than mere ego and million dollar judgments. Few lawyers in America are more thoughtful, or more constructive, about the problems facing society today. In numerous books Spence has laid out his life and his philosophy in a manner that has won considerable acclaim.

Gerry Spence. (AP Wide World Photo/Adam Nadel)

He is, in a profession not noted for its humility, capable of the most scalding self-flagellation. Such an instance arose from his appointment as special prosecutor in the 1979 trial of suspected murderer Mark Hopkinson. As a ploy, to impress upon the jury just how dangerous the defendant was, Spence wore a bullet-proof vest and placed bodyguards around the courtroom. He got his conviction and a death sentence, but it was victory at a price. So appalled was Spence by his own trial conduct—"It was the worst thing I ever did," he said, describing his emotion-packed summation to the jury—that he joined efforts to get Hopkinson reprieved. To no avail. In 1992, Hopkinson became the first person to be executed in Wyoming for twenty-six years. He went to the electric chair cursing Spence to the end.

For overblown personalities like Spence, controversy comes with the territory. The eldest of three children, he was eighteen years old when his mother, a fervently religious teacher, shot herself. For years Spence blamed himself, theorizing that his wild behavior caused her to feel she was a failure as a parent.

Spurred on by such uncertainties, he graduated top of his class at the University of Wyoming Law School. Then came eight years with the county prosecutor's office, during which time he moonlighted on behalf of insurance companies, fighting liability claims, until a chance encounter with a crippled litigant, whom he had recently defeated, changed him forever. It was a conversion of Damascene proportions. Thereafter Spence was inextricably linked to the underdog. These came in all shapes and sizes: the estate of alleged nuclear martyr, Karen Silkwood; Imelda Marcos, widow of the former Philippines president, and one of the most unpopular defendants ever to sit in an United States courtroom.

And then there was Randy Weaver. Spence loathed everything this ex-Green Beret turned fanatic stood for—racial bigotry, intolerance, contempt for the law—but he also knew that denying a decent defense to someone just because of their beliefs was an unforgivable renunciation of that person's civil rights.

II. Randy Weaver (1993)

At age forty-five Randy Weaver had abdicated from conventional society. He lived with his forty-three-year-old wife Vicki and their four children in a tiny shack with no running water in the sparsely populated woods of northern Idaho, growing his own food, finding occasional work as a logger. Self-sufficiency was his watchword. As a member of the Christian Identity sect, he believed the federal government was controlled by Jews, and he wanted nothing to do with it or any of its employees. Ironically, such views, so vocally expressed, guaranteed that he would be pestered by those whom he despised the most.

For the Bureau of Alcohol, Tobacco and Firearms (BATF), Weaver was just one of possibly thousands of subversives who inhabit the wilds of Idaho, Montana, and other remote Western regions. Falling under the collective umbrella of the Aryan Nation, this band of self-proclaimed patriots had irked the BATF for years, and in Randy Weaver the government agents recognized a golden opportunity to smash the organization once and for all.

The intention was to "turn" Weaver, make him spy on his cohorts, and to achieve this goal, BATF agents first sent in an informant who persuaded the unsuspecting Weaver to saw-off two shotgun barrels, thus making them 1/4 inch shorter than the minimum eighteen inches allowed by federal law. This transaction—caught on tape, along with Weaver's gloating admission that he hoped the sawed-off guns would be used by street gangs—provided the ammunition for BATF agents to threaten Weaver with imprisonment unless he became an informant. When he refused, they slapped him with weapons charges.

In 1991 Weaver failed to appear in court[1] and a fugitive warrant was issued. For BATF agents this was the precursor to Operation Northern Exposure. Costing $13,000 a week and lasting eighteen months, this mission involved air reconnaissance of Weaver's property, night vision equipment and 160 hours of high resolution video surveillance of the cabin, taken from more than a mile away.

Then, on August 21, 1992, six marksmen from the U.S. Marshals Special Operations Group (SOG) team, wearing camouflaged combat fatigues and carrying silenced submachine guns, went in to arrest Weaver. Immediately, the farm dogs began barking. Weaver, alarmed by the ruckus, grabbed his gun and went to investigate. With him was his fourteen-year-old son, Samuel, and a friend, Kevin Harris, aged twenty-five. They were just in time to see one of the dogs, a yellow Labrador, being shot to death by the intruders. In a reflex action Samuel Weaver began shooting at the assailants, who had still not identified themselves as U.S. Marshals. Their return fire first shattered Samuel's arm, and then, as he turned to run, caught him full in the back. The boy fell dead.

A. Deadly Fusillade

Kevin Harris saw all of this, feared for his own life, and began firing. A bullet from his rifle struck one of the hidden intruders, William Degan, a member of the SOG team, and killed him. Leaving Samuel where he lay, Harris and Weaver ran back to the shack, where they holed-up with the rest of Weaver's family.

Within days the Idaho mountainside was swarming with more than 400 federal agents and members of the National Guard. According to one government

---

[1]*It later emerged that Weaver had been given an incorrect court date.*

Randy Weaver holds the door of his cabin, which sustained bullet holes during the seige of his home. (AP Wide World/Joe Marquette)

spokesman, a "hostage rescue" mission was being mounted over concerns for the children, even though no evidence existed to suggest that the Weavers would harm their own children.

Some time later, when Weaver, his daughter Sara, and Harris left the cabin in an effort to recover Samuel's body, an FBI sniper, acting on orders to shoot any armed individual, fired at the gun-carrying Harris. The bullet passed through Harris's arm. As he and the others ran back to the shack, the sniper shot again. By this time Vicki Weaver was in the doorway of the cabin, holding her ten-month-old baby in her arms. The bullet tore through Vicki's face and hit Harris. Dripping blood, he helped the rest of the Weaver family drag Vicki inside and bolted the door.

The standoff lasted eight days. On August 28, Weaver's former commander in the Green Berets, James (Bo) Gritz, visited the shack, in an attempt to mediate the situation. The next day the group emerged. Harris and Weaver were given medical treatment and taken into custody, Harris facing charges of murder and Weaver accused of aiding and abetting.

During the negotiations, Gritz told Weaver that Gerry Spence would examine his case with a view to providing representation, and that night Spence visited Weaver in jail.

After his ordeal, Weaver cut a sorry figure. Spence made his own position clear. "If I defend you I will not defend your political beliefs or your religious beliefs, but your right as an American citizen to a fair trial."

Weaver nodded, "That is all I ask."

Spence's decision was not taken lightly. His own sister pilloried him for defending this "racist," and others begged him to steer clear. In answering one such plea, Spence wrote, "If I were to withdraw from the defense of Randy Weaver as you request, I would be required to abandon my belief that this system has any remaining virtue. I would be more at fault than the federal government that has murdered these people . . . I would be less of a man than my client who had the courage of his convictions. I would lose all respect for myself."

Then it was down to the nuts and bolts of organizing a defense. As soon as Spence takes a case he begins drafting his opening statement, searching for a single phrase that will hook the jury's imagination. So it was that Samuel Weaver, far from being a teenager who had opened fire on U.S. Marshals, became "little Sammie Weaver." (Later, in another trial, Imelda Marcos would metamorphosize into "a small, fragile woman" whose sole crime was that she was "a world-class shopper.")

A lawyer who knows Spence well, John J. Bartko, says, "He is probably better in a case with a moral dimension as opposed to a complex, difficult one," and early on in this trial Spence set out his stall for the jury, telling them that this case was a "watershed," a chance to send the government a message on the permissible use of deadly force. The Weavers, he said, had been "murdered" by federal agents, and all because Randy Weaver "was a little guy who just wanted to be alone."

B. Evidence Tampering

But it wasn't just emotive rhetoric; Spence knew he was holding all of the high cards, as it soon became apparent that the prosecution case was hopelessly flawed. Whole chunks of evidence had been tampered with, either first removed from the cabin, then returned and photographed, or else, in the case of one photograph of a bullet, fabricated entirely. On his first visit to the witness stand, Agent Greg Rampton failed to disclose that the photograph had been staged. Now, when re-examined by Spence, the whole sordid story spilled out.

"You knew before the trial," said Spence, "that the pictures I had were reconstructed when I cross-examined you the other day, isn't that true?"

"You never asked me about that," Rampton replied lamely. "And I tried to stick with the questions you asked."

In a humiliating moment, prosecutor Ronald Howen was forced to admit to the court that, eight weeks before the trial, he knew that the suspect photograph had been staged, yet said nothing.

Spence also induced further damaging revelations from Dick Rogers, agent in charge of the mission, who admitted that the rules of engagement had been altered at the scene. Previously they stated that an agent may only shoot if his life or someone else's life is in danger. On this occasion federal snipers were given clear orders to fire on any armed adult.

Despite producing fifty-six witnesses over thirty-six days, the prosecution collapsed. At one point, while the jurors were absent, Judge Edward Lodge expressed his belief that seventy-five-percent of prosecution testimony had aided the defense. So overwhelming was the rout that Spence rested his case without producing a single defense witness. After three weeks of deliberation, the jury found both men not guilty of murder, ruling they had acted in reasonable self-defense. They did, however, convict Weaver of weapons charges and on October 18, 1993, he received an eighteen-month sentence.

In a later interview, Spence said, "What can happen to Randy Weaver can happen to anybody in this country." Describing his own beliefs as "about as far left of Randy Weaver as anyone's can be," he said that, during the trial, "It was the most important thing in my life that he get justice."

Nowadays Spence is a wealthy man. He lives in rural splendor on thirty-five heavily wooded acres just outside Jackson, Wyoming, and nearby is another ranch, most of which he has donated as an elk refuge.

He remains, above all, an individual, someone who fights the system single-handedly, rejecting such modish developments as jury consultants. "I don't care whether jurors are rich or poor, black or white, male or female, old or young, or what they do. I want to know if it's someone I can bare my soul to, someone who will listen to me, someone I can be a friend to, or if it's some cynic or jerk who's full of hate."

It's a wholeheartedness others can only dream of emulating. During the Weaver trial, David Z. Nevin, who defended Kevin Harris, got plenty of opportunity to study Spence at first hand. Says Nevin, "A beginning lawyer's pitch is 'My client isn't guilty because it's not logical that he's guilty.' But a Gerry Spence says 'My client isn't guilty because I say he's not.' Gerry puts his integrity on the line."

Spence's pose as the last gunfighter might draw sniggers from some, but not from Nevin. His overall view of Gerry Spence pulls everything into focus, "There really is a good person under that hat."

OTHER NOTABLE CASES:

Ed Cantrell (1979); Mark Hopkinson (1979); Silkwood v. Kerr-McGhee (1979); Imelda Marcos (1990); USX Corp. (1992)

Max Steuer

(1871–1940)

I. Career

When Max Steuer first set foot in America he was just three years old, the son of a poverty-stricken Austrian immigrant. When he died, some sixty-six years later, the mourners at his funeral read like a Who's Who of New York politics. Among the pallbearers who carried Steuer to his final resting place were Governor Herbert H. Lehman, Senator Robert F. Wagner, and Mayor Fiorello LaGuardia. All came to honor the man they called "The Magician," an attorney whose power and influence extended far beyond the courtroom and into every corner of New York life. While the days when poor Jewish immigrants would routinely pack the courtrooms to hear their idol deliver one of his spell-binding summations were long gone—in his later years, the little attorney with the quicksilver memory and languid tongue preferred the less-publicized world of civil litigation—the reputation lived on.

And Steuer was a man who had prospered greatly from his reputation. His fondness for money was well-documented. One client came to Steuer with a problem and readily agreed when Steuer announced that he would require $10,000 as a retainer. When the animated client then went on to discuss details of the case, Steuer cut him off sharply, reminding him about the fee. Undeterred, the client insisted that the funds would be forthcoming, but Steuer was adamant, snapping, "I can't even think about the case until I've had the money!"

During the 1920s it was rumored that his annual income exceeded $1 million, a staggering sum at the time. With this success came a strange liability; people began to suspect that anyone desperate enough to pay Steuer's going rate must have a shaky case, to say the least. Of course, this was untrue, but this perception might help explain why, of all the great early twentieth century lawyers, Steuer suffered more courtroom reversals than most.

Early in his career it looked as though no one would ever beat him, as he went six years without tasting defeat. His rise had been stratospheric, from grinding poverty on the Lower East Side, where he sold matches at age ten to swell the flagging family coffers, to Columbia Law School, and then admittance to the New York bar—all before the age of twenty-one! Trial, corporate, and civil law, it was all the same to him, and he mastered every branch.

But it was in the criminal court where Steuer first made his name. Like most great advocates his memory was phenomenal, honed by the deliberate avoidance of note-taking, and it was these immense powers of recall that allowed him the flexibility to engage his real specialty: cross-examination. Of all the advocates mentioned within these pages, his was the lightest touch. He was never a bully in court; he didn't need to be with his mesmeric powers of persuasion. Witnesses expecting to be browbeaten into submission often found themselves thrown by Steuer's kindly paternalism, a comforting mix of blandishment and sympathy that encouraged them to loosen their tongues and not notice the contradictions in their testimony. Only later, as Steuer expanded on these contradictions, making them apparent for all to see, did the witnesses realize that they had been duped.

Never was this mastery of witness psychology more evident than during the Triangle Shirtwaist Fire Trial (1911), when Steuer successfully defended two sweatshop owners accused of causing the death by fire of 146 workers. Had it not been for Steuer's kid-glove treatment of the female witnesses, which completely changed the mood of the trial, both defendants would probably have faced long jail terms.

Hand in hand with Steuer's courtroom success went progress up the greasy pole of Democratic politics. A stalwart of the Tammany political machine that had controlled New York's civic government since the early nineteenth century, Steuer attained a rank second only to that of John F. Curry, the so-called

"Boss of Manhattan." With credentials like that, Steuer was expected to deliver whenever one of the Tammany faithful found themselves in legal distress. Such a crisis came in late 1929.

II. Albert H. Vitale (1930)

On December 7, 1929, members of the Tepecano Democratic Club gathered in the upper room of a Bronx restaurant for a testimonial banquet honoring local magistrate, Albert H. Vitale. It was a convivial affair that lasted into the early hours, at which time Vitale, a close ally of New York Mayor Jimmy Walker, rose to make his thank-you speech. Suddenly, seven armed men stormed into the room and began relieving everyone present of their money and jewelry. Then, as quickly as they appeared, the thieves vanished into the night. In all, the sum stolen only amounted to $4,500, but the ramifications from this otherwise commonplace robbery spread far and wide, especially when New York's Commissioner of Police, Grover A. Whalen, discovered that among the guests was one of his top detectives, Arthur Johnson. Sadly for Johnson, others gathered at the table included the likes of Ciro Terranova, a racketeer known as the "Artichoke King" and also the Savino brothers, John and James, two thugs with close ties to mobster "Dutch" Schultz. The press, smelling blood, circled like sharks.

They learned that Vitale had been particularly anxious to stop details of the robbery leaking out. Stranger still were rumors that the heist had been engineered by Terranova himself, a possibility that seemed to account for the curious lack of resistance on the part of the guests. Only one, Johnson, had put up any kind of struggle, drawing his gun, which was then grabbed and taken by the robbers. Three hours later the bemused Johnson stood gaping as Vitale handed back the missing weapon, with the suggestion that the entire incident be buried and forgotten.

Which was, of course, the very last thing that the press intended. Graft and corruption were endemic in New York politics; just recently Fiorello LaGuardia, called the "Little Flower" and running on a ticket of cleaning house, had failed by only the smallest of margins to defeat the incumbent Walker. And now here was one of Walker's closest supporters, Magistrate Vitale, openly consorting with known racketeers. It was too good an opportunity to miss.

The newspapers ran rampant, with inflammatory demands for a purge of political corruption. One of their first victims was Detective Johnson, demoted and put back in uniform. Still the clamor mounted. Tammany Hall reeled as citizen pressure groups took up the cry, insisting on Vitale's removal from office.

Max Steuer, "the Magician," with Charles E. Mitchell. (UPI-Corbis-Bettman)

Eventually, unable to resist the protests any longer, the New York Bar Association drew up charges against the hapless magistrate and preparations were made to hold the proceedings before the Appellate Division. Levying charges on behalf of the Bar Association was George Z. Medalie, the brilliant Republican lawyer who would later hire Thomas Dewey (q.v.) to the post of assistant U.S. Attorney. Facing him was Max Steuer.

As always, Steuer sifted through every grain of evidence. It was this laser-like attention to detail that often led him to decline briefs, as he was disinclined temperamentally to argue hopeless cases. Here, though, he was Tammany's hireling and expected to produce.

A. Suspicious Business Transaction

The hearing began in March 1930, and it was soon clear that Steuer faced an uphill struggle, as Medalie introduced evidence that cast Vitale in the murkiest of lights. It all centered around the activities of the Rothermere Mortgage Corporation, a company owned by late gambler Arnold Rothstein, who had been shot to death in November 1928. Among the many letters found in the dead gambler's files was one recording a loan of $19,940 from Rothermere Mortgage Corporation to Vitale. At the very least, prosecutors claimed, in taking out the loan Vitale exhibited judgment unbecoming in a judicial appointment; at worst, it could be construed as a bribe. There were other charges as well, but it was this connection to Rothstein that would decide Vitale's future.

As Steuer rose to make his representations there was little about him that commanded attention. He was a tiny man, almost frail looking, with a bald, egg-shaped skull, but the brain behind that nondescript appearance was turbo-charged and running in top gear. Outlined by his persuasive tongue, the loan seemed commonplace, as he reduced accusations of malpractice to the simplicity of just an ordinary business transaction. To hear Steuer's version of events, the City of New York was taking a very picayune course in harassing a jurist simply because he had borrowed a trifling twenty thousand dollars.

"It was not an act or transaction which Magistrate Vitale was called upon to perform in connection with his judicial office. There is no allegation that there was any inducement of any kind held out to the Rothermere Mortgage Corporation, to Rothstein, or to anyone else, and no suggestion of any promise of any kind to anyone which would affect the future conduct of the Magistrate."

As to the charge that Vitale had known Rothstein to be a gambler when he obtained the loan, Steuer declared that the Rothermere Mortgage Corporation was in the business of lending money, and at the time of Rothstein's murder, the corporation had $1 million out in loans to about 400 persons. Steuer contended that the loan was from the corporation, not a personal loan from Rothstein.

"Well," said Justice Victor Dowling, "the fact is that he obtained the loan, and that the person from whom he obtained it was a person of evil repute—that is the fact, is it not?"

"Yes, but that does not change the fact that it was a loan transaction, pure and simple. Does a judge have a right to borrow money? Courts heretofore have always determined that acts complained of were committed in a judicial capacity, or that the acts would impair the Magistrate's integrity or the integrity of his office."

B. The Weight of Public Opinion

There was no denying the impeccable logic of Steuer's reasoning, or that no direct evidence of wrongdoing was ever actually laid at his client's door, but it was impossible to resist the weight of public opinion. The League of Women Voters was just one of the many organizations that passed resolutions demanding Vitale's neck, and supportive petitions landed daily on the desk of Mayor James J. Walker. Magnificent though it had been, Steuer's silken discourse was drowned out by the roar of self-righteous populism, and Vitale was ousted.

During the 1930s Steuer became a popular radio broadcaster, renowned for his on-air stamina (he once talked for almost two hours without a pause); and, of course, he did nothing to allay perceptions that he was the consummate insider.

So how good was he? There is a story told—it may be apocryphal—of how the Chase National Bank found itself being threatened with a serious suit, one which challenged the company's very being. An anxious board of directors gathered together.

"Gentlemen," said the chairman to others, "we must have the best lawyer in the world. I am going to pass out twelve cards, and I want each director to think of the man he believes to be the world's best lawyer and write that lawyer's name on the back of the card."

The cards were handed out and the table became a patchwork quilt of knitted brows and furrowed expressions. When, eventually, the cards were collected and given to the chairman, he spread them all out on the table in front of him. On each of the twelve cards was written: Max Steuer.

OTHER NOTABLE CASES:

Frank J. Gardner (1910); Triangle Shirtwaist Fire Trial (1911);
Hartog v. Murphy (1923); Stokes v. Stokes (1923);
Croker v. Croker (1923); Harry M. Daugherty (1927);
Isidor Kresel (1931); Charles Mitchell (1933);
Joseph Broderick (1932); Vallee v. Vallee (1935)

Lloyd Paul Stryker
(1885–1955)

I. Career

Both in temperament and talent, Lloyd Paul Stryker, one of the twentieth century's most distinguished criminal lawyers, was born about 200 years too late. By almost any yardstick he belonged to the age of Patrick Henry and Andrew Hamilton, when high-flown oratory was something to be prized and principle mattered above all. Stryker loved the law. But many of its aspects disturbed him. In his eyes, the law was fashioned for courtroom conflict, and he could be scathing in his opinion of those attorneys who shied away from criminal practice in favor of the safer and infinitely more remunerative civil litigation. "Drawing up corporate mortgages," he called it, curling his lip around the phrase as if it were some foul emetic.

In 1954 he attempted to reverse this stampede into civil practice by publishing *The Art of Advocacy,* a plea for more attorneys to undertake trial work. It remains a classic of its kind, an outstanding volume that convinced many young lawyers, among them the young F. Lee Bailey (q.v.), where their destiny lay.

"A trial," Stryker observed, "is still an ordeal by battle. For the broadsword there is the weight of the evidence; for the battle-ax, the force of

District Attorney William F. X. Geoghan, his counsel, Lloyd Paul Stryker, and Captain John McGowant (left to right, in foreground) examine documents by which Governor Lehman seeks to determine Geoghan's fitness for office. (AP Wide World)

logic; for the sharp spear, the blazing gleam of truth; for the rapier, the quick and flashing knife of wit."

He was always going to be a great speaker. When his father, M. W. Stryker, a Presbyterian preacher and fiery sermonizer, left the clergy to become president of Hamilton College in New York, he daily urged his young son to practice public speaking in the huge barn that stood at the rear of the presidential mansion. The lad learned his lessons well, and after graduation from the New York Law School, and with a little help from Nobel prize-winning statesman, Elihu Root, he secured his first job, as assistant district attorney to Charles Whitman, later to be governor of New York.

It was a period of his career that he rarely looked back upon with unalloyed pride. Between 1910–12 he was usually to be found prosecuting cases at the nagging behest of Anthony Comstock and the New York Society for the Suppression of Vice, an outfit of self-righteous busybodies that trawled for prurience in the unlikeliest settings. Stryker soon tired of such pettiness and entered private practice. His only stab at public office came two years later when he ran unsuccessfully as a Republican for City Court. One year after that came the trial that made his reputation.

II. Rocco Carnivale (1915)

In 1915, New York City experienced a political convulsion of seismic magnitude when a long-running feud between arch rivals Tom Foley and Michael Rofrano erupted into bloodshed with the murder of Foley's longtime ally, District Captain Mike Giamari. At a subsequent trial, hired gunman Gaetano (Tony) Montimagno was convicted of the murder and sentenced to death. But that wasn't enough to placate the vengeful Foley, who saw to it that conspiracy to murder charges were leveled at another Rofrano associate, Rocco Carnivale.

Stryker spent many hours with Carnivale in the Tombs prison, trying to fashion some sort of defense. According to the state, Rofrano, Deputy Street Cleaning Commissioner in Mayor John Purroy Mitchel's cabinet, had paid Carnivale to hire someone to shoot Giamari. They further contended that Carnivale held a meeting at his Brooklyn apartment at which Montimagno agreed to carry out the killing.

Carnivale admitted to Stryker that a meeting had taken place at his apartment, but he insisted that murder had not been discussed and that Montimagno was not present. Indeed, he had never met him before! Stryker asked who was present. Carnivale wracked his brain and came up with half a dozen Italian names, including, almost as an afterthought, Tony Mongano. Stryker noticed the similarity between the names and filed it away for future reference.

When the trial opened in June 1915, fellow Tombs inmate Joseph La Salle testified that the defendant had confessed behind bars. "Carnivale told me that Rofrano wanted to get rid of Giamari because he was too popular," alleged La Salle, adding that Carnivale admitted receiving $50 a week from Rofrano to "get Giamari." This was a fine act of betrayal on La Salle's part. Earlier, while on the run himself for murder—the crime for which he was now serving a life term—La Salle had taken refuge at Carnivale's home.

But none of that mattered now. He was implacable in his insistence that Carnivale had figured in the Giamari slaying. Another of Carnivale's jailhouse visitors who testified, saloon owner Michael Santangelo, vigorously denied Stryker's suggestion that his trip had been undertaken in order to urge the defendant to rat on Rofrano.

It was time for the prosecution to turn the screws. Rofrano, subpoenaed to explain phone records that showed a dozen calls between his office and Carnivale's home, admitted knowing the defendant for twenty-four years, but denied any knowledge of the calls. Most he had alibis for; the rest, well, he could hardly be held responsible for every single call to his busy office, could he?

With considerable trepidation, Stryker called Carnivale to the stand. In his broken English the semi-literate Italian denied participation in any murder conspiracy, as well as any discussion of his case with any other Tombs inmate. About the meeting in his Brooklyn apartment he was just as emphatic. Yes, it had taken place: no, there had not been any talk of murder. Stryker then asked him to name those present, feeling that a stronger impression would be made upon the jury by having him tell those who were there, rather than asking first if Tony Montimagno had been present.

A. Deadly Pause

Carnivale began quite confidently, reeling off half a dozen Italian names, then he slowed, "also present Tony Mon—" The court was galvanized as the defendant, red-faced and snapping his fingers to jolt his faulty memory, appeared on the verge of saying Tony Montimagno. Those gathered around the prosecution table beamed at the jury in triumph.

It was the dramatic flashpoint of the trial. Stryker knew that a moment's further pause would mean the electric chair for his client. He had to repair the damage. Now!

"Rocco," said Stryker, "in telling us who was present at that conference, you just said 'there was Tony Mon—' and then you stopped. Were you about to say Tony Mongano?" Instantly a smile of recognition came over the defendant's face. The sun seemed to break through his dark clouds and he became a relaxed and different person who answered, "Yes." Then, in order to emphasize the similarity between the two names and the occasion for his confusion, Stryker went on, "You said Tony Mongano was there; was Tony Montimagno also there?" To which, with a clear and steady voice, he answered "No."

Stryker's quick thinking gave his client at least the glimmer of a chance. It was an advantage that he carried into his closing speech, when he reiterated the claim that this was purely a show trial, staged by cronies of Tom Foley, to blacken Rofrano's reputation. How much bearing Stryker's intervention had on the jury's decision can only be guessed at, but he saved Carnivale's life. The conviction was for murder in the second degree, and with it a life sentence. Stryker wasn't done yet. He later obtained a reversal by the Appellate Division which the Court of Appeals upheld, and Rocco Carnivale went free.

With successes like these, Stryker's future seemed assured, but the outbreak of World War I put all career aspirations on hold. He combined the duties of artillery officer with those of acting counsel at countless court martials. After demobilization he returned to New York, determined to rebuild his criminal practice.

In 1928, he was offered the vacant chair of Criminal Law at Harvard University Law School. The prestige of such position had its attractions for Stryker, yet not enough to lure him from the courtroom. A rather more difficult offer to refuse came in 1929 when he was named to a federal judgeship. Stryker's sense of *noblesse oblige* virtually demanded that he accept. However, when the Senate adjourned without confirming him, Stryker sighed quietly with relief and the matter was never raised again. The bench's loss was advocacy's gain.

Stryker continued his trial work, and he continued to write, five books in all. One, a monumental biography called *Andrew Johnson—a study in courage,* affected him so much that he changed his affiliation from Republican to Democrat.

B. International Success

He became one of the busiest and best lawyers of the 1930s, often crossing swords with Thomas Dewey (q.v.), as the latter pursued his campaign against organized crime in New York. Success on the international stage came in 1949 at the first trial of alleged traitor, Alger Hiss, where Stryker's blistering cross-examination of chief prosecution witness Whittaker Chambers drew no less than half a dozen admissions of false testimony in a single day.

Whenever Stryker's name is mentioned, people recall his gift for language. That great champion of the spoken word, Alexander Woollcott, said of him in 1939, "There is no more effective speaker at the New York bar." It was a talent that, at times, he found difficult to harness. Once, when lamenting the caliber of testimony brought against his client, Stryker seemed so overcome by indignation that he paced the court, bellowing repeatedly, "Dirty business! Dirty business!" It was too much for the judge, who looked up wearily and groaned, "Don't make so much noise. I can hear you."

An embarrassed hush fell over the courtroom. Then, in a small yet defiant voice, Stryker spoke: "I am very sorry that the tone of my voice should have been such as to annoy Your Honor. I regret it. Perhaps my fault lies in the fact that I have never been able to encounter outrage with complacence. Nor have I yet achieved that poise which would allow me to speak in the quiet tones of equanimity about an effort to strip an American citizen of his liberty by perjured testimony. And yet I have consolation. As I think back to that little Boston State House in February 1761, when James Otis before a hostile court thundered against the Writs of Assistance, I am satisfied that he, too, on that occasion raised his voice."

The creator of this unscripted little masterpiece died of a cerebral hemorrhage on June 21, 1955.

OTHER NOTABLE CASES:

Charles Becker (1912); William Geoghan (1938); James Hines (1939); Alger Hiss (1949)

Michael Tigar
(1941-)

I. Career

When Michael Tigar was twelve years old and growing up in Glendale, California, he announced that he wanted to be a lawyer. His father, an executive secretary of Local 727 of the Machinists Union at Lockheed, encouraged the young boy's ambition by handing him a copy of Irving Stone's book *Clarence Darrow for the Defense*, with the words, "This is the kind of lawyer you should be. He fought for people's rights." Despite the impossibility of the goal, no one can say that Michael Tigar hasn't tried.

For thirty years he has battled his way through courtrooms all across America, arguing unpopular causes in much the same way as Clarence Darrow (q.v.), winning some, losing a few, always fighting. Like Darrow, he has gained a reputation as a champion of the underdog, but this particular blue-collar advocate has also represented an impressive list of blue-chip clients whose social standing fixes them right at the heart of the American establishment. Tigar, quite properly, sees no conflict of interest in this—after all, even the rich are not entirely immune to the sting of injustice—and treats every case on its merits. Anyone searching for a common denominator in all of these cases, might find it in Tigar's antipathy to heavy-handed state oppression of the individual.

He fortified his politics in the radical maelstrom that was Berkeley University in the '60s, and then on to its associated law school, Boalt Hall, where he was editor-in-chief of the law review and class valedictorian in 1966. An early setback came while he was still at college. An outstanding academic record had earmarked him for a clerkship with Supreme Court Justice William J. Brennan, Jr., in the fall term of 1966, but then Brennan got wind of Tigar's radical views. Asked to detail his political activities, Tigar said he would only do so if Brennan agreed not to share it with anyone, and the job offer was withdrawn. Later, Brennan conceded, "I must say I've had a number of second thoughts [about not hiring Tigar]."

Instead, Tigar cut his legal teeth at the Washington-based law firm of Edward Bennett Williams (q.v.), where, besides obtaining access to many of Williams' highest-profile cases, he learned firsthand from an acknowledged master just how to structure and win a case. At the same time he maintained his contact with the political left. David Dellinger of the Chicago Seven, Angela Davis, and accused bombers from the Students for a Democratic Society were just a few of the many radical clients that passed through Tigar's hands during this period.

Michael Tigar talks to reporters outside the Federal Courthouse in Denver. (AP Wide World/Ed Andrieski)

When Tigar founded his own small law office in 1977, he insisted that all of the associates devote at least one-third of their time to pro bono cases. Some years later he abandoned full-time criminal work in favor of a professorial post at the University of Texas (UT) law school. In his spare time he writes essays under the pen name of Edward Michaels about a fictitious Texas lawyer named Henry Charles, and has also become an accomplished playwright, with dramatizations of celebrated legal cases from the past. One features Tigar's lifelong hero, Clarence Darrow, while another recounts the historic John Peter Zenger trial (1735) that laid the ground rules for freedom of the press.

Although still on the faculty at UT, Tigar is that rare animal, a legal academic prepared to argue criminal cases in open court, as he demonstrated to such good effect in August 1996.

II. Debra Meeks (1996)

Just three weeks before she was due to retire on February 29, 1996, after twenty-two years honorable service in the Air Force, Major Debra Meeks, forty-one, learned that her retirement had been suspended and that she would face criminal charges. These arose from an accusation made in December 1994 by a civilian named Pamela J. Dillard, that Meeks, her landlord, had threatened her with a gun. The following month, after this original complaint was found wanting, Dillard expanded her complaint to allege that she and Meeks had been involved in a two-year lesbian relationship.

In 1993 the U.S. Military Services had instituted a policy of "Don't Ask, Don't Tell," in response to the question of homosexuality among its officers and recruits. As its name implies, the policy treated sexual preference as a private matter, and one which could only be made an issue if such conduct became public knowledge.

A. Court-Martialed

As a consequence of Dillard's accusations, Meeks was charged under Article 125 of the Uniform Code of Military Justice with consensual sodomy (oral sex), and Article 133, Conduct Unbecoming an Officer, a reference to the alleged gun threat. Before the case came to court-martial the military offered Meeks a plea bargain, guilty to assault. Bravely, she refused, choosing to fight on, at immense personal peril: if convicted she faced dismissal from the service, eight years imprisonment, and loss of all military benefits. As her pension amounted to $1,800 per month, this alone could prove to be a calamitous, open-ended fine.

Meeks' military record was exemplary. She enlisted in 1974 and served two years as an airman, then joined the Reserve Officer Training Corps to pursue a college degree. After graduating from Troy State University in her home state of Alabama, she was gradually promoted through the ranks. For most of her career

Major Debra L. Meeks, left, leaves Lackland Air Force Base Law Center in San Antonio, Texas, August 14, 1996, with her attorney Michael Tigar and assistant defense counsel, Major Dawn R. Eflein. (AP Wide World/Gloria Ferniz)

in the 319 Training Squadron she had worked in personnel without ever receiving any disciplinary citations.

Amid great public interest the court-martial sat at Lackland Air Force Base, San Antonio on August 12, 1996. Tigar slid smoothly into gear. One of his great strengths is the way he is able to shift the trial focus from the behavior of his client to the misbehavior of the authorities. Here, he claimed, the military acted improperly because, not only did Meeks deny the lesbian relationship, she also refused to discuss her sexual orientation, and therefore not contravened the 1993 directive. Additionally, the investigation into Meeks was initiated by an Air Force official who wasn't her commander, a clear violation of military procedure. One of the military prosecutors, Vance H. Spath, countered that the inquiry began because of gun-threat allegations, not homosexual accusations.

B. Intimate Relationship

Dillard was the chief prosecution witness. She detailed an intense two-year affair with Meeks that included oral sex, saying that Meeks sent her cards and letters about their liaison. The relationship, she said, began in Virginia in 1992, and continued after Meeks transferred to Texas. After claiming that she moved to San Antonio at Meeks' request, Dillard denied defense claims that she acted out of a desire to establish residency rights for a Texas medical school.

Tigar was ruthless in his depiction of Dillard as a vengeful woman, laying siege to her credibility, arguing that she concocted allegations of a romance with Meeks because she had been rejected. Even when the prosecution produced explicit love letters from Meeks to Dillard, Tigar questioned their relevance, arguing that written words were hardly evidence that homosexuality had occurred.

The prosecution had no doubts whatsoever. "Those are not the letters that a friend would send to a friend," said co-prosecutor James L. Flannery. "They were passionate letters that one lover would send to another. Sodomy? You betcha!"

In the absence of any defense witnesses, Tigar argued that even if the jury believed Meeks to be homosexual, there was no proof that she had committed sodomy, and that she was entitled to be acquitted. He was also able to portray Meeks to the seven member jury—all colonels—as very much one of their own, implying that only military personnel truly understood the meaning of civil rights.

The gambit worked. On August 16, 1996, Major Debra Meeks was acquitted on all charges. Afterwards Tigar told waiting reporters, "This is a proud day for justice in the military. Major Debra Meeks had the courage to refuse to accept an offer to plead guilty to something she did not do . . . I hope it encourages others who may be the victims of charges to stand up and fight." Asked why he took the case, he replied, "I was offended by what happened to her and how she had been treated. It seemed to me that having a pajama police force was a waste of money."

At the time of writing, Tigar, who has argued seven cases before the Supreme Court, is embroiled in perhaps the toughest fight of his career. He has been engaged to defend Terry Nichols, accused with Timothy McVeigh of blowing up the Alfred P. Murrah Federal Building in Oklahoma in April 1995, killing 168 people, and injuring more than 500. This trial, scheduled for late 1997, is guaranteed to keep Tigar's name right at the very forefront of American jurisprudence.

Sadly, the father who handed his son a book about Clarence Darrow all those years ago, never lived to see the fruits of his dream. He died when Tigar was just fifteen. Had he lived, he probably would have thought that the kid did just great.

OTHER NOTABLE CASES:

Fernando Chavez (1971); Angela Davis (1971);
Cameron David Bishop (1975); John Demjanjuk (1988);
Kay Bailey Hutchison (1995); Terry Nichols (1997)

Howard Weitzman
(1940–)

I. Career

When British actor Hugh Grant found himself facing a morals charge in Los Angeles in 1995, he did what dozens of the anxious and the affluent in California have done over the years: he hired Howard Weitzman. Ever since the mid-1960s, this stocky, tenacious figure with the high-powered courtroom delivery has handled some of the West Coast's most sensational cases. Rock legends, movie superstars, drug dealers both accused and actual, even Manson family members, all have benefited from Weitzman's aggressive style of advocacy, and few have had cause to complain.

Intimate contact with so many household names has given him a unique insight into the workings of the superstar psyche. "Sometimes the image—and how the public perceives the client—is more important than winning or losing a case," he once commented. "My experience with high-profile people is that their career really comes first—even in family law matters."

His own family background provides the clue to the self-professed restlessness of someone who says he "never lived in a real house until I was thirty-one." His father was a buyer for grocery stores in South-Central Los Angeles, and that was where the young Weitzman grew up.

His first love was baseball, and he was a second baseman for the 1961 USC team which won the NCAA championship. He could turn a double-play as slickly as most, and he was good for the occasional double, but the statistics did not reveal Weitzman's true forte. As a bench jockey he was dynamite! A constant stream of motivation or sarcasm flowed from his whiplash tongue, forever encouraging teammates, haranguing the opposition. Sadly, Weitzman never realized his ambition of playing in the majors, and he was forced to find another outlet for his prodigious verbal skills.

Salvation came in a change of course and in 1965 the ex-ballplayer graduated from USC Law School. After a year spent fighting civil cases for an insurance company, he took the big plunge, opening a private practice in L.A., concentrating on criminal law, handling everything that came his way and soon carving out a reputation as a tough courtroom battler. His first major case, in 1971, involved Mary T. Brunner, member of the Manson family, who was accused of murder and robbery. Weitzman did manage to gain an acquittal on the murder charge, but lost two counts of robbery that led to long jail terms for Brunner.

By the mid-1980s Weitzman was amongst the very top flight of California attorneys, able to pick and choose his cases. Nobody, though, expected even this courtroom wizard to pull John DeLorean's fat out of the fire, when the failed automaker found himself facing drug-dealing charges and a possible seventy-two-year jail term.

II. John DeLorean (1984)

Throughout 1982, Wall Street had buzzed with rumors that the motor company founded by John DeLorean in Northern Ireland, and which bore his name, was teetering on the brink of bankruptcy. But nobody was quite ready for the stunning events of October 19. That day, DeLorean was arrested in Los Angeles and charged with conspiracy to distribute $24 million worth of cocaine! Furthermore, smirked jubilant federal officials, they had the evidence on videotape! More than 100 hours of audio and video surveillance had culminated in the fifty-seven-year-old automaker being shown taking delivery of the cocaine from undercover cops.

It looked like the perfect sting.

And that's the way it appeared when the trial opened on April 18, 1984, as jurors heard how FBI agent Benedict Tisa, posing as James Benedict, a crooked banker, met with DeLorean at a bank in San Carlos, California on September 8,

1982. In their taped conversation he told DeLorean about a prospective investor who had "all these profits from his cocaine deals," to which DeLorean replied, "It looks like a good opportunity." On a later tape DeLorean was shown raising a glass of champagne and describing cocaine as "better than gold."

Tisa testified how he had heard from James Hoffman, a convicted drugs smuggler and government informant, that DeLorean had $2 million "he wanted to invest in a narcotics transaction" that would turn a fast profit. The deal proposed DeLorean invest $1.8 million with Hoffman to buy thirty-four kilos of coke that they hoped to sell for $5.1 million. Through other Hoffman connections, DeLorean then hoped to raise a $15 million loan routed through the San Carlos bank, and parlay his money.

Each day of the trial, Weitzman and his partner, Donald Re, held a press conference outside the federal courthouse on Main Street. The "Howard and Don Show" became so regular, that TV technicians laid down markers in red and yellow electrical tape, reading "R" and "W." But there was a serious point to all of this. It allowed Weitzman to fight the case in the court of public opinion. When, in one tape, DeLorean could be heard telling Tisa he no longer had the money to buy into the deal, Weitzman proclaimed that this was his way of telling Tisa to "get lost . . . It's a clear indication that John doesn't want to participate in a narcotics transaction."

John DeLorean speaks to reporters outside the Federal Courthouse in Los Angeles. (AP Wide World)

A. Withering Attack

Meanwhile, in court, Weitzman was giving Tisa a torrid time. After extracting an early confession from the witness that he lied in telling another contact that he already received money from DeLorean, Weitzman turned the screws. He wanted to know about the case notes Tisa made. Finally, after three days of relentless questioning, Tisa admitted, "I may have rewrote the pages, [sic]."

Weitzman, adamant that the only reason for such actions was to alter evidence, looked askance. "And you destroyed the original?"

"Yes, a portion of them," confessed Tisa.

Weitzman threw his hands up in disbelief. "How do we know what you changed, what you added, what you took out and what you threw away? How do we know that?"

It was a bravura performance, one which moved DeLorean to tell waiting reporters that night, "I only got one thing to say [sic], 'Thank God for Howard.'"

For his part, Weitzman admitted that the tapes showed his client discussing coke. "Clearly his judgment was not only poor, it was non-existent," he said, but added that DeLorean had been pushed into it by government pressure.

B. A Hired Gun

When James Hoffman took the stand, tapes had already been played in court showing him drinking and making bawdy comments about women, so nobody was expecting too much cerebral content. Despite this perception he still managed to resist Weitzman's penetrating cross-examination. Then came a sensational turning point. Suddenly, it became known that Hoffman was trying to work a deal with the government. Judge Robert Takasugi exploded. Blasting the witness as a "hired gun," Takasugi found it "offensive" that the prosecution failed to reveal sooner that Hoffman "demanded" a share of any money seized in the case. Although said out of the jury's hearing, this revelation brought about a marked change of courtroom atmosphere.

Weitzman declined to call DeLorean because "we don't believe he [has] anything to defend. . . . The burden is on the Government to prove their case beyond a reasonable doubt, I don't think they've done that."

All through the trial, Weitzman varied his pose, at times friendly, informal, almost folksy, then sarcastic when necessary. But in closing he was at his most aggressive, comparing the case to George Orwell's novel, *1984*. "The whole premise is that the Government rewrites history, the government controls people, the Government stifles people." He said the government knew DeLorean was in trouble but went after him anyway. "Somebody should have said, 'Step back here,

Howard Weitzman at a press conference. (Archive Photos)

this is wrong.'" Weitzman said the government went to his client "and promised to save his dream, and there's something wrong with that."

On August 16, the jury acquitted DeLorean of all charges. They felt he had been entrapped and that the Government had not proved the trafficking charges. Weitzman snatched a famous victory. Such work deserves stellar rewards, and he is rumored to have received, among other things, a $2.5 million San Diego ranch in payment from DeLorean.

Since those days, like most attorneys in his position, Weitzman has ridden the highs and lows of celebrity. For a brief period he represented O.J. Simpson, and it was he who allowed the ex-football star to make a statement to the police, a decision deplored by his colleagues. In the Monday morning quarterbacking that lawyers are so fond of, they noisily raked Weitzman over the coals for allegedly putting his client at risk.

Others bemoan how he handled the Michael Jackson affair, where, against the advice of other parties who believed they had a winnable case, Weitzman arranged for a settlement believed to be in the region of $20 million to be paid to the family of a young boy who made allegations against the superstar.

But Weitzman's confidence remains unshaken, and just recently he has appeared in a new guise, as legal consultant to the epic TV crime series *Murder One*.

OTHER NOTABLE CASES:

Mary Brunner (1971); Tom Dragna (1981); Richard Miller (1984); Barbara Mouzin (1984); Kim Basinger (1993); Michael Jackson (1993); O.J. Simpson (1994); Hugh Grant (1995); Duke Estate (1995)

Edward Bennett Williams
(1920–1988)

I. Career

When former Senator Edmund S. Muskie once remarked, "Anyone who is fortunate enough to get close to Ed Williams is well served," he merely acknowledged one of the eternal verities of American law: in matters of criminal trial procedure, Edward Bennett Williams had no peers. In little more than three decades, he soared from Depression-era hardship to a position as one of the most powerful men in Washington. Along the way he advised mobsters and ministers, presidents and plunderers, and—like the clients of a certain well-known stockbroking firm—they all listened.

No less a colleague than Alan Dershowitz (q.v.) described Williams as "the acknowledged master of criminal trials," an advocate capable of speaking for hours without recourse to a note. Every detail of the brief was filed away in his megabyte memory, and with almost instant powers of retrieval he rarely found himself in the awkward position of having to fumble for the next sentence. Such courtroom mastery proved overwhelming to many of his opponents. Some sneered that he was ready to defend anyone if the price was right, and none too fussy about what kind of tactics were necessary to get his client acquitted. They cited his defense of Teamster boss Jimmy Hoffa in 1957 on charges of bribery. First, Williams picked an eight black, four white jury, and then, during a brief recess, he managed to get ex-world heavyweight boxing champion Joe Louis—a black American icon—to hug Hoffa in full view of the jury. As a result of that acquittal Williams received a $50,000 annual retainer as counsel to the Teamsters and a mountain of complaints.

He shrugged off the criticism. "If the day ever comes when lawyers grow timid about taking unpopular cases," he said, "the whole criminal procedure under our Constitution is in pretty serious trouble." In 1953 many expressed repugnance at his defense of disgraced senator Joseph McCarthy on tax and libel charges, while ignoring the fact that, at the same time, Williams also acted for two of McCarthy's victims, Hollywood screenwriters Robert Rossen and Sidney Buchman, who were cited for contempt of Congress after refusing to answer questions about alleged communist activities.

Williams saw no conflict in this duality. His job was to provide a defense: it was up to others to decide justice. He became the consummate courtroom performer, and yet originally it was politics, rather than the law, that attracted him. Born in Hartford, Connecticut, he reached his maturity at a time when America was still struggling to shake off the worst slump in living memory. When his father got laid off from his job as a department store floorwalker, the young Ed Williams pumped gas at a local station to help stretch the depleted family coffers. At the same time, he studied hard and earned a scholarship to College of the Holy Cross in Worcester, Massachusetts, graduating just in time for World War II. Like millions of others he enlisted in the Army. Two years later, a training plane crash left him with such serious back injuries that he was discharged.

Still intent on a career in politics, he enrolled at Georgetown Law School, where his outstanding record brought him to the attention of a prominent Washington law firm, Hogan and Hartson.

"I went there in my third year of law school," recalled Williams. "I began sitting at the table everyday with great trial lawyers. I became so taken with it that

Attorney Edward Bennett Williams is pursued by reporters as he leaves his Washington, D.C. office. (AP Wide World)

I just abandoned the idea of going back to Hartford and entering politics. I like the idea of being a trial lawyer in Washington."

In 1945 he joined Hogan and Hartson full-time, defending corporate clients against liability suits, but by 1949 he had decided there were "only a certain number of ways to get hit by a streetcar," and switched to trial law. It was a decision he would never regret.

His speed of thought and shrewdness at judging character made him ideally suited to the cut-and-thrust of adversarial courtroom combat. Neither did he waste time. The modern practice of psychological profiling to sift out potential jurors was not for him. "I have never taken more than half a day to pick a jury," he said, "and I have never lost a case because I didn't have time to pick a jury." It was a self-assurance born from experience. With his impressive appearance and a beautifully modulated voice that rarely rose above normal conversational levels, Williams felt confident of being able to woo any panel, irrespective of background or belief. A good chance to test that sangfroid came in 1975 when one of the most famous politicians in America found himself facing charges of bribery.

II. John B. Connally (1975)

Of all the many dislocations wrought by the Watergate scandal, the trial of John B. Connally was one of the easiest for the general public to understand and assimilate. The issue was clear-cut: had the fifty-eight-year-old former Texas governor taken kickbacks when he was Secretary of the Treasury? The charge had its genesis in the infamous Nixon Tapes, when Watergate Committee members uncovered conversations that appeared to reveal lobbying irregularities by the Associated Milk Producers Inc. (AMPI). An investigation of those suspicions led to the 1974 conviction of AMPI attorney Jake Jacobsen on charges of bribery. However, the matter did not end there.

According to the government, on March 19, 1971, Jacobsen went to Connally, whom he had known for twenty-five years, asking that he use his influence on behalf of the milk producers when the question of subsidies was discussed at a forthcoming Cabinet meeting. Records showed that, four days after meeting Jacobsen, Connally did indeed urge President Nixon and other officials to raise the federal price support-level from $4.66 to $4.92 per hundredweight of milk.

A. A Test of Credibility

That much could be corroborated. What brought this matter to court could not. For it was Jacobsen's contention that, in May 1971 and again the following September, as a reward for services rendered, Connally was paid thousands of dollars in cash. While Connally admitted that he lobbied for the increase, he denied that any money changed hands. If convicted he faced a possible two years imprisonment and $20,000 fine.

The trial came to court on February 28, 1975. In his opening address, and in total contrast to the prosecution's rather prosaic opening, Williams was highly animated, pacing up and down in front of the jury-box, engaging everyone's attention. Jacobsen was, he claimed, an inveterate perjurer who "embezzled" the funds that allegedly went to Connally; and he cautioned the jury not to prejudge the case until they heard from the defendant, observing that "as the old mountaineer says about his pancakes, 'No matter how thin I make them, there's always two sides to them.'"

Williams moved on, telling how Jacobsen had been indicted twice by federal grand juries because of "frauds, crooked loans, [and] crooked deals" arising from a Texas banking scandal. And yet, noted Williams in mock amazement, all but one of the seven charges levied against Jacobsen were dropped, in return for a single plea of guilty to bribery and cooperation with the prosecution. Was this a witness whose evidence could be trusted? Williams' expression of contempt said it all. Everything, he suggested to the jury, boiled down to a test of credibility—Connally or Jacobsen?

Jacobsen came under scrutiny first. He told the court he went to Connally's office on May 14, 1971, and handed over an envelope that contained $5,000 in cash, saying "here's some of the money." Connally reportedly pocketed the cash and replied, "Thanks very much." Jacobsen then described a similar meeting on September 24. To back up his claim that influence-peddling took place, the prosecution played a taped discussion between Connally and Nixon. Although the quality was scratchy, Connally could be clearly heard spelling out the level of AMPI's political clout and arguing for increased milk support. After considering the arguments from every angle, Nixon told Connally to "make the best deal you can."

B. Shifting Testimony

When tackled by Williams, Jacobsen began piling up the equivocations thick and fast. He admitted that he might have once claimed to have given Connally a third $5,000: but he couldn't actually remember doing so. He freely acknowledged receiving the money from AMPI, insisting it had been passed on to Connally. Throughout his ordeal Jacobsen maintained an uneasy composure that only lapsed when Williams taunted him with suggestions that he was prepared to incriminate anyone—even longtime acquaintance, ex-President Lyndon Johnson—to save his own skin. Angrily, Jacobsen retorted that this was untrue. Then Williams quizzed him about the physical dimensions of $10,000 in Treasury notes. How big was the pile? How had it been transferred? Again, Jacobsen's memory became conveniently hazy.

Bob Lilly, a former assistant to the general manager of AMPI, testified that he handed $10,000 to Jacobsen for onward transmission to Connally. But as Judge George L. Hart, Jr. was quick to remind the jury, this did not amount to proof that Connally received the funds.

A string of character witnesses took the stand on Connally's behalf. Drawn from the great and the good, they formed an imposing lineup: Dean Rusk, Robert McNamara, even Lady Bird Johnson, who brought chuckles to the crowded courtroom with her wry description of the defendant, "Now, some folks don't like him, but I don't think any of them doubt his integrity."

But it was evangelist Billy Graham who provided the clearest indication of the verdict to come. Asked by Williams to describe his job, he replied, "I teach the gospel of Jesus Christ across the face of the earth." Williams said later that when he overheard one juror murmur "Amen" in response, he knew he had it in the bag.

First, though, he had to present Connally in the best light possible. This was easily achieved. Coached for hours by Williams and his associates, the defendant smoothly refuted every one of Jacobsen's allegations on a date-by-date basis. He admitted that Jacobsen had mentioned political contributions from the milk people, only for him to reject them. One by one Williams fired the prosecution's allegations at Connally, and to each he replied in the negative.

Under cross-examination Connally repeated his insistence that he had not taken a bribe. He did concede that some testimony he had given earlier to the grand jury and the Watergate Committee had been erroneous, but blamed that on a faulty memory. In his closing speech Williams pointed out that out of thirty-six prosecution witnesses only Jacobsen was able to link Connally with money. Again, whom should the jury believe?

This was emphasized by Judge George L. Hart, Jr., in his final charge to the jury, "You should scrutinize the testimony of an informer carefully to determine whether it is slanted in such a way against the defendant to further his [the witness] own interests . . . you should receive such testimony with suspicion and act on it with caution."

Connally was duly acquitted of all charges. For Williams, this was a great triumph. Eight years earlier he lost the Bobby Baker trial amid rumors that he devoted too much attention to the Washington Redskins football team, which he part-owned. Now he was back on top. The cases flooded in. His interest in sports continued to thrive—he bought the Baltimore Orioles—and so did his contributions to charity. The Edward Bennett Williams Law Library at Georgetown University is a lasting memorial to his great career. On August 13, 1988, after a long battle with cancer, Edward Bennett Williams died. The plaudits he earned in his career are as diverse as they are plentiful. One associate said of him, "What he has done is make the practice of criminal law respectable." Another, Mafia mobster Frank Costello, was more heartfelt, "I've had forty lawyers, but Ed's the champ."

OTHER NOTABLE CASES:

Jimmy Hoffa (1957); Georgetown College v. Jones (1963);
Robert Baker (1967)

Index

The names of the lawyers featured in *SuperLawyers* are listed in boldface and all capitals; cases are listed in all capitals; boldfaced numerals indicate photographs.

A

B

INDEX

C

G

H

I

J

M

V

W

Z